D0281104

ᶠK L

STRATEGIC MANAGEMENT ACCOUNTING

CONCEPTS, PROCESSES AND ISSUES

SECOND EDITION

ZAHIRUL HOQUE PhD, CPA, FCMA
Professor of Management Accounting
Northern Territory University, Australia

© 2003 Zahirul Hoque

All rights reserved. No part of this publication may be reproduced, stored in a retrieval system, or transmitted in any form or by any means, electronic, mechanical, photocopying, recording, or otherwise, without written permission of the publisher.

Senior Acquisitions Editor: Karen Hutchings
Editorial Coordinator: Laura Chapman
Project Editor: Chris Richardson

Printed in Malaysia (CTP-V VP)

2 3 4 5 10 09 08 07 06

ISBN 10   0 7339 8445 2
ISBN 13   978 0 7339 8445 7

Learning Resources
Centre

1293318X

Pearson Education Australia
Unit 4, Level 3,
14 Aquatic Drive
Frenchs Forest NSW 2086
www.pearsoned.com.au

An imprint of Pearson Education Australia
(a division of Pearson Australia Group Pty Ltd)

This book is dedicated to Shirin, my wife and best friend,
for her enduring support

Preface to the Pearson Education Australia second edition

Spiro Press—a subsidiary of Capita Services in the UK—has been publishing my book since 2004. In April 2006 I was notified that Capita Services had decided to close its publishing business, Spiro Press and that all rights in the text reverted to me. I then decided to approach Pearson Education Australia as an alternative publisher as a logical first choice. They are a large tertiary textbook publisher specialising in accounting, with extensive sales and marketing resources. Also, as an international company, they have the ability to market and distribute the title internationally.

Pearson Education Australia's senior acquisitions editor Karen Hutchings agreed to publish this title in time for second semester adoptions in 2006. For the sake of speed to market this edition is a 'sprint print' meaning that the design, content and format remain the same as the Spiro edition. However there are plans for a fully revised new third edition to publish in the near future.

Zahirul Hoque
May 2006

Contents

• •

Foreword

It is evident, certainly in Anglo-American companies, that the job of management accountant is disappearing or, more commonly, being drastically reconstituted. The demand for scorekeepers of manufacturing achievements detached from line management and strategic planning is diminishing. Costing remains important, but its procedural techniques are easily reproduced through imported software. This, and the rise of computer-based control systems that combine physical, financial and qualitative data in real time has meant that non-accounting managers often control information systems that previously lay within the domain of accountants. The significance of traditional budgetary controls has declined in importance in parallel with these changes: manufacturing costs are a declining proportion of total costs whereas service industries and activities have risen in importance. The emphasis today resides in identifying and improving the value added of service activities deemed to deliver customer satisfaction, product differentiation, and more skilled, committed employees with problem-solving and team working abilities. Cost management rather than conventional costing is a prime managerial concern: the focus of cost management residing in pre-production and strategic decisions rather than tight control of operational costs. Although the latter remains important, operational controls now incorporate a series of non-financial indicators of performance, for example quality, downtime, lead times to customers and employee satisfaction. The trend towards broader planning and control systems has been aided and abetted by flatter, more process-oriented organisation structures to cope with increasing global competitiveness and shorter product life-cycles.

Accountants have always been skilled in adapting their skills and roles to new opportunities and environmental changes. The dramatic changes occurring in organisations today present a fresh challenge. If management accountants fail to acquire new skills and techniques, then emerging roles of hybrid accountants, sometimes called business analyst, management controller or strategic analyst, will be filled by MBAs or engineers, or some function other than accountants. To survive, accountants must acquire not only more multidisciplinary, cross-functional knowledge and practices, but also develop personal skills necessary for involvement within general management. In short, management accountants need to retool if they have not already done so.

This book is directed at these issues. It maps out contemporary changes and explains the major new techniques, practices and philosophies associated with the rise of strategic management accounting. Within a short space it gives a broad résumé of issues at the forefront of best practice and academic research. Students and practitioners seeking information on how management accounting is being reconstituted in today's rapidly changing environment will find much of interest and value.

Trevor Hopper
Professor of Management Accounting
Manchester School of Accounting and Finance
The University of Manchester
Manchester
United Kingdom

Preface to the second edition

Management accounting exists to help managers make better decisions. Changes in the way managers operate require re-evaluating the design and operation of the management accounting systems themselves. The most significant change is the redirection of the reference point from a short-term focus to a long-term focus. This concept has taken on radical new meanings recently, where the focus is now on 'strategic relevance'. This book will reinforce the view that today's companies should realise that traditional management accounting systems are no longer sufficient for strategic decisions in the longer term, and they should adopt a new focus, oriented towards today's competitive strategy and environment. I wrote this text to have these focuses.

This text is intended for practitioners (such as accountants, auditors, financial analysts, managers), executives, management accounting students and researchers. The primary focus of this text is not on techniques, but on understanding and using the concepts of contemporary management accounting for strategic business decisions.

I have organised this text into 15 chapters. In Chapter 1, after providing an introduction to the roles of management accounting in the contemporary business environment, I provide a description of a number of dominant theoretical perspectives on management accounting, followed by a conceptual framework of the text. In Chapter 2, I provide the basics of organisational goals, objectives and strategic choices. In Chapter 3, the fundamentals of management control systems are discussed. Chapter 4 presents the processes of conventional cost allocation and activity-based costing. In Chapter 5, I present the roles of cost and management accounting in advanced manufacturing technologies. In this chapter, I also discuss JIT and other manufacturing practices in organisations. In Chapter 6, the concepts of quality costing and total quality management are introduced. In Chapter 7, I provide an analysis of the role of accounting in the value-chain analysis. In Chapter 8, I give practical advice on how a customer accounting or customer profitability analysis can be undertaken. Chapter 9 presents the processes of competitor accounting or competitor analysis. In Chapter 10, I discuss the conventional performance measurement system and transfer pricing. In Chapter 11, the non-financial performance measurement system is introduced. In Chapter 12, I present the balanced scorecard philosophy. In Chapter 13, the role of management accounting in the benchmarking process is discussed. In Chapter 14, I present several forms of incentive plans. Finally, in Chapter 15, I present the nature of management accounting and controls in the public sector.

In this text, a general knowledge of undergraduate cost accounting is assumed. Nevertheless, students without a background in cost accounting should find all of my discussion and analyses easily understandable.

Changes to the second edition

New format

Each chapter of this second edition contains the following:

- learning objectives;

- discussion questions;

- references for further reading;

- up-to-date literature on the topic.

Case studies

This second edition contains a number of practical case studies from a variety of settings, which can be used as bases for group discussion in lectures, tutorials, seminars or workshops. Within each case study, you will learn how to (a) analyse a business problem, (b) identify the strengths and weaknesses of the organisation, (c) design an alternative system, and (d) suggest for further improvement.

The case method will help you to develop the following six major skills:

- analytical skills;

- application skills;

- creative skills;

- communication skills;

- social skills;

- self-analysis skills.

Cases incorporated into this second edition will provide a useful forum for analysing students'/readers' values. For a detailed discussion of the case method and its usefulness, refer to Geoff Easton's *Learning from Case Studies*, Englewood Cliffs, NJ: Prentice-Hall International, 1991.

Teaching supplements

Solutions manual for instructors

This supplement contains the solutions for end-of-chapter questions in CD-ROM format.

Who would benefit from this book and how to use it

This text has several potential uses.

Undergraduate programmes

This text can be easily used as the basis of a one-semester advanced management accounting course for students in undergraduate programmes in accounting, finance and business. Because this text contains 'Discussion questions' and 'Further reading' at the end of each chapter, tutorial/workshop/seminar work may be set with a mixture of discussion questions, journal articles and case studies.

Master's degree, MBA or executive MBA

As the principal focus of this text is on conceptual foundations, I believe that the text would also be ideal for courses in graduate programmes such as a master's degree, MBA or executive MBA. The case studies that are included in this text would best fit the above courses' goals.

Professional courses

Strategic management accounting now becomes one of the elective segments offered in the professional accounting programmes. In Australia, it is listed as an elective offered in the CPA programme. 'The principal objective of this segment is to introduce candidates to contemporary management accounting developments and to provide some tools that can be used by management accountants in practice.' This second edition perfectly fits into this goal of the CPA programme. CPA and other accounting professional students will gain the most from the materials covered in this edition.

Practising accountants, executives and managers

The book will serve as a reference source for practising accountants, senior executives and managers working in human resources, operations and accounting divisions.

Research higher degree students

This book is different from other management accounting textbooks in that it places emphasis on understanding contemporary accounting issues from wider economic, social, political and institutional contexts. It is based on the idea that accounting has multiple roles to play in organisations and society. It focuses on symbolic, economic, political and institutional roles of accounting control systems in organisations. Research higher degree students may find this book useful for it will serve as a reference source for literature reviews and future research issues.

Zahirul Hoque

Excerpt from the preface to the first edition

This book is about accounting for strategic decisions. It is intended for practitioners (such as accountants, auditors, financial analysts, managers), executives, management accounting students and researchers. The primary focus of this book is not on techniques, but on understanding and using the concepts of contemporary management accounting for business decisions. This book will be a very useful addition to various texts on the subject of management accounting, where the focus is on 'strategic relevance'. In addition, the book will serve as a reference source for practitioners, research higher degree students and academics alike.

In recent years the traditional role of management accounting as a rational system providing information for economic decision-making has been expanded and challenged. Apart from their role in promoting organisational efficiency and effectiveness towards profit-maximisation goals, management accounting systems are advocated, in recent writings, for their social, economic, cultural, political, institutional and administrative values. Some of the many roles ascribed to management accounting systems include:

- providing information for resource allocation decisions;

- motivating managers to perform certain actions;

- aiding the exercise of influence and control;

- increasing confidence in decisions made in uncertain and ambiguous situations;

- performing functions to legitimate organisations;

- performing sociopolitical and institutional roles within and outside organisations.

Management accounting exists to help managers make better decisions. Changes in the way managers operate require re-evaluating the design and operation of the management accounting systems themselves. The most significant change is the redirection of the reference point from an internal one to an external one. This concept has taken on radical new meanings recently. This book will reinforce the view that today's companies should realise that traditional management accounting systems are no longer sufficient for strategic decisions in the longer term, and they should adopt a new one oriented, towards today's competitive strategy and environment.

Zahirul Hoque

Acknowledgments

Several people have provided useful comments and suggestions. Manzurul Alam (James Cook University, Australia), Trevor Hopper (University of Manchester), Bhagwan Khanna (Victoria University of Wellington, New Zealand), Lokman Mia (Griffith University – Gold Coast) and Sue Jackman (Christchurch College of Education, New Zealand) have provided excellent and invaluable feedback. I wish to also thank Jo Burling (School of Accounting and Finance at Griffith University) for her logistic assistance at various times during preparation of the second edition.

The following three individuals deserve my special thanks for their help in making improvements in the second edition: John Sands (School of Accounting, Banking and Finance, Griffith University, Brisbane, Australia), Jodie Moll (School of Accounting and Finance, Griffith University, Gold Coast, Australia) and Lanita Winiata (Satya Wacana Christian University, Salatiga, Indonesia).

Thanks are also due to Glyn Jones and Carl Upsall of Spiro Press and Peter Williams (freelance editor) for their support during preparation of this edition. I am also grateful to the Institute of Management Accountants for its permission to use some cases in this textbook. I am indebted to my parents, father-in-law Abdul Hoque Miazi, brother-in-law Aminul Hoque Miazi, and my elder brother Shah Alam, for their continued support. Also, to my mother-in-law (1947–2000) and younger brother Salah Uddin Salim (1964–1994), who departed forever. Finally, I would like to thank my wife, whose forgiveness I will continue to beg, for being distant and forgetful. I dedicate this book with my love to her.

Zahirul Hoque

List of abbreviations

ABC	activity-based costing
ABM	activity-based management
ADM	assistant deputy minister (Canada)
AMT	advanced manufacturing technology
BSC	balanced scorecard
CAD	computer-aided design
CAE	computer-aided engineering
CAM	computer-aided manufacturing
CC	capital charge
CDS	Chief of the Defence Staff (Canada)
CEO	chief executive officer
CFBS	Canadian forces bases
CIM	computer-integrated manufacturing
CIMA	Chartered Institute of Management Accountants
CNC	computerised numerical control
CPA	customer profitability analysis
CQI	continuous quality improvement
CVP	cost-volume profit
DFM	design for manufacturability
DLH	direct labour hour
DM	deputy minister
DND	Department of National Defence (Canada)
EBU	engine build-up
EPS	earnings per share
ERP	enterprise resource planning
EVA	economic value added
FAA	Federal Aviation Administration
FMS	flexible manufacturing systems

GDP	gross domestic product
HR	human resources
HRM	human resource management
JIT	just in time
MAS	management accounting systems
MCS	monitoring and control system; management control system
MRP	manufacturing resources planning
MVA	market value added
NAA	National Association of Accountants
NATO	North Atlantic Treaty Organisation
NC	numerically controlled
NDHQ	National Defence Headquateres (Canada)
NIBT	net income before tax
NOPAT	net operating profit after taxes
NPM	new public management
O&IRs	operations and inspections records
OPT	optimised production technology
PE	political economy
PER	price-earnings ratio
PEU	perceived environmental uncertainty
PGA	pin grid array
PPBS	planning programming budgeting systems
PRP	performance-related pay
PVA	process value analysis
R&D	research and development
RI	residual income
ROA	return on assets
ROE	return on equity
ROI	return on investment
QLF	quality loss function
SBU	strategic business unit
STEP	sociological, technological, economic and political
TPM	total productive maintenance
TQM	total quality management
UN	United Nations (The)
WIP	work in progress
ZBB	zero-base(d) budgeting

The author

Zahirul Hoque, BCom (Hons) (Dhaka), MCom (Dhaka), PhD (Manchester), Grad. Cert. Higher Edu. (Griffith), FCMA (Bangladesh), CPA (Australia), CMA (Australia) is Professor of Management Accounting within the School of Business at the Northern Territory University in Darwin, Australia. He has held faculty positions at the Gold Coast Campus of Griffith University in Queensland, Australia (1996–2003), Victoria University of Wellington, New Zealand (1994–96) and the University of Dhaka, Bangladesh (1986–93). He also has been a visiting professor at American International University – Bangladesh and King Fahd University of Petroleum and Minerals in Saudi Arabia during 2001–02.

Zahirul earned a PhD in public sector management accounting and control from the University of Manchester in 1993 under the supervision of Professor Trevor Hopper. He is a fellow of the Institute of Cost and Management Accountants of Bangladesh and a member of CPA Australia. He is also associated with the following professional bodies: the Institute of Certified Management Accountants in Australia, Accounting and Finance Association of Australia and New Zealand, American Accounting Association, British Accounting Association, European Accounting Association and the International Association for Accounting Educators and Research (IAAER).

He has been on the editorial board of *Accounting, Accountability and Performance* since January 2000 and an associate editor of *AIUB Journal of Business and Economics*. He has served as a joint guest editor (with Trevor Hopper) of a Special Supplement of *Research in Accounting in Emerging Economies* on 'public sector reform, privatisation, and changing forms of accounting and accountability within emerging economies' published by Elsevier Science in 2003. Currently he is working on his second book *Value for Money Auditing* with the publisher of this book.

Zahirul's research interests include the design and use of performance management systems, particularly balanced scorecard implementations in organisations, both in the public and private sector, public sector reforms and accounting change, industrial relations and management controls in mining companies, value for money auditing, and management accounting in emerging economies. He has published widely in these fields in leading journals, including *Journal of Management Accounting Research, Accounting and Business Research, Accounting, Auditing and Accountability Journal, Management Accounting Research, Critical Perspectives on Accounting, The British Accounting Review, Advances in Management Accounting, Public Administration and Development, The International Journal of Accounting, Journal of Accounting Education, International Journal of Public Sector Management* and *The Journal of Cost Management.*

The author may be contacted by e-mail or directly as follows:

E-mail: zahirul.hoque@ntu.edu.au
Tel: +61 8 8946 6017
Fax: +61 8 8946 6777

CHAPTER 1

Accounting for strategic management: introduction and the conceptual framework

Key learning objectives

After reading this chapter you should be able to:

- explain the concept of 'strategic management accounting';
- describe similarities and differences between management accounting and strategic management accounting;
- describe the concepts of broad-scope management accounting systems (MAS) information;
- describe the relations among financial accounting, cost accounting, cost management and strategic cost management, and strategic management accounting;
- explain the two competing models of business;
- demonstrate an understanding of the dominant theoretical perspectives (or viewpoints) of management accounting.

Introduction

Organisations must establish *key success factors* that allow managers to see how strategies are or are not leading to achieving organisational goals and objectives. More and more management accountants are being required to move outside the realm of financial (or quantitative) measures. Being involved in an external and internal analysis allows management accountants to increase their skills in non-financial and qualitative areas. As business environments or conditions change, management must make sure that the management accounting system changes too. Because management accounting plays an important role in many of the decisions that managers make, this book will focus on how management accounting can provide relevant data for guiding line personnel's strategic decisions. This component of management accounting is commonly known as *strategic management accounting*. This chapter provides some definitions of the key terms used in the management accounting literature.

Strategic management accounting: what is it and what does it offer?

This book is about strategic management accounting: but what do I mean by that? I define strategic management accounting as follows:

> Strategic management accounting *is the process of identifying, gathering, choosing and analysing accounting data for helping the management team to make strategic decisions and to assess organisational effectiveness.*

The emphasis is on continual feedback to ensure that when conditions and needs change, strategic management accounting continues to meet the organisational objectives of information provision, control and performance evaluation. Strategic management accounting is oriented towards the long term. That is, it concerns issues that stretch beyond the organisation's annual budget period. Strategic management accounting can be thought of as accounting systems for managing strategies and the competitive advantage of the organisation. This book focuses on both private and public sector organisations.

Today's businesses operate in a dynamic, complex environment as they are affected by *STEP* (sociological, technological, economic and political) factors, internal competition and, increasingly, the bargaining power of suppliers and customers. These forces have radically altered today's business environment. In order to survive in the changing business environment, organisations should rethink their strategic philosophy and the role of management accounting therein.

Managers set objectives, form plans to achieve the objectives, implement the plans, and finally evaluate their progress towards accomplishing their objectives. The management accounting system (MAS) provides information on these matters. In preparing and assessing their strategic plans, organisations need information on many areas of their business environment. Consistent with the changing environment, management accounting is also in a process of change. While some businesses continue to use conventional methods of costing, performance measurement and cost analysis, increasing numbers are adopting activity-based costing, strategically-oriented performance measurement systems and strategic cost analysis. Without such a strategy- and environment-oriented MAS, an organisation will not be able to track its performance in comparison to its competitors. Scholars label this discipline *strategic management accounting.*

This discipline builds on many of the contemporary techniques and considers the skills and competencies management accountants and practitioners need to develop in the new millennium to reap the many opportunities offered by these new techniques and systems. Strategic management accounting is built upon the view that accounting should be tailored specifically to the strategies and environment of the business, and this is the key focus of this book.

Financial accounting, cost accounting, cost management, management accounting and strategic cost management: how do they relate?

It is important to understand the relations among financial accounting, management accounting, cost accounting, cost management and strategic cost management, in order to appreciate the emergence and importance of strategic management accounting ideas.

Financial accounting originated to fulfil the stewardship function of businesses. It measures and records business transactions and provides financial statements that are based on generally accepted accounting principles as well as relevant accounting standards. It mainly concentrates on external reporting. Financial accounting prepares such reports as income statements (or profit and loss accounts), balance sheets (or statements of assets and liabilities), cash-flow statements and changes in equity.

Management accounting, in a general sense, identifies, collects, measures and reports information that is useful to managers in planning, controlling and decision-making. This is commonly known as the technical-rational (or conventional) role of management accounting. It is based on the basic premise that a business has (a) preset unitary goals, (b) utility/profit maximisation goals, and (c) an efficiency and effectiveness focus. Management accounting textbooks identify the following two key points concerning managers and accounting information:

- Managers need information, need to understand its usefulness and need to know how to use it.

- Management accounting information can contribute to the following management areas: policy formulation, planning and controlling the activities of the firm, decision taking on alternative courses of action, and so on.

It is often claimed that conventional management accounting systems (MASs) are heavily technical and focus mainly on short-run decisions. By conventional MASs, this book refers to systems of product costing and quantitative systems of planning and control, such as volume-based cost allocations, cost-volume-profit analysis, budgetary control and standard costing.

In general, scholars identify the following major limitations of conventional MASs:

- *their technical orientation* – placing heavy emphasis on technical (or computational) aspects of accounting;

- *they ignore human-relations aspects* such as employee morale, attitude, perceptions and motivation;

- *they ignore business context* such as strategy, organisational culture, management/leadership style, external environment, government regulation, politics and power.

Research has shown that MASs are not always embraced warmly by organisational managers, and the magnitude of the unintended negative consequences is alarming (for further details see Kaplan, 1983; Kaplan and

Norton, 1996; and Simons, 2000). There is the view that if we could somehow get the human relations aspects right, then our accounting and information systems would work as they are supposed to do (Macintosh, 1985). More recently scholars take the view that accounting and accountability may be embedded in virtually all forms of internal and external environment. Strategic management accounting is the primary means available to managers to deal with the increased scale and pace of change within and outside organisations. As such, to deal with today's complex and uncertain business environment, conventional approaches to management accounting are no longer sufficient for their heavy emphasis on financial, quantitative and historical information.

Cost accounting is a hybrid of financial and management accounting. It is concerned with the ascertainment and control of costs. It provides information on a company's costs and may be used for both external and internal purposes. When cost accounting is used for financial accounting (or external purposes), it measures the cost of production and sales in accordance with generally accepted accounting principles. When used for internal purposes, cost accounting information provides the basis for planning, controlling and decision-making. Cost accounting includes such topics as cost-volume-profit (CVP) analysis, budgeting, relevant costing, job costing, process costing, activity-based costing (ABC), activity-based management (ABM) and cost allocation processes.

Cost accounting and management accounting are closely related. A basic requirement for management accounting is the existence of a sound costing system to provide data for internal planning, control and decision-making purposes.

Cost management requires a deeper understanding of the cost structure of the firm; it combines elements from three older fields: management accounting, production and strategic planning. Horngren, Foster and Datar (2000) use this term to describe the activities of managers in short-run and long-run planning, and control of costs. Cost management not only focuses on cost reduction, but also on cost control and management. Thus, it has a broad focus.

Strategic cost management provides costing information for strategic decisions. It helps formulate and communicate strategies. It has a long-run focus. It carries out tactics that implement those strategies. It develops and implements controls that monitor success at achieving strategic objectives.

Financial accounting, cost accounting, cost management, strategic cost management, management accounting and strategic management accounting all contribute to the information (financial and non-financial) system of an organisation and increasingly in practice are totally integrated.

Two competing models of business: accounting and economic

The accounting model

The accounting model mainly focuses on 'bottom line figures' (i.e. profits), which are determined by traditional accounting, irrespective of whether they affect the business cash flows or whether transactions are recorded on the balance sheet or off-balance sheet. Examples include net earnings, earnings per share, return on investment (ROI) and price earnings ratio (PER). These accounting models suffer from limitations because they are all faulty, as they are dependent on subjective accounting methodology for determining earnings in the first place. Additionally, there is no distinction between operating and financial results (Ireland, 1992).

The economic model

The economic model is concerned with two issues: the cash flows generated over the life of a business, and the risk of the cash receipts. The first is embodied in the corporate plan, and the second is determined in the marketplace.

'What cash (or capital) has been invested in the business and what are the related cash returns?' is an example of an accounting model while under the economic model the accounting income statement and the balance sheet are treated as one account, 'Sources and uses of cash' (Ireland, 1992).

Broad-scope MAS information

The recent suggestion in management accounting literature is that MAS should be developed to focus on an organisation's value-added activities, relative to its competitors (Bromwich, 1990). This type of MAS produces what is called broad-scope MAS that allows managers to obtain information necessary to make successful economic decisions in the long run. Research has shown that managers' greater perceived environmental uncertainty (PEU) implies greater difficulty in predicting future events; therefore, they need timely, relevant and accurate information to deal with uncertain operating situations (Gordon and

Narayanan, 1984; Chenhall and Morris, 1986). The suggestion is that in PEU situations, elaborate and sophisticated accounting and reporting systems are required, which should focus information on the sources of uncertainty. Recent studies (Mia, 1993; Mia and Chenhall, 1994; Libby and Waterhouse, 1996) suggest that organisations, where managers have greater PEU, experience more complex communication and coordination problems, thus causing them to place greater emphasis on a sophisticated information system, which is broad in scope and multidimensional.

No business decision should depend solely on financial information; managers should rely on a wide range of both financial and non-financial information for day-to-day business operations. Based on prior research, Gordon (1998) has identified the following eight information attributes of such broad-scope MAS information:

1. Financial, ex post internal – e.g. a firm's actual cost of producing a specific product.

2. Financial, ex post external – e.g. a competitor's actual price for a specific product.

3. Financial, ex ante external – e.g. a firm's expected cost of producing a specific product.

4. Financial ex ante external – e.g. a competitor's expected price for a specific product.

5. Non-financial ex post internal – e.g. a firm's unit sales volume for a given product over the past year.

6. Non-financial ex post external – e.g. an industry's unit sales volume for a given product over the past year.

7. Non-financial ex ante internal – e.g. a firm's expected unit sales volume.

8. Non-financial ex ante external – e.g. an industry's expected unit sales volume.

From a public sector accounting perspective, Hoque and Mia (2001) suggest that traditional MAS such as budgets have previously been mainly input-based. Budgets were generally only concerned with the cost of inputs necessary to maintain current spending programmes and no linkage was required to how this spending related to outcomes. Broad-scope MAS information deals with a wide range of non-financial matters, as outlined above; it looks forward and deals with issues not only internal, but also external to the organisation.

Simons (2000) suggests that management accounting plays a central role in mapping future direction by giving managers a variety of information for setting strategies and the ability to ensure that inputs, processes and outputs are aligned to achieve organisational goals. In a public sector context, there is one important additional use of this information – for *external communication* to users who have a vested interest in the direction and success of the entity. These users fall into three groups: resource providers (employees, lenders, creditors, suppliers), recipients of goods and services (ratepayers, taxpayers and members of professional associations) and parties performing a review or oversight function (parliaments, governments, regulatory agencies, analysts, labour unions, employer groups, media and special interest community groups).

Theoretical perspectives (or viewpoints) of management accounting

Over the past decades, a large literature has evolved in the area of management accounting in organisations. Researchers seek to understand and examine management accounting systems in organisations from a variety of theoretical approaches on management accounting. Subsequent sections describe those approaches that were found to be widely used in management accounting research.

Technical-rational view of management accounting

The technical-rational approach originates in economics. Based on neoclassical economic theory, the technical-rational approach presumes management accounting as a computational decision-making tool that helps maximise the goal of the organisation. According to management control theorists a technical-rational approach helps organisational managers make rational types of decisions to maximise the goal of the organisation (Anthony, 1965).

The technical-rational approach has the following key features. First, it assumes a preset goal or consistent goal sets. There is the view that rationality emphasises consistency among goals and objectives concerning a particular action and consistency in the application of principles to select the optimal alternative. The technical-rational perspective also assumes that alternatives are mutually exclusive, separate and easily identified. Thus this approach deals with unitary goals, identification of the range of possible options, their likely consequences and the selection of an alternative that maximises the goal of the organisation. Most management accounting textbooks are built on these assumptions.

Within such technical-rationality, accounting is used as an internal decision-making tool. Accounting information thus can be used to measure the efficiency of resource allocations at an organisational level. It also provides a record of organisational choices and actions.

The technical-rational model assumes that it is always possible to improve accounting information through the introduction of new technical developments. An example of this in the recent public sector is the introduction of accrual accounting. Accrual accounting was introduced in the public sector to improve the accounting information produced and therefore lead to better decision-making. Additionally, technical rules such as legislation, regulation or rules set by Standards Setting Bodies have been linked to changes in public sector accounting to improve the decision-making ability of public sector organisations (Moll, 2000).

Further, the underlying assumptions grounded in the technical-rational choice model focus on bureaucracy, hierarchical controls and optimal resource allocation. In its purest form, the technical-rational choice model suggests that accounting information leads to rational decision-making. For instance, organisations use budget control systems to set budgetary standards, to collect cost revenue information and to report variances. The budgets are therefore used for decision-making purposes and for performance measurement. Simply put, the information provided by the MAS aids in the efficient and effective allocation of resources. This assumption also implies that when organisations change, the MAS will also change to reflect the new operating environment so that it will continue to provide information that will assist in the decision-making process (Moll, 2000).

Mouritsen (1994) suggests that applying the technical-rational choice model in organisational decision-making can hinder the development of organisational systems when textbook systems are adopted. In addition to this, he argues that organisations are rarely managed using rational choice and therefore the technical-rational choice model is unrealistic. Feldman and March (1981), March (1989) and March and Olsen (1989) support this argument, claiming that organisations rarely use information for the purpose of making rational decisions. From a public sector context, it can be suggested that recent reforms in the public sector are not completely rational, but rather a 'window dressing' of organisations. This implies that the public sector is undergoing significant reform, not to achieve greater efficiency, but for the purpose of legitimising themselves to ratepayers.

To sum up, despite some useful insights, the technical-rational approach has the following weaknesses. First, it ignores the wider social, economic and political context in which organisations operate. Second, the technical-rational perspective fails to assess the effect of individual values and beliefs, organisational conflicts and the divergence of goals in the organisation upon decisions. It emphasises the internal operations of the organisation to the neglect of external social and institutional factors.

Weber's bureaucratic rational-legal authority

Some have taken Weber's classical theory of bureaucracy (1947) to represent a technical-rational perspective, in the sense of rational goal maximisation. Weber sees bureaucracy as an organisational form to achieve rational-legal authority. He argues that authority structures in organisations are dependent on meanings and the prevalent mode of control and power in society. To Weber, bureaucracy is a means of domination; its use and direction are distinct; and, its consequences for social actions are central to organisational analysis. Organisational literature finds two notions of rationality in Weber's theory of bureaucracy:

- The attainment of an end by means of precise calculation of means. The focus is on the means, their adequacy or inadequacy to an end, even if this end has a religious or mystical basis.

- The second meaning of the term refers to the kind of rationalisation the systematic thinker imposes on the image of the world: an increasing theoretical mastery of reality by means of increasingly precise and abstract ideas. In a negative sense, this process of rationalisation leads to the rejection of all religious, metaphysical or traditional values and explanations of the world.

Bureaucracy can attain the highest degree of efficiency within an organisation. However, Weber is careful to point out that bureaucratic administration means the exercise of control, based on certain beliefs and knowledge. This makes Weber's bureaucracy specifically rational in the sense of the organisation meeting its ends according to rational-legal authority. According to Weber, bureaucratic rationality includes universalistic criteria, formalisation of rules and procedures, a well-defined channel of communication and the hierarchy of authority in the organisation.

The human relations view of management accounting

There is the view that participation in the budget process may have either a positive or negative effect on individuals' behaviour, motivation and satisfaction. The human relations view suggests that personal relations among organisational members are critical to performance. Several strands have emerged from accounting studies, based on the human relations approach. Human relations studies can help explain the operation of accounting and control systems according to individuals' attitudes, behaviour and job satisfaction. Research suggests that individuals' behaviour influences the way managers do process information in control systems and increased satisfaction can sometimes result in increased productivity. Human relations studies have contributed to a broader understanding of how a variety of human aspects can affect the operation of accounting and control systems in organisations. These include: the effects of participation/consultation in decision-making processes; motivation, satisfaction and reward systems; leadership effects; organisational slack practices; and the effect of interpersonal relations among organisational members (see Macintosh, 1985, 1994).

Through the human relations approach, researchers discovered: how superior managers use accounting information to express their own styles of leadership; how subordinates react to budget-related pressure and the association of budgets with pressure, aggression, conflict, inefficiency and staff–line clashes; and how managers use budgets in response to prevailing environmental circumstances. Other factors studied include: personality and attitudinal variables; the influence of personality factors in participative budgeting; dysfunctional aspects of participative budgeting; and the phenomenon of budgeting and organisational slack (for details, see Macintosh, 1985, 1994).

Studies have shown when budget participation is high (low), a high (low) budget emphasis is associated with enhanced managerial performance. When budget emphasis is high (low) and task uncertainty is low (high), job-related tension is minimised.

Despite its contributions the human relations approach has weaknesses. First, human relations studies on accounting and control systems provide inconsistent results. Second, by adopting scientific methods (e.g. structured questionnaires, tests of hypotheses and establishing statistical relationships), the human relations work can neglect the import of individuals' understanding, values, meanings and culture. Finally, this approach fails to explain how accounting and control systems may be products of the socioeconomic and political contexts in which the organisation operates.

Contingency view of management accounting

The central idea of contingency theories of organisation is that there is no universally acceptable model of the organisation that explains the diversity of organisational design (Lawrence and Lorsch, 1967; Woodward, 1965). It claims that organisational design depends on the contingent factors relevant to the situation.

Under contingency theory the type of accounting and control system varies according to the specific circumstances or situations in which the organisation operates. There is the view that 'there is no universally "best" design for a management control system, but that "it all depends" upon situational or contextual factors' (for details see Otley, 1980; Chapman, 1997).

Several studies have tried to establish which factors shape management accounting systems in organisations (for references see Otley, 1980; Chapman, 1997; Kingfield-Smith, 1997). Researchers have identified a range of variables implicated in the design and use of accounting and control processes in organisations. These include the influence of the organisation's culture, technology and market on budgetary control systems; the size of an organisation, its technology and structure; decision-making styles; organisational values and motivation; and management aspiration for profit growth. Daft and Macintosh (1978) investigated why accounting practices differ from situation to situation and what factors influence the design and functioning of accounting and control systems in organisations. Research studies by Hopwood (1973) and Otley (1978) show how the structure of the organisation affects the way in which management accounting systems function. Hayes (1977) studied reporting systems in different subunits and their interrelationships with environments.

Nevertheless, contingency theory is subject to criticisms from a range of sources. These criticisms relate to the theoretical deficiencies and methodological assumptions of this approach. The critics argue that contingency theories are based on a highly technical view of organisational choice. As Hopper and Powell (1985, p. 441) put it:

Contingency theory thus represents a holistic apotheosis of the functional approach rather than a major new departure.

Scholars expressed reservations concerning a contingency approach. First, the conceptualisation, definition and measurement of key variables within contingency theory have not been adequately elucidated – they require greater theoretical and empirical attention. Second, correlations reported in most contingency studies are small and not always consistent; and, finally, contingency theory fails to incorporate the wider context of the organisation, i.e. the social, political, economic and institutional aspects (Hopper and Powell, 1985; Chapman, 1997).

Agency view of management accounting

Agency theory is concerned with the delegation of decision-making authority by a principal (e.g. an owner) to an agent (e.g. a manager). More simply, an agent's performance is evaluated based on the agent's performance, and reward is dependent on the agent's performance.

Agency literature suggests that the agent will not always take actions that are in the principal's best interests (for details, see Macintosh, 1994; Gordon, 1998). Jensen and Meckling (1976) suggest that the owner can limit such aberrant behaviour by incurring auditing, accounting and monitoring costs, and by establishing, also at a cost, an appropriate incentive scheme. Agency theory is built around the key ideas of self-interest, adverse selection, moral hazard, signalling, incentives, information asymmetry and, most pervasively, the contract (for details see Macintosh, 1994).

Interpretive approach to control

The research approaches outlined above are essentially functionalist and treat the social world as objective. Little is provided on the actual functioning of accounting and control systems in their organisational contexts (Burchell et al., 1980). Thus conventional research of the 'the scientific variety' enables the scholar to remain unconcerned that he has little direct familiarity with the sphere of life being studied (Blumer, 1978).

Many accounting scholars (for instance, Burchell et al., 1980; Colville, 1981; Tinker et al., 1982; Tomkins and Grove, 1983; Cooper, 1983; Cooper and Sherer, 1984; Chua, 1986a, 1988) have questioned the relevance to practice of conventional academic research based upon economic rationality. These researchers have argued traditional approaches to control, eliminate, de-emphasise, or even denigrate the importance of the social and political contexts in which they are located.

To overcome such drawbacks, accounting scholars have begun to see accounting and control as socially and politically constructed phenomena (as opposed to the technical–rational role of accounting in organisations). Researchers have called for more interpretive studies to gain a 'better' understanding of accounting and control systems in organisations: how to best pose the problem; how to identify which data is most relevant; and how to interpret individual meanings and people's perceptions of 'reality' in an organisation. Hopper and Powell (1985, p. 446) remarked thus:

> People constantly create their social reality in interaction with others. It is the aim of an interpretive approach to analyse such social realities and the ways in which they are socially constructed and negotiated.

Interpretive researchers attempt to make sense of observed phenomena by uncovering the meanings those phenomena have for individuals (for details, see Blumer, 1978; Tomkins and Groves, 1983; Hopper and Powell, 1985). The social world is thus seen as essentially one of social construction, achieved through individuals negotiating with each other. An interpretivist focuses on the way people manage impressions of themselves through the meanings they attach to acting out prescribed rules and even sometimes creating their own scripts (Goffman, 1959).

Weber's theory of bureaucracy is also related to the interpretive approach to the study of control. To Weber 'bureaucracy' in the 'interpretive' sense refers to the beliefs underpinning people's ways of acting and thinking in the organisation's decision-making processes. According to Weber these permeate all aspects of social life.

Weber (1968) sees bureaucracy as a means of political domination arising from what are perceived as legitimate sources of authority. According to Collignon and Covaleski (1991, p. 151):

> Although Weber does not treat the subject directly, his framework implies the possibility of analysing the members' resistance to domination and its mechanisms, i.e. accounting practices.

However, Mouzelis (1975) views the political domination of bureaucracy as problematic and dependent upon the external forces of every particular situation. He argues that Weber's ideas are often imprecise and one cannot be sure in what way the ideas are linked with the social reality that Weber wants to express. Thus Weber's theory of bureaucracy seems to formulate oversweeping generalisations and are half-truths (in the sense that they are only valid under certain conditions, which remained unspecified by Weber's classic theory of bureaucratisation).

Research adopts an interpretive approach to accounting research in the belief that it can better identify the social, economic and political aspects of management control systems in the organisation from the perspective of actors involved in their operations.

Political economy view of management accounting

The above approaches to management accounting fail to explain fully the relationships between polity, state, economy and organisational processes (Tinker et al., 1982; Cooper and Sherer, 1984). It has been suggested that traditional approaches based on neoclassical economics assume away the linkages between polity, state, society and economy (for a review see Scapens, 1994). There is the view that there are many different variants of the political economy (PE) perspective. The central thrust of this approach is to understand the close interdependence of economy, polity and society.

The PE approach emphasises the historical nature of the social world. It attempts to understand a particular phenomenon from its socio-political contexts that exist at a time and place. The role of history is treated as significant in explaining the changing roles of economic systems and why and how these changes occurred. From this philosophical line of thought, the PE approach, relying on the historical context of the inquiry, helps capture the action, conflict and social problems through an account of the past. Political economists view an economic process as part of the total system consisting of economic, social and political factors. Thus the PE approach states that an understanding of the structure, meaning and significance of an economic activity or behaviour requires, among other things, an understanding of the constituent elements of its social framework.

From the PE approach society is being viewed as composed of individuals whose performance is to predominate in social choices. Because of power and conflicts, organisational members within and outside the organisation may try to influence the decision-making process in organisations. Here the PE approach helps reconcile conflicting interests through negotiations: a series of compromises and alliances can emerge in the organisation.

Another major feature of the PE approach is that it takes into account the institutional legitimacy of the society in explaining management processes in an organisation. 'Institutions' are patterns, which define what are felt to be proper, legitimate or expected modes of action in a given society. Institutional aspects cover various social and economic institutions: state, markets, legal systems, religions, law and order, political processes, governmental administration, labour unions, and cultural rules and customs. These regulate or dictate organisational activities and human behaviour (see Scapens, 1994).

The concept that the state influences shaping and legitimating organisational activities is fundamental to the PE approach. Legal systems, fiscal and taxation policies, foreign trade policies, trade union legislation and investment in public sector services are common features of the economic role of the state.

A political economist clearly distinguishes between ceremonial and instrumental values in a society. Ceremonial values (e.g. using deceit, coercion and historical status or power to manipulate the behaviour of others) correlate behaviour within the institutions by providing the standard of judgement for invidious distinctions. These prescribe status, deferential privileges and master–servant relationships, and warrant the exercise of power by one class over another. In contrast, instrumental values (e.g. using scientific knowledge) correlate behaviour by providing the standards of judgement. These employ tools and skills in the application of evidently warranted knowledge to the problem-solving process.

According to the PE approach, economic activities in a society tend to display a social character; actions and practices of economic agents are structured and moulded in social processes. Research has viewed that understanding these actions and practices requires an understanding of the economic, cultural, social and political processes within the organisation itself and of its relations to other organisation and the society at large.

In summary, the PE approach helps an understanding of the mutual relationships between polity, state, economy and organisational processes, such as the design and use of management accounting systems. Issues of power and conflict, and historical, social, economic, political, cultural and institutionalised rules and regulations are key variants of the PE approach. The PE approach explains how these affect or dictate the operation of management processes in organisations. Accounting research suggests that a PE approach can better capture these phenomena by tracing the socio-political underpinning of economic phenomena to patterns of state involvement and the interaction between legal and economic processes upon and within the organisation. It is also suggested that accounting is essentially a naturalistic phenomenon, influenced by the individual and class behaviour inside and outside the organisation. Several themes have emerged from accounting studies using a PE approach including: how accounting systems are shaped by the interrelationships between political and economic forces in organisations and society; and how the meanings, culture, ideology and the organisational contexts dictate the operation of accounting and control systems in the organisation.

Organisation change literature

Organisations change their organisational structure and cultures to become more effective and efficient, thereby gaining a larger market share and ensuring the survival of the firm. There is the view in the organisation literature that organisations change in response to existing problems and for continuous improvement. Senior suggests that change in organisations arises from many different sources, temporal, external and internal. These are briefly outlined below.

Temporal sources relate to the historical development of an organisation that results in change over time. Temporal sources have been limited to the industry cycles and the use of firm-specific history as forces of change. The external forces of change can be categorised according to socio-cultural changes, political/legal changes, economic conditions or technological developments. A socio-cultural change refers to those changes in a society's beliefs, attitudes, opinions and lifestyles. For instance, demographic trends, skill availability and concern for the environment are possible socio-cultural influences that may force organisations to change. Political and legal changes are often a result of a change in government, such as government legislation and government ideologies to wars, local regulations and taxation. On the other hand, economic conditions affect all organisations, regardless of industry. Examples of economic influence could include competitors, suppliers, employment rates, government economic policies and changes from public to private ownership. Finally, technological factors that force organisations to change include new production processes or the computerisation of processes (Senior, 1997).

Three types of organisational change were identified in a literature review, those being developmental, transitional and transformational (Costello, 1994). Developmental change can be defined as improving the organisation through practices such as team building, expanding into the markets, or introducing new technology. Developmental change is more easily managed in the workplace as it is perceived as less threatening by employees. Transitional change refers to the implementation of a new structure or new method. It requires a reorganisation of the entity, the introduction of new techniques, methods and procedures, or new products and services. Employees perceive these changes as threatening and often tend to resist them. Lastly, transformational change refers to the introduction or evolution of a new structure, which also results in a change in the organisational strategy and vision. This is the most complex form of change as it results in a highly uncertain environment. Consequently, it receives the most resistance from employees. Examples of transformational change include mergers, consolidations and restructuring efforts.

Organisational change tends to dominate two organisational properties: the structure of the organisation and the cultural characteristics of the organisation. Organisational structures define job activities, responsibilities and accountabilities. They enable managers to organise and distribute resources and they also establish the power hierarchy of the organisation. Emmanuel, Otley and Merchant (1990) claim that the design of the organisational structure can significantly influence and control the behaviour of employees. Senior (1997) claims that organisations change their structures for successful performance and as a coping mechanism for change. Organisational structures can be defined in terms of centralisation or decentralisation, efficiency or effectiveness, professionalism versus management, control versus commitment and change versus stability (Carnall, 1990).

In organisations that are highly decentralised, the decision-making process is highly autonomous, employees tend to be more motivated, such large organisations are capable of dealing with higher levels of uncertainty and lines of accountability are clearly identified. Centralised organisations or highly bureaucratic organisations are the opposite. They operate according to clearly defined rules and regulations, senior managers are held accountable for the progress of the organisation and all decisions are made at the management level (Carnall, 1990).

Daft (1992, p. 317) defined organisational culture as 'the set of values, guiding beliefs, understandings and ways of thinking that is shared by members of an organisation and is taught to new members as correct.' Changes to the organisational culture then refer to changes in the perceptions, assumptions and behaviours of employees, the ethical codes, symbols and actions. Smith (1998) claims that the organisational culture impacts on the change process and that it is the manager's responsibility to change the culture so that it is conducive to meeting the organisation's initiatives. In addition to this, Schneier (1995) claims that managers also have to change the focus of the firm or the corporate practices of the organisation so that the organisational goals are able to be achieved.

Schwartz and Davis (1981) claim that when an organisation changes without assessing the organisational culture, it can hinder that firm's ability to achieve their desired result. In an article written by Argyris and Kaplan (1994), it was suggested that managers can overcome resistance to change using three processes: education and training; sponsorship of the change process; and alignment of incentives. Similarly, Smith, Swaffer and Gurd (1998) claim that management commitment, strong leadership, education and training programmes and customer focus can all be used to produce a positive change environment. Additionally, Kelaher (1991, p. 44) suggests that organisations need to address their operating environment during periods of change including: decentralising management authority, redesigning the organisation, defining the core business, creating business structures, appointing governing boards, rationalising business operations, developing commercial skills and modifying the values of the organisation to change the organisational culture. Subsequently, a failure to assess organisational culture results in resistance to change, because the strategic focus of the firm and the culture are not aligned (Senior, 1997).

Organisational culture is a key component of the monitoring and control system (MCS). The organisational culture can be used to control change when the MCS is aligned with the norms of the organisation. Birnberg and Snodgrass (1988) suggest that culture can affect the effectiveness of the MCS in two ways: the way aspects of the control system are viewed; and also opinions about those aspects of the control system.

The MCS of an organisation is not limited to accounting, but also encompasses such concepts as market share, employee commitment and morale, and research design and development. Otley (1987) argues that the management control process requires individuals to modify their behaviour to ensure that the organisation goals are achieved. It is for this reason that the behavioural issues surrounding the changes to an organisation should be explored to achieve a more in-depth view of the impact of the change on organisations.

Change can have significant social implications on organisations, especially when management does not adequately plan it. Emmanuel et al. (1990) claim that one of the objectives of the MCS is to compel individuals to behave in a manner that will contribute to the overall success of the organisation. Therefore, when an organisation changes, the MCS should also change to motivate employees to continue to behave in a manner that is conducive to achieving the organisation's goals.

People react to change in different ways. Some view change as positive; others view change as negative. Either way, individual perceptions on change and how it is managed determine their reaction to that change. Greenberg (1996) contends that individuals resist change at both an individual and organisational level. At an individual level, employees tend to resist change because of economic insecurity, fear of the unknown, threats to social relationships, habits, lack of trust and failure to recognise the need for change. Other causes of individual resistance include revenge, surprise, poor timing, poor approach and misunderstandings, absent benefits or phariseeism. Further individual responses to change are dependent on their personal attitudes. Their response will depend on whether they view change as positive or negative. At an organisational level employees resist change because of a change in the balance of power, previously unsuccessful change attempts, work group inertia and structural inertia (Greenberg, 1996). Resistance to change is projected by employees through absenteeism, decreased productivity and regression in behaviour, resignations, transfers and sabotage.

Careful planning and sensitivity to employees is the key to managing employee resistance. Greenberg (1996) suggests that resistance can be overcome by educating employees on the expected change and the effects of that change. In addition to this, methods for dealing with change include facilitation and support, negotiation and agreement, manipulation and cooperation and implicit or explicit coercion. The literature also suggests that resistance can be overcome by employing devices such as survey feedback, quality of work–life programmes, management by objectives (MBO), sensitivity training, team building and participative goal setting.

In a study conducted by George (1983) it was argued that providing employees with accounting information during periods of change can reduce resistance to change. This argument was further supported by Parker (1976), who claims that providing employees with management accounting information can lead to a positive self-image. More recently, Johnson (1992) claims that empowering employees with accounting information such as performance targets can lead to improved efforts and greater commitment, involvement and output from employees.

Chapter summary

This chapter introduces the concepts of strategic management accounting, outlines its key features, defines key terms and outlines the major views of management accounting. It has been suggested that conventional MAS are increasingly subject to criticism from a range of sources. Most criticism points largely to the deficiencies of these systems to satisfactorily capture important dimensions of company performance and information under conditions of managers' greater perceived environmental uncertainty. Partly in response to such criticism, a growing number of accounting researchers have explored the need to develop different sorts of management accounting systems that provide timely, relevant and different kinds of information for operational control that are not well-covered by conventional MAS such as standard costing and variance analysis. There is the suggestion that organisational and environmental factors have a major bearing upon characteristics of accounting and control systems, and organisational performance. Research has shown that the amount of MAS information that managers use for decision-making is a function of their perceived environmental uncertainty (PEU) and organisational strategic orientation.

It is good to reinforce again here that strategic management accounting is future-oriented and any strategic management accounting system must also be flexible enough to let managers know when changes are necessary. Strategic management accounting is built around the key ideas of strategy, structure, responsibility accounting, costing and cost management, performance measurement, reward systems and organisational effectiveness. Figure 1.1 outlines the book's theoretical framework. The next chapter is devoted to dealing with strategic issues that have significant effects on organisational activities, performance and strategic management accounting.

Key terms to learn

Agency theory	Financial accounting
Broad-scope MAS information	Human relations
Contingency view	Management control
Cost accounting	Political economy
Cost management	Strategic management accounting
Economy	Strategic planning
Effectiveness	Technical-rational
Efficiency	Traditional management accounting

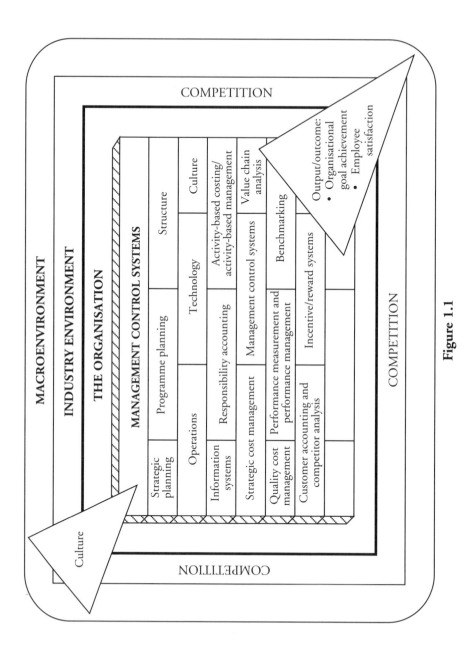

Figure 1.1

Discussion questions

1.1 How would you define the term 'strategic management accounting'? How does it differ from conventional 'management accounting'? Explain and give examples.

1.2 What is the role of strategic management accounting?

1.3 How do financial accounting, cost accounting, cost management and strategic cost management relate to each other? Explain with examples.

1.4 What are the two types of MAS information discussed in this chapter? Discuss each of them in terms of their importance to managerial decision-making.

1.5 Describe the purpose for which management uses cost information.

1.6 What are the major differences between management accounting and financial accounting?

1.7 What is meant by the term 'technical-rational choice models' of organisations? Briefly discuss its relevance to management accounting.

1.8 What are the main issues discussed in 'contingency theory' of organisations? Briefly discuss.

1.9 Discuss, with examples, how contingency theory differs from institutional theory.

1.10 Describe some of the changes that have altered the business environment.

1.11 What kinds of information do organisations require to compete in the new business environment?

1.12 What are the conventional methods of management accounting? Provide examples.

1.13 Discuss why managers should not rely solely on financial information for maintaining competitive advantage in the new business environment.

1.14 What is the difference between information use in the public sector and private sector?

1.15 Explain how the agency view of management accounting applies to the public sector.

1.16 Compare and contrast the technical-rational view of management accounting with the contingency view of management accounting. Use examples to explain.

1.17 Describe the relationships among organisational change, management control systems and management accounting systems.

1.18 Discuss the types of organisational change and provide examples of each.

1.19 Organisational change tends to dominate two organisational properties. What are these? Discuss each property and explain how it is affected by change.

Further reading

Boer, G. (1996) 'Management accounting beyond the year 2000', *Journal of Cost Management*, Winter, pp. 46–9.

Bromwich, M. (1990) 'The case for strategic management accounting: the role of accounting information for strategy in competitive markets', *Accounting, Organisations and Society*, vol. 15, nos. 1 and 2, pp. 27–45.

Chenhall, R. H. and Morris, D. (1986) 'The impact of structure, environment and interdependence on the perceived usefulness of management accounting systems', *Accounting Review*, vol. 61, January, pp. 16–35.

Freeman, T. (1998) 'Transforming cost management into a strategic weapon', *Journal of Cost Management*, November/December, pp. 13–26.

Tymon Jr, W. G., Stout, D. E. and Shaw, K. N. (1998) 'Critical analysis and recommendations regarding the role of perceived environmental uncertainty in behavioral accounting research', *Behavioral Accounting Research*, vol. 10, pp. 23–46.

CHAPTER 2

Vision, mission, goals, objectives and strategy typology

Key learning objectives

After reading this chapter you should be able to:

- describe the concepts of 'vision', 'vision statement', 'mission' and 'mission statement';
- explain the concept that forms competitive strategy;
- describe the similarities and differences between 'goals', 'strategic goals' and 'objectives';
- describe strategic decisions;
- outline the types (or levels) of competitive strategy;
- outline Simons' strategy, Miles and Snow's strategy typology, Porter's competitive strategy and Mintzberg's five Ps for strategy;
- describe the concepts that form Porter's structural analysis of industry;
- demonstrate an understanding of the relation between strategy and environmental uncertainty.

Introduction

Strategy plays an important role in the choice of management accounting systems and an effective management accounting system must be able to assess the organisation's progress on strategic priorities. The question is then: do management control systems need to vary according to the strategy being pursued by a firm? This chapter will be devoted to addressing this issue.

Chapter 1 suggests that an organisation's strategy be supported by a suitably focused management control system (MCS) within the context of the particular competitive environment facing the organisation. Developing and implementing the MCS necessary to evaluate and control the competitive strategies of their organisations is the major opportunity and challenge facing today's management accountants. With today's intense competition, it is the management accountant's responsibility to design systems that can provide the extra edge to win, as organisations with different strategies need different MCSs. This chapter focuses upon defining some key terms and concepts that are related to strategic management accounting and organisational effectiveness.

What is a vision statement?

An organisation's vision statement provides the vision of what top management sees as the reason for the firm's existence. That is, it describes what the firm would like to become. It is a description of the ideal, and as such is a picture of the potential future which it is hoped employees, perhaps scattered around the world, can rally round, understand, be committed to, and be motivated to help attain. Vision is the 'dream' that people in the organisation can relate to and commit their time and efforts to achieve (Digman, 1999). Apple Computers put forward in 1980 its vision as making a contribution to the world 'by making tools for the mind that advance humankind'. Walt Disney is a little bit more down to earth in simply being 'to make people happy'. The Commonwealth Bank of Australia put forward its vision as 'to be the best brand in helping customers manage and build wealth'. Another example of a vision statement is that of an Australian university shown in Figure 2.1, while the vision statement of a New Zealand plastic packaging company is shown in Figure 2.2.

ABC University, a multi-campus, learning-centred, research university, will be acknowledged as an outstanding university, which combines the best university traditions and values with the innovation necessary for success.

Ideally positioned for the 21st century in the fastest growing region in Australia, the university will build on its reputation for responding creatively to local, national and global change by embracing diversity and nurturing innovation.

Figure 2.1 Vision statement of ABC University.

Our vision

'To build a long-term profitable future for Alpha Food Packaging's employees and stakeholders by striving to be the "Highest Value Supplier" of packaging solutions to domestic and international markets.'

Figure 2.2 Vision statement of Alpha Packaging.

What is a mission statement?

An organisation's mission statement portrays its long-term concrete ends to be achieved. It reflects *what* the organisation is now and the perceived needs of its customers or constituents. Every corporation and their major business units have either an explicit or implicit business mission. This business mission enables today's management to select strategies to accomplish organisational objectives. The mission statement provides a short, written description of the organisation's overall purpose. One company defines its mission as 'to develop leading-edge businesses across a myriad of total systems fronts, from industrial automation to aerospace to medical systems.' Figure 2.3 outlines the mission statement of a multinational cereal company, which is the world's leading producer of ready-to-eat cereal and a leading producer of grain-based convenience foods, including pastries, frozen waffles and cereal bars. Figure 2.4 presents the mission statement of a local government water corporation in Australia and Figure 2.5 presents the mission statement of an Australian university.

Wheelen and Hunger (1998) have classified an organisation's mission statement as 'broad' or 'narrow'. A broad mission statement refers to the organisation's general statement: 'to serve the best interests of shareholders, customers and employees', while a narrow mission statement describes the organisation's primary business.

> **Our mission**
>
> ABC is a global company committed to building long-term growth in volume and profit, and to enhancing its worldwide leadership position by providing nutritious food products of superior value.

Figure 2.3 Mission statement of a multinational cereal company.

> **Our mission**
>
> Alpha Water exists to operate a successful commercial business which supplies safe water and removes sewage and storm water at an acceptable cost and in an environmentally sensitive manner for the benefit of present and future Alphanians.

Figure 2.4 Mission statement of a local government water corporation.

> **Our mission**
>
> In the pursuit of excellence in teaching, research and community service, ABC University is committed to:
>
> - innovation
> - bringing disciplines together
> - internationalisation
> - equity and social justice
> - lifelong learning
>
> for the enrichment of Queensland, Australia and the international community.

Figure 2.5 Mission statement of ABC University.

Organisational strategy

Strategy has been defined (Mintzberg, 1978) as: 'a pattern or stream of decisions about an organisation's possible future domains'. Strategy is the process by which organisational managers, using a time horizon of three to five years, evaluate external environmental opportunities and also internal strengths and resources to decide on goals, as well as a set of action plans to accomplish these goals. Chandler (1962, p. 13) defines strategy as 'the determination of basic long-term goals and objectives of the enterprise and the adoption of courses of action and the allocation of resources necessary for carrying out these goals.'

Thus strategy can be seen as an integrated set of actions aimed at securing a sustainable competitive advantage. Strategy focuses the firm's attention on those aspects of its products and services that it must rely on to drive the firm towards achievement of its goals. It can be seen then that, overall, strategy is the process of building defences against competitive forces or the finding of positions in the industry where the forces are weakest. Therefore any sensible competitive strategy should be designed to build on the relative competitive advantages of the business. Figure 2.6 illustrates the competitive strategy of a New Zealand plastic food packaging company.

Our strategic priorities

- To provide excellence in customer service and ongoing quality improvement.
- To focus on the development of long-term partnerships with company customers and suppliers.
- To strive to be proactive towards consumer needs, environmental and community issues.

Figure 2.6 Competitive strategy of Alpha Plastic Food Packaging Company.

Goals/strategic goals

Goals are specific concrete targets. The term 'goal' is often used to describe an open-ended statement of what one wants to accomplish with no quantification of what is to be achieved and no time criteria for completion. A firm's goal(s) is a specific outcome that it seeks to attain or maintain. Goals are chosen to implement the firm's strategy or to align the firm more closely with its vision and mission. One example of an organisational goal is to 'increase profitability'. An organisational goal does not specifically quantify or state how much to make the next year.

A firm works back from mission to goals. In commercial firms, where financial objectives dominate, goals are in terms of return on investment (ROI) or return on equity (ROE), earnings per share (EPS), and so on.

When an organisation's goals are set for a longer term, say for a period of between three and five years, they are then termed *strategic goals*. One example of strategic goals is that of a multinational cereal company:

- *People:* attract, select and retain top-quality people; provide training, development and growth opportunities; promote from within whenever possible; recognise achievement and reward performance.

- *Profit and growth:* grow and expand core business; strengthen global leadership; excel in the introduction of products that meet consumer needs.

- *Consumer satisfaction and quality:* strive for excellence, as defined by internal and external customers; pursue partnerships with company customers, suppliers and company employees to achieve common goals.

- *Integrity and ethics:* engage in fair and honest business practices; show respect for each other, company customers, suppliers, shareholders and communities within which the company operates.

- *Social responsibility:* produce quality products and market them in a responsible manner; encourage company people to participate in community programmes and invest company resources, human and financial, in organisations that benefit the community.

A leading Australian commercial bank states its strategic goals as follows:

A set of business goals underpins the achievement of the group's vision. Each operating division in turn has a series of strategies that are consistent with, and directed at, the collective achievement of those business goals, which are:

- attract more customers and revenue per customer;
- best value service through innovation and on-line leadership;
- best team;
- develop offshore opportunities;
- global best-practice costs.

Objectives

Objectives are the future results sought or the aims and expectations as to the future state desired. Objectives are the end results of an organisation's planned activity. Objectives are the desired targets within the scope of the vision to realise the mission (Viljoen and Dann, 2000). Objectives state what is to be accomplished by when, and should be quantified if possible (Wheelen and Hunger, 1998). An organisational goal is broken down into objectives – measurable accomplishments to be implemented within a specific period of time. An objective for increased profitability might be an increase of 6 per cent within six months to one year.

At the corporate level objectives can be split into vision and mission statements and a statement of goals, each reflecting different levels of abstraction and precision.

Strategic decisions

Mintzberg, Quinn and Voyer (1995, p. 7) describe strategic decisions, as follows:

> Strategic decisions are those that determine the overall direction of an enterprise and its ultimate viability in light of the predictable, the unpredictable, and the unknowable changes that may occur in its most important surrounding environments.

In formulating an organisation's strategy, three main types of strategic decisions are made:

1. What business will the organisation operate in?

2. How should the organisation compete in that business?

3. What systems should the organisation have in place to support its competitive strategies?

Effective strategic decisions within an organisation:

- deal with the organisation's boundaries;

- relate to the matching of the organisation's activities with the opportunities in its substantive environment;

- require the matching of an organisation's activities with its resources;

- have major resource implications for organisations;

- are influenced by the values and expectations of those who determine the organisation's strategy;

- affect the organisation's long-term direction.

The primary stages of strategic decisions are as follows:

1. formulating strategies of the business;

2. communicating those strategies throughout the organisation;

3. developing and carrying out tactics to implement the strategy;

4. developing and implementing management control systems to monitor the success of the implementation steps, and hence the success in meeting the strategic objectives.

Cost information plays a significant role at each of these stages. It is in this area that strategic management accounting systems are important.

What is a strategic business unit?

This book defines a strategic business unit as follows:

> A strategic business unit (SBU) *is an organisational operating or subunit that has a distinct set of products or services sold to a customer/group of customers, facing a well-defined set of competitors, and a mission distinct from those of the other operating units in the firm.*

According to Lynch and Cross (1991), SBUs are separate businesses in large, usually diversified companies, have distinct business concepts and missions, have their own competitors – mainly external – and make independent management decisions (see also Miles and Snow, 1978). Note that SBUs may or may not be part of a larger corporation.

Types (or levels) of strategy

Typical business firms use three types of strategy: corporate, competitive (or business) and functional (or operational):

- *Corporate strategy* describes how a company determines what business it wants to be in. Corporate strategy deals with three key issues: directional strategy (growth, stability, or retrenchment); portfolio strategy (industries or market for products); and parenting strategy (systems of allocation of resources and coordinating activities among product lines of business units. An example of a corporate strategy would be whether a big multinational corporation, Coles Myer, periodically considers whether it should continue to operate in the discount store market (Kmart and Target) and the departmental store (Myer and Grace Brothers) and grocery business (Coles Supermarket and Bi-Lo Supermarket).

- *Competitive (or business unit) strategy* occurs at the business unit, division or product level, and it refers to how an organisation competes within each type of activity and tries to achieve competitive advantage relative to its competitors. Coles Myer's supermarkets may compete on the basis of low price, while the Myer departmental stores may focus on providing superior quality products and customer service.

- *Functional (or operational) strategy* is concerned with the firm's strategy relating to its various functional or operational activities such as recruitment, marketing, distribution and advertising. Coles Myer Supermarkets would periodically review its marketing and distribution functions or sales strategy relative to its competitors such as Woolworth.

Various types of strategy typology

The following sections focus upon generic strategies identified by scholars. These strategic alternatives are termed *generic* because any type of business unit can adopt them, whether it is a traditional manufacturing company, a high-technology firm or a service organisation.

Simons' strategy typology

Simons (1990) breaks down the concept of a firm's strategy into the following four distinct areas:

1. *Strategy as process.* This strategy describes the managerial activity inherent in shaping expectations and goals and facilitating the work of the organisation in achieving these goals.

2. *Strategy as competitive position.* This refers to how the firm competes in its markets, that is the product and market characteristics chosen by the firm to differentiate itself from its competitors and gain an advantage.

3. *Business level strategy.* This refers to how a company competes in a given business and positions itself among its competitors.

4. *Corporate level strategy.* This is concerned with determining what business or businesses the organisation chooses to compete in and the most effective way of allocating scarce resources among business units.

In each of the areas described above there are 'strategic uncertainties'. Simons (1990, p. 136) argues that:

> Although firms competing in the same industry face the same set of potential uncertainties (changes in government regulation, intensity of competition, advance of new technologies, nature of customers and suppliers, product life-cycles and diversity in product lines), the strategy of the firm strongly influences which uncertainties are critical.

Managers must rank information from most critical to least critical; this allows management to attend to strategic uncertainties that they feel they must monitor to ensure that the goals of the firm are achieved (Simons, 1987, 1990).

Miles and Snow's (1978) strategy typology

Miles and Snow (1978) suggest that organisations consciously develop an image to demonstrate how and why the organisation's structure and processes reflect decisions about the market and how these decisions 'pave the way' for future development. This image development can be seen to be the organisation's attempt to adapt to its environment by following a cycle that involves decision-making regarding the following three potential problems:

- *Entrepreneurial problems* involve deciding the strategic management of its product markets.

- *Engineering problems* relate to creating a system for producing and distributing the firm's products.

- *Administrative problems* involve the 'structure-processes and innovation' areas of the firm.

Miles and Snow also believe that organisations 'enact in their own environment' and that no two organisational strategies are the same, i.e. each organisation has its own set of products or services and hence decisions will be supported by an organisation's own technology, structure and processes. Despite this individuality, Miles and Snow have identified patterns of behaviour within single industries and have developed four archetypes of firms, which follow particular behaviour types. These are discussed in turn.

- *Defender-type strategy.* Organisations that adopt a defender-type strategy have constricted product-market areas and managers are generally specialised in the product or service type that the organisation produces.

Defenders have a narrow product range, search little for new products, aggressively compete on price, quality and services, concentrate on product improvement, and rarely make major adjustments to their technology, structure or methods of operations. Their primary attention is on the efficiency of their operations, emphasising stability and earning the best profit possible, given their internal environment.

- *Prospector-type strategy.* Prospector-type organisations search continuously for new market opportunities and regularly experiment with possible new trends and innovations. They are 'creators of change' and as such generally focus attention on product innovation and market opportunities, emphasising creativity over efficiency and maintaining flexibility.

- *Analyser or mixed strategy.* Analyser or mixed strategy firms are those that operate in two types of product-market domains. The first is one that is relatively stable and the other dynamic. This then seems to incorporate both the 'defender' and 'prospector' type of organisation, in so much as the first area concentrates on being efficient and the second area concentrates on watching their competitors closely so as to determine the possibility of introducing new products or services as rapidly as possible.

- *Reactor strategy.* Reactor-type organisations appear to be inefficient in so much as they 'rank below' the defender in their attitude regarding growth and the intensity of the market. Miles and Snow suggest that the reactor is a residual strategy, arising when one of the other three strategies is improperly pursued; they appear to be aware of environmental uncertainty, but are unable to respond effectively. This type of organisation, because it has no direct strategic direction, tends to make no adjustment until absolutely necessary by being forced to do so by environmental pressures.

Porter's (1980) competitive strategy

Michael Porter (1980) believes that there are many strategic types, which vary the specifics of the control systems employed. He proposes, however, two 'generic' business unit strategies for outperforming other organisations in a particular industry: *lower cost* and *differentiation*.

- *Lower cost (or overall cost leadership) strategy* is the organisation's ability to produce and market a comparable product at a lower price than its competitors. It focuses on low cost, high market share, standardised products, economies of scale and tight cost control. Firms using lower cost strategy produce no-frills products industry-wide. One example is that of Franklin Superstores. They address a mass market comprised of price-sensitive customers.

- *Differentiation strategy* is the organisation's ability to produce and market unique and superior quality products. It focuses on product uniqueness, brings brand quality, emphasis on marketing and research and has superior after-sales service. Examples include BMW, Mercedes Benz and Alfa Romeo quality car producers. Their prices range from average to high.

Porter further proposes another strategic focus some organisations may have. This is *focus strategy*, which concentrates on a defined buyer group, product line or geographic market and quick response (or niche strategy).

Porter's structural analysis of industry[1]

Michael Porter identifies five basic competitive forces that determine the intensity of competition in an industry: entry, threat of substitution, bargaining power of buyers, bargaining power of suppliers, and rivalry among current competitors. These are outlined below:

- *Threat of entry.* New entrants to an industry bring new (or similar) products and services, thus increasing market competition. However, such a threat depends on six major sources of barriers to entry: (1) economies of scale; (2) product differentiation; (3) capital requirements; (4) access to distribution channels; (5) cost disadvantages independent of scale; and (6) government policy.

- *Pressure from substitute products.* All firms in an industry face this sort of pressure. Substitutes limit the potential of an industry by placing a ceiling on the prices firms can charge. For example, products made from natural fibres (e.g. jute goods) face serious pressure from synthetic substitutes. According to Porter, substitutes not only limit profits in normal times, but they also reduce the bonanza an industry can reap in boom times.

- *Bargaining power of buyers.* Buyers compete with the industry by forcing down prices, demanding higher quality or more services and playing competitors off against each other – all at the expense of industry profitability (Porter, 1980). According to Porter, a buyer group is powerful if: (a) large volumes of purchases are made; (b) products represent a significant fraction of the industry's costs; (c) products are standard or undifferentiated; (d) it faces few switching costs; (e) it earns low profits; (f) buyers pose a credible threat of backward integration; and (g) the industry's product is unimportant to the 'quality' of the buyers' products or services.

- *Bargaining power of suppliers.* A supplier group can exert bargaining power if (a) it is dominated by a few companies and is more concentrated than the industry it sells to; (b) it is not obliged to contend with other substitute products for sale to the industry; (c) the industry is not an important customer of the supplier group; (d) the supplier group's products are differentiated or it has built up switching costs; and (e) the supplier group poses a credible threat of forward integration.

- *Rivalry among existing competitors.* Rivalry among existing competitors occurs when competitors are numerous in an industry. These firms compete for everything – price, advertising, product introduction, distribution channels and after-sales services. This pattern of action affects organisational performance.

Given the above forces, in order to be competitive and to survive in the market it is essential that firms in an industry pay a great deal of attention to structural analysis and strategic choices. Structural analysis helps reduce the need for debates on where to draw industry boundaries (Porter, 1980). Also, by doing so, firms can make a choice of where to draw the line between established competitors and substitute products, between existing firms and potential entrants and between existing firms and suppliers and buyers (Porter, 1980).

Mintzberg's five Ps for strategy

Mintzberg describes organisational strategy by using five Ps. According to him, strategy is:

- a *plan* when it provides a consciously intended course of action as a guideline to deal with a situation;

- a *ploy* when it is an intended specific manoeuvre to outwit competitors;

- a *pattern* in a stream of actions for an intended strategy to be realised;

- a *position*, that is a means of positioning firms within their business environment;

- a *perspective* – an ingrained way of perceiving things that exist only in the minds of interested parties.

Note that this description of strategy takes it beyond the corporate and business levels of strategy into the functional/operational levels. Porter's five forces of competitive strategy do not drop down to this operational/functional level.

Naturally, Mintzberg's descriptions reflect the theme of his 1978 paper that intended strategies are realised strategies and that strategy formulation and implementation were separate and sequential processes. As dynamic global business environment factors have led to firms recognising the need for employee empowerment (internal business process and learning and growth perspectives) in the strategy decision process, the broadness of MAS's measures/information must be suitable for the new, less sophisticated (from an accounting perspective) users of that information (for details, see Mintzberg et al., 1995).[2]

Business mission typology

Business mission typology relates to the nature of the strategic goals pursued. It constitutes a continuum with pure *build* at one end and pure *harvest* at the other end. Market share is a paramount objective where the strategic goal is to build, even if at the cost of short-term financial results. At the other end of the continuum a harvest mission aims at maximising short-term earnings and cash flow, even if loss of market share results (Govindarajan and Gupta, 1985).

Organisations using a build mission are more likely to experience greater dependencies with external individuals. A build mission signifies additional capital investment (greater dependence on capital markets), an expansion of capacity (greater dependence on the technological investment), an increase in market share (greater dependence on customers and competitors) and an increase in production volume (greater dependence on raw material suppliers and labour market). In the long run, competitive market forces prevent the firm from passing cost increases on to customers, and sustainable competitive advantage arises only by having higher productivity than competitors or by offering specialised products and services that competitors cannot match. Thus costs might be less significant in build than in harvest situations; build units therefore are more likely to place greater emphasis on keeping production up to budgeted levels and identifying bottlenecks than are harvest units. Conversely, harvest firms operate in a stable and narrow product market (Hoque, 2000b).

Strategy and environmental uncertainty

In this book, environmental uncertainty refers to the firm's inability to predict accurately the effects of various aspects of the firm's external environment, such as customers, suppliers, deregulation and globalisation, technological processes, competitors, government regulations/policies, the economic environment and industrial relations. Emphasis is placed on top managers' perceptions of their organisation's economic, political, legal, technological and competitive environments, rather than the actual environmental uncertainty (see Gordon and Narayanan, 1984; Tymon et al., 1998).

Contingency theory literature (Thompson, 1967; Gailbraith, 1977) suggests that there is no 'best' way to approach organisations, but that the organisational design should reflect the environment in which it is found. The greater the environmental uncertainty, the greater the difficulty in predicting future events (Lawrence and Lorsch, 1967; Duncan, 1972). Hence, greater care must be taken in designing the appropriate MCS, which is essential to organisational effectiveness. There is the view that an organisation's survival depends upon 'fitness' for the changing environment. Research has shown that environmental uncertainty is a major influence on managers' use of accounting information and control systems (Gordon and Narayanan, 1984; Chenhall and Morris, 1986; Mia and Chenhall, 1994; Hoque, 2000b).

The current literature in this area suggests that the environmental uncertainty of most companies has been increasing rapidly in the 1990s driven by factors like an acceleration in the rate of technological dissemination, greater deregulation and globalisation (Hamel and Prahalad, 1994; Cooper, 1995; Goldman et al., 1995). Companies are adapting to this uncertainty by adopting strategies, structures (including size, 'downsizing' and 'right sizing') and systems (including performance evaluation) that allow flexibility, keep options open and support a fast response capability.

Whittington (1993) suggests that various approaches to strategy formulation differ widely in their advice to management under conditions of greater environmental uncertainty. He suggests that management's strategic choices are directly associated with their perceived environmental uncertainty. According to Whittington, this linkage, however, is positively associated with management's choice and use of organisational control systems. Scholars also suggest that although firms competing in the same industry face the same set of potential environmental uncertainties, management's strategic choice strongly influences which uncertainties are critical and which accounting information system is appropriate for managerial planning and decision-making. There is an association between strategy and environmental uncertainty. For example, since defender (or harvest) firms focus on searching ways to reduce production and distribution costs, to cut marketing expenses and to improve product quality to maximise short-term financial goals, they tend to experience low uncertainty. Since prospector (or build) firms compete in a broad product market domain, by introducing new products and developing new markets they are likely to face high uncertainty. Thus the level of uncertainty is high for firms following a 'prospector' (or build) strategy and it is relatively low when a 'defender' (or harvest) strategy is pursued (Hoque, 2000b).

Chapter summary

A business unit strategy focuses on two interrelated aspects: (1) its mission or goals; and (2) the way the business unit chooses to compete in its industry to accomplish its goals. Studies have shown the management control systems (MCS) need to reflect and be able to adapt to the differing strategies. Studies have concluded that MCS are contingent upon strategy and differing degrees of uncertainty attach to differing strategies.

Key terms to learn

Goals

Miles and Snow

Mission statement

Objectives

Porter's competitive strategy

Strategic business unit

Strategic decisions

Strategic goals

Strategy

Vision

Discussion questions

2.1 Why do you think it would be important for you as a manager to understand issues of strategy choice in organisations?

2.2 What factors might influence the way an organisation formulates its business strategy? Discuss.

2.3 Explain how vision, mission and strategy relate to each other. Provide examples.

2.4 How does the organisational environment affect the organisational strategy?

2.5 Assume you are a manager in the hotel industry. Develop your own company vision, mission and strategy.

2.6 How would the vision, mission, goals and strategy differ for a non-profit organisation?

2.7 What is a strategic business unit?

2.8 Explain the types or levels of strategy.

2.9 What is the difference between the build and harvest strategies?

2.10 Organisations can adopt a number of strategies to compete in the business environment including:
- quality
- cost
- customer service
- product differentiation
- technology.

Provide examples of companies that may use the strategies for competitive advantage (e.g. McDonald's requires a cost strategy).

2.11 Explain why different companies require different strategies.

2.12 Discuss how a company can use strategy to create barriers to entry. Give examples.

2.13 'By improving supplier relations the organisation can reduce the bargaining power of their supplier.' Critically evaluate this statement.

2.14 Discuss the relationships among the uncertain environment, strategy, management control system and management accounting system.

Notes

1. The discussion contained in this section is based, in part, on Michael Porter (1980). A detailed discussion on the topic is beyond the scope of this book. Readers are therefore advised to consult Porter's book for further details on the topic.

2. The author wishes to thank John Sands at Griffith University School of Accounting, Banking and Finance, Brisbane, Australia, for his insightful advice on this issue.

Further reading

Hoque, Z. (2000) 'Matching productivity measures with business mission and uncertainty', *Advances in Management Accounting*, vol. 9, pp. 109–25.

Govindarajan, V. and Gupta, A. K. (1985) 'Linking control systems to business unit strategy: impact on performance', *Accounting, Organizations and Society*, vol. 10, no. 1, pp. 51–66.

Simons, R. (1987) 'Accounting control systems and business strategy: an empirical study', *Accounting, Organizations and Society*, vol. 12, no. 4, pp. 357–74.

Simons, R. (1990) 'The role of management control systems in creating competitive advantage: new perspectives', *Accounting, Organizations and Society*, vol. 15, nos. 1 and 2, pp. 127–43.

CHAPTER 3

The basics of management control

Key learning objectives

After reading this chapter you should be able to:

- explain the concept 'management control';
- outline the emergence of the concept of 'control';
- describe the differences between planning, strategic planning, strategic management and programme planning;
- demonstrate an understanding of the effectiveness of a management control system;
- describe the differences between economy, efficiency and effectiveness;
- demonstrate an understanding of the empirical evidence on the relation between business unit strategy and management control systems.

Introduction

Over the past decades, a large amount of literature has grown up around the area of management control systems (MCS) in organisations. The subject 'management control' is rapidly approaching a theoretical and practical watershed. The myths and traditions of management control systems design and practice are all facing profound changes simultaneously. Social expectations of employing organisations and the managerial tasks within them are changing rapidly. All these, however, raise profound questions about the traditional concept of management control systems within organisations. This chapter attempts to review briefly various approaches to date to defining 'management control' and also suggests a wider definition of control in its social organisational context. This attempt perhaps will help managers, academics and students interested in this area to understand the key issues in the current debate concerning theories of management control 38 years after the publication of Robert Anthony's (1965) control models of organisation.

Management control: what is it?

The term 'control' originated from the French word 'controller', which means 'inspection' or 'to check or verify'. According to Weber's Dictionary, control means:

> Application of policies and procedures for directing, regulating and coordinating production, administration and other business activities in a way to achieve the objective of the enterprise. (Cited in Otley and Berry, 1980, p. 232)

The management control system (MCS) has traditionally been viewed as an analytical and calculative process to make decisions in the accomplishment of an organisation's objectives. In his seminal book, Professor Robert Anthony (1965) defined management control as 'the process by which managers assure that resources are obtained and used effectively and efficiently in the accomplishment of an organisation's goals'. Horngren, Foster and Datar (2000, p. 4) define 'control' as '(a) deciding on and taking actions that implement the planning decisions and (b) deciding on performance evaluation and the related feedback that will help future decision making'. Feedback refers to the examination of past performance and systematically exploring alternative ways to make better informed decisions in the future (Horngren, Foster and Datar, 2000).

Much of the literature has been devoted to exploring the rational processes of controlling people, things and events within organisations. These processes have three common elements: (a) a process of comparing performance with standard; (b) a process of feedback; and (c) corrective actions to change the process if necessary to maintain its performance as near as possible to the standard. Such a rational control model stresses the technical aspects of control systems with the aim of rationality fostering efficiency, order and stability within organisations, and it forms the basis of the range of formal coordination and control systems that exist within organisations.

In summing up, the MCS is a means of gathering data to aid and coordinate the process of making planning and control decisions throughout the organisation. The literature focuses on a number of interrelated components that comprise an organisation's MCS:

- strategy, strategic planning and strategic management;

- accountability structure (corporate governance);

- responsibility accounting (such as budgeting);

- performance measurement;

- direction;

- motivation;

- incentives.

The key to formulating an MCS is in understanding the interdependence of the components. None can effectively be managed without considering its impact on other components and how they support each other (Rotch, 1993). According to Emmanuel et al. (1990), a complete MCS will encompass internal functions, people's reaction and controls design. Ansari (1977) proposes integrating structural and behavioural views in relation to an effective MCS. He suggests that the structural view is concerned with informational content, while behavioural views reflect the relationship between managers and subordinates, and the interaction needed to achieve desired outcomes. It is also suggested that if these two views are not considered in unison, there may be problems associated with the neglect of either. Therefore management must choose a suitable mix of MCS, whereby the cognitive conflict between managers and subordinates is minimised (for a good review of the MCS literature, see Rotch, 1993 and Simons, 2000).

The emergence of the concept of 'control'

There are a number of conflicting views regarding the best manner in which to manage an organisation. However, theorists as well as practising managers agree that good management requires effective 'control'. A combination of planned objectives, organisation structure, capable direction and motivation has little probability of success unless there exists an adequate system of control. There are many factors that make control a necessity in today's organisations. They include the changing environment of organisations, the increased complexity within organisations, the fallibility of organisational members and the need of managers to delegate authority.

Control is closely interrelated with organisations, as traditional theorist Arnold Tannenbaum (1968), while studying the control of many different types of organisations, argues: *organisation without some form of control is impossible.*

A general nature of control is that it places emphasis upon performance and the monitoring of activities that facilitate the accomplishment of an organisation's objectives. The concept 'control' within organisations as a tool of management accounting emerged a long time ago from the management writer, F. W. Taylor (1949), who considered 'control' to be a scientific form of management, whereby rules of thumb are applied to all organisational actors, including the workers. Later, Alfred Sloan (former president of the General Motors Corporation) also, among others, contributed to the emergence of the concept of 'control' in organisations.

In the early part of this century, General Motors faced serious problems in its survival in the economy due to the failure of its management systems to cope with rapid growth, large size and a volatile environment. Sloan formulated a philosophy of management, 'decentralised with coordinated control', which proved central to General Motor's survival in industrial history. Sloan (1963) in his book *My Years with General Motors* noted: 'If we had the means to review and judge the effectiveness of operations we could safely leave the prosecutions of those operations to the men in charge of them' (p. 140; quoted in Macintosh, 1985, p. 239). The traditional thoughts of effectiveness in financial controls became known later as 'management controls' (Macintosh, 1985).

Management theorists (such as Koontz and O'Donnell, 1972) as well as accounting scholars (such as Anthony, 1965; Ijiri, 1965) view control as a feedback process, so that objectives are maximised. They view management control as a subset of the total of managerial activity (planning, motivating, coordinating, staffing, directing, controlling), designed to ensure that individuals, organisations and societies satisfy their goals.

Thus management controls have tended to concentrate on the optimal means–end relationship. Such a relationship focuses on economy, efficiency and effectiveness within an organisation. However, these views are regarded as problematic, because of their restricted conceptions of the social world and their assumptions of objectivity and economic rationality (Chua, 1989).

A number of accounting researchers have used alternative approaches, such as the open systems and cybernetic approaches, to study control systems in organisations (Otley and Berry, 1980; Hofstede, 1981). When viewed from an 'open systems approach', organisations are being seen as organisms that process inputs from the environment back as outputs (Ansari, 1979). Such an approach provides a means of viewing and describing environmental influences and interdepartmental dependencies.

Cybernetic notions are central to the open systems approach (Ashby, 1956). Viewed as a cybernetic concept, management control has been defined as the process of ensuring that the organisation is adapted to its environment and is pursuing courses of action that will enable it to achieve its purposes (Otley and Berry, 1980, p. 233). From the work of Tocher (1970), Otley and Berry (1980) derived a model of the cybernetic control process having identified four necessary conditions that any control system must include:

- the existence of an objective or standard that is desired (otherwise control has no meaning);

- the measurement of process outputs along the dimension specified by the objective (output of the process must be measurable);

- the ability to predict the effect of potential control actions (a predictive model of the system is required);

- the ability to act in a way that will reduce deviations from the objective (a selected action requires to be implemented).

Of the four necessary conditions stated above, the construction of predictive models for control is likely to be a central concern of the control system design. Having identified a discrepancy between actual and standard outcomes, a predictive model process is necessary for a control action to be determined. According to Otley and Berry (1980), this predictive model provides a means for forecasting the likely outcomes of various alternative courses of action; without such a model, control is impossible and may be counterproductive (p. 236).

From the cybernetic viewpoint, Hofstede (1981) argues that different forms of activities may demand quite different forms of control. Based on this notion he formulated a cybernetic control model, which he believes can be applied to public and not-for-profit activities. He proposes six types of control (e.g. routine, expert, trial and error, intuitive, judgmental or political control) applicable to an organisation, depending on the nature and type of activities within it. It is thus clear that the nature of the activities is fundamental to the adoption of any control mechanism (for details, see Hofstede, 1981).

The fundamental concern of the cybernetic model of control is negative feedback controls. The basic control is therefore to reduce differences that may occur between actual outputs and those considered desirable.

In recent years, scholars have focused on social interactions and decision-making in organisations within the broad framework of impersonal forces such as uncertainty, interdependence among organisational components, specialisation arrangements, integrative mechanisms and technology. As discussed in Chapter 1, scholars have labelled this the 'contingent approach'. According to this approach, an MCS depends upon certain contingent variables. In other words, the control system must be matched with environmental circumstances and also with different parts of the organisation. Viewing from such a perspective, accounting scholars have investigated why accounting and control practices differ from situation to situation and what factors influence the design and functioning of accounting and control systems in organisations.

Some scholars (e.g. March and Simon, 1958; Lindblom, 1959; Cyert and March, 1963; March, 1989) have advocated a more realistic approach to control, labelling it 'political' or 'pluralistic' control. This model suggests that control within an organisation can be achieved by maintaining a network of rules and regulations that permit bargaining between groups. Following this approach, management control is seen to be within the wider context of the diversity of interests among organisational members, their conflicts and the power structure prevailing in the organisation.

As opposed to the presumptions of traditional control models, the pluralistic approach assumes the organisation to be pluralistic and divided into various interests and subunits. Thus, in viewing organisations as coalitions, this approach provides a source of ideas and insights into organisational control to show how control is achieved through political processes within organisations. Seen in such a context, political models attempt to diagnose the power distribution in an organisation, that is they consider who the players are and what their relative positions should be.

Planning, strategic planning, strategic management and programme planning: how do they relate?

Planning is the making of decisions that determine *what* the company will do and *how* it will do it – *what* products to sell, *where* to acquire them, *how* to market them and *where* and so on. Planning, therefore, can be defined as choosing goals, predicting results under various alternative ways of achieving those goals and then deciding how to attain the desired goals. Planning isn't a single process – it is a series of related processes, some with long time horizons, some focusing on the immediate future.

Strategic planning is the process of deciding in broad terms how to implement the organisation's goals, that is the reasons why the organisation exists. Anthony, Dearden and Vancil (1965, p. 4) provide a comprehensive definition of strategic planning:

> Strategic planning is the process of deciding on the objectives of the organization, on changes in these objectives, on the resources used to attain these objectives and on the policies that are to govern the acquisition, use and disposition of these resources.

Thus, strategic planning includes decisions about the types of businesses and markets that an organisation operates in and decisions about how those businesses and activities will be financed. Strategic planning helps managers formulate the plans and activities that will bring their organisation closer to its goals.

Strategic management is the process of analysing and practising strategy, including the implementation of strategic plans.

Programme planning is the process by which management decides how best to implement its strategy, given the resources available to it in a specified time period. If the time period is a year or less, we refer to programme planning as *budgeting* and its output as a *budget*; for longer periods, the term is long-term planning and the product is a *long-term plan*.

Taylor (1975), in his article 'Strategies for planning', discusses the main differences between strategic and operational planning. These are summarised in Table 3.1.

Table 3.1 Strategies for planning

	Strategic planning	**Operational planning**
Focus	Longer-term survival and development	Operational problems
Objective	Future profits	Present profits
Constraints	Future resources environment	Present resource environment
Rewards	Development of future potential	Efficiency, stability
Information	Future opportunities	Present opportunities
Organisation	Entrepreneurial/flexible	Bureaucratic/stable
Leadership	Inspires radical change	Conservative
Problem solving	Anticipates, finds new approaches High risk	Reacts, relies on past experience Low risk

Source: Adapted from Taylor, B. (1975), 'Strategies for planning', *Long Range Planning*, vol. 8, no. 4, p. 38.

Effectiveness of management control systems

There are many factors that make control necessary in today's organisations. They include: the changing environment of organisations; the increased complexity within organisations; the fallibility of organisational members; and the need of managers to delegate authority.

Thus, an organisation's MCS is influenced by the behaviour of competitors, the nature of the industry within which the organisation operates, and changes in its business environment. The system effectiveness depends on how well its components are responded to. An effective MCS should demonstrate the following attributes:

- *Goal congruence.* To what extent the MCS contributes to the goal congruence of the corporate company. Goal congruence refers to the consistency between the personal goals that a manager has because of the control system's influence and the goals of the organisation that derive from its strategy. For example, if the performance measure is not suitable, it may result in agency costs to the organisation as the manager attempts to achieve his own goals rather than the strategic goals set by management. This in turn leads to goals being incongruent. Therefore it is necessary to select appropriate measures that give appropriate directions to the manager. If these directions are not consistent with corporate strategy, the control system has promoted incongruence and led to goal incongruence in the organisation.

- *Employee motivation.* An employee's desire to achieve a selected goal (set by management). An MCS should focus on how well it motivates individuals to strive towards achieving organisational goals. This is often achieved through the selection of related performance indicators and setting appropriate rewards for achieving the desired result.

- *Formal and informal control mechanisms.* What sorts of formal and informal control mechanisms are in place in the organisation? For example, reward systems, culture, etc.

- *System goals and risk sharing.* Is there a system of risk sharing among various divisions of the organisation? For example, what team performance measurement systems and subsequent reward systems are in place?

Merchant (1982) suggests that good control can be achieved by avoiding behavioural problems and/or by implementing one or more types of the following tools:

- *Control-problem avoidance.* Managers can avoid some control problems by allowing no opportunity for improper behaviour. One example of this action would be automation. Other options include centralisation, risk-sharing schemes and elimination of a business or an operation entirely.

- *Control of specific actions.* This type of control attempts to ensure that employees and workers perform (or do not perform) certain actions that are desirable (or undesirable) by management. Other control tools may include feedback control (action plan), direct supervision, formal planning and review.

- *Control of results.* This type of control focuses on actual outcomes or results.

- *Control of personnel.* This emphasises a reliance on the personnel involved to do what is best for the organisation. It includes such actions as improved communications, peer review and education and training.

A general guideline for comparing alternative systems is to focus on predicting how each system will affect the collective actions of managers. The management accounting literature suggests that the highly competitive environment in which companies operate and their complex organisational structures may cause a company to fail if the interrelated components are not working in unison.

Economy, efficiency and effectiveness: what are they and how do they relate?

Economy concerns inputs. In a broad sense it means the acquisition of sufficient quality and quantity of financial, human, physical and information resources at the appropriate times at the lowest cost (Parker, 2001).

In contrast *efficiency* concerns both inputs and outputs. It means the use of financial, human, physical and information resources so that output is maximised for any given set of resource inputs, or input is minimised for any given quantity and quality of output (Parker, 2001).

Effectiveness refers to the performance or actual outcome of an organisation. It is the achievement of the objectives or other intended effects of activities.

Organisational effectiveness depends on how well changes in the microenvironment (industrial structure) and macro-environment (social, technological, economic and political factors) are responded to. In addition to financial performance, organisations must look at non-financial performance, such as customer and employee satisfaction, because they are important organisational elements. The customer has a strong desire to obtain 'high-quality' products or services, but now the major focus is also on 'high value'. This means that the customer wants what is perceived as high quality, but it must be available for what is perceived as a fair price (Hansen and Riis, 1996). However, the biggest challenge to the organisation is how to motivate employees to perform very well so that it can achieve this goal. This means that this new corporate culture must be related to the rewards. Employees have to be educated in achieving customer satisfaction. To yield a high-quality product or service, they will need to be educated in the principles of customer satisfaction and will have to be shown its benefits for their organisation as well as themselves. The main focus of strategic management accounting is to help the management team by providing the relevant accounting information for the achievement of economy, efficiency and effectiveness.

Business unit strategy and management control systems: empirical evidence

Defenders tend to have a functional structure and formalised hierarchical information flows, are planning intensive and are centralised; finance and production are the most important functions and controls emphasise efficiency. On the other hand, prospectors tend to have a flexible structure, that is low formalisation and low division of labour, are decentralised and have lateral information flows; marketing and research and development are the most important functions and performance measures stress effectiveness in innovation.

Simons (1987) found that prospector firms use a high degree of forecast data in their MCS, emphasise tight budget goals and outputs are closely monitored. Defender firms use budget systems less intensively, like little change in systems and managers' rewards are related to budget achievement. Simons found a negative association between profit performance and tight and close budget controls.

Interestingly, in his 1990 case study of top managers' use of controls in two large companies (one defender and one prospector), Simons found similar MCS but used differently by managers. His results are summarised in Table 3.2.

Competitive strategy and costing systems: empirical evidence

Research (Shank and Govindarajan, 1989) has found significant variation in cost systems between strategic emphases by firms. Table 3.3 summarises these below.

Table 3.2 Managers' use of management control tools in defender and prospector firms

Management control systems	Defender firm	Prospector firm
Strategy reviews	Sporadic, little debate	Intensive, annual, debated
Financial goals	Set by top management	Established by strategic business units and intensive reviews
Budget preparation	Must meet financial targets	Prepared by segments, strategic
Finance coordinate meetings	Focus, coordinated in meetings	Little formalisation
Budget review	None in year	Rebuilt three times a year
Programme review	Product and process programmes monitored and cut at all levels	Programmes limited to R&D
Rewards	Bonus on profits over target	Subjective evaluation in MBO (management by objectives)

Table 3.3 Cost systems and strategic emphasis

Cost systems	Product differentiation strategy	Cost leadership strategy
Standard costs and performance evaluation	Not very important	Very important
Use of costing, e.g. flexible budgeting, for manufacturing cost control	Moderate to low	High to very high
Perceived importance of meeting budgets	Moderate to low	High to very high
Importance of marketing cost analysis	Critical to success	Often not done formally
Importance of product costing for pricing decisions	Low	High
Importance of competitor cost analysis	Low	High

Business unit mission and incentive systems: empirical evidence

Govindarajan and Gupta (1985) found significant variation in the use of incentive plans and performance measurement systems between the build strategy and harvest strategy. Their results are summarised in Table 3.4.

Table 3.4 Incentive plans and performance measurement systems in build and harvest firms

Strategy	Incentive plans	Performance measures
Build (increase market share in growing market, low profits and cash flow)	Long-run focus	Subjective (mostly non-financial)
Harvest (high but declining market share, maximise short-run earnings and cash flow	Short-run focus	Objective, mainly budget-based

Chapter summary

This chapter has reviewed the body of research and issues that have emerged in the area of MCS in organisations since the 1920s. It has critically examined the various approaches to control with a view to more clearly focusing on the key issues in this body of knowledge.

During its formative years MCS theory concerned itself with the development of general principles and ideal types of control systems. It was believed that once these principles were developed, they could be applied universally. This line of reasoning, however, is giving way slowly to a different idea. A behavioural approach suggests that human forces within organisations influence organisational processes. Many studies in the 1940s and 1950s followed this lead. In the 1960s, a separate line of inquiry emerged integrating various approaches to organisation. This approach argues that environment and technology have a good deal of influence on the structure of control systems. This body of knowledge establishes the influence of several contingent variables on the control systems in practice within organisations. Another group of scholars view the organisation as a coalition and stress the diversity of interests, the conflicts between and the power structure of individuals within organisations, which may impinge upon the functioning of control processes in the organisation.

Key terms to learn

Economy	Planning
Effectiveness	Programme planning
Efficiency	Strategic management
Incentive systems	Strategic planning
Management control systems	Strategy

Discussion questions

3.1 What is the management control system (MCS)? Describe how the components of the control system are interrelated.

3.2 Why do you have to consider behavioural views when designing the MCS?

3.3 Discuss the relationships among strategic planning, strategic management and programme planning.

3.4 Describe how goal congruence relates to MCS effectiveness.

3.5 What are the relationships between economy, efficiency and effectiveness? Define each of these concepts and discuss.

3.6. What is the difference between the formal and informal control system? Provide examples.

3.7 Discuss why informal systems are important?

3.8. Develop the cost system strategy for a retail company such as Coles Myer Supermarkets.

3.9 What factors do you have to consider when designing incentive systems?

3.10 Why is it necessary to have a long-term focus for incentive plans?

3.11 Performance measures should include non-financial and financial measures. Critically evaluate this statement.

Further reading

Gosselin, M. (1997) 'The effect of strategy and organisational structure on the adoption and implementation of activity-based costing', *Accounting, Organizations and Society*, vol. 22, no. 2, pp. 105–22.

Langfield-Smith, K. (1997) 'Management control systems and strategy: a critical review', *Accounting, Organizations and Society*, vol. 22, no. 2, 207–32.

CHAPTER 4

Cost allocations and activity-based costing and activity-based management

Key learning objectives

After reading this chapter you should be able to:

- demonstrate an understanding of how organisations allocate costs to products or services;
- explain the role of activity-based costing (ABC) and the use of ABC information in decision-making;
- outline the basic steps in the ABC methodology;
- demonstrate an understanding of how organisations classify their activities within an ABC methodology;
- explain the difference between traditional cost systems and ABC;
- identify the limitations of an ABC system.
- Explain the concept 'activity-based management' (ABM) and illustrate its basic elements.

Introduction

The use of modern manufacturing practices such as automation, computer controlled machines, robotics and just-in-time (JIT) manufacturing can significantly change the structure of the costs of production – with very large changes in the relative proportions of direct materials, direct labour, inventory holding costs and the costs of technology. Management accounting literature has seen the development of an alternative approach for allocating costs to individual products in the 1980s; this is commonly known as ABC or activity-based costing, or more recently as ABM or activity-based management. This chapter is devoted to discussing these developments in management accounting.

Cost allocation to products and services: how do organisations do it?

Traditional cost systems use volume-driven allocation bases, such as direct labour hours and machine hours, to assign common organisational expenses to individual products or services. Such allocations are needed for, among other things, inventory valuation in the financial accounts. In practice, many of the organisational resource demands by individual products and customers are not proportional to the volume of units produced or sold (Cooper and Kaplan, 1992). Consequently, the above conventional cost allocation practice suffers from the following limitations:

- It ignores non-volume-related support activities, such as material handling, material procurement, set-ups, production scheduling and inspection activities.

- Assumption that products consume *all* resources in proportion to their production volumes may result in distorted product costs.

- It is inappropriate in today's organisational environment where companies produce a wide range of products and experience intense global competition.

Traditional manufacturing involves routine manufacturing processes with high-labour content which are relatively simple. In such an environment, cost allocation using direct labour hours or direct labour costs are adequate. However, in a highly technical manufacturing environment, the labour content is declining rapidly. Consequently, product costing based on traditional costing systems involve very high overhead allocation rates.

Activity-based costing: what is it and what does it offer?

In recent years there has been considerable comment expressing concerns with traditional costing systems, which focus on volume-based cost allocations and short-term cost information usage in organisations (Hoque, 2000a). The changing manufacturing environment requires a concomitant shift from traditional cost accounting methods to ones that capture and reflect the firm's manufacturing environment.

This traditional cost system assumes that products consume all resources in proportion to their production volumes. But many organisational resources exist for activities that are unrelated to the physical volume of units produced. Consequently, traditional volume-based cost allocation practices may report distorted product costs. Cost accounting literature has proposed a shift to an alternative basis for costing – activity-based costing (ABC) – which assumes that activities cause costs and that products (and customers) create the demands for activities. Under an ABC system, costs are assigned to products based on individual products' consumption or demand for each activity.

The Chartered Institute of Management Accountants (CIMA) defines ABC as:

> Cost attribution to cost units on the basis of benefit received from indirect activities, e.g. ordering, setting-up, assuring quality.

ABC endeavours first to establish the cost of the activities going on in the various factory departments, which are creating the overheads and then relating these activities to the products. Under ABC, a cost driver is used, which is simply a driver of the work being created or generated, in other words the activity that drives the costs. CIMA defines a cost driver as an activity that generates cost. Cost pools or cost centres are activity accounts (the general ledger cost accounts) set up to collect the costs created by each activity.

Steps in the ABC methodology

Figure 4.1 sums up the ABC process.

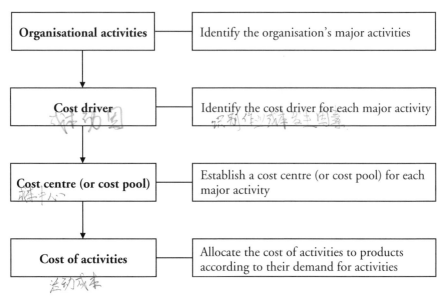

Figure 4.1 Steps in the ABC methodology.

Classification of organisational activities for an ABC system

Under an ABC system, the following activities can be identified (Cooper, 1990):

- *Unit-level activities* relate to the number of units produced. Related expenses include direct labour, direct materials, energy costs and expenses (depreciation and maintenance).

- *Batch-related activities* include setting up a machine or processing a purchase order, production scheduling, and material handling, movement and inspection.

- *Product-sustaining activities* are supporting activities to different products in the product line (e.g. engineering activities). Expenses include engineering costs, design development, tests, etc.

- *Facility-sustaining (or service-sustaining) activities* relate to administration, plant management, accounting services and lighting and heating of the factory that cannot be traced to individual products or services, but support the organisation as a whole. Expenses include costs related to these activities.

Table 4.1 gives a list of potential costs drivers in a manufacturing context.

Table 4.1 Potential cost drivers

Manufacturing activity	Potential cost drivers
Unit level	Weight of direct material used Number of direct labour hours Number of machine hours Number of kilowatt-hours used
Batch level	Amount of material handling Number of setups Number of inspections Amount of production scheduling
Product-sustaining (or service-sustaining) level	Hours of engineering labour Equipment maintenance hours The time spent by designers
Facility-sustaining level	General administration hours Building security and rent (Note: It is difficult to find good cause-and-effect relationships between these costs and a cost-allocation base. So some companies may use direct labour hours to allocate facility-sustaining related costs to products or service. For details, see Horngren et al., 2000.)

Traditional cost systems and activity-based cost systems: how do they differ?

Traditional costing systems measure accurately volume-related resources that are consumed in proportion to the number of units produced of the individual products. Such resources include direct labour, materials, energy and machine-related costs. However, many organisational resources exist for activities that are unrelated to physical volume. Non-volume-related activities consist of support activities, such as material handling, material procurement, set-ups, production scheduling and inspection activities.

ABC assumes that activities cause costs and that products (and customers) create the demands for activities. ABC analysis focuses on how costs react to changes in activity level. Costs are assigned to products based on individual products' consumption or demand for each activity.

(ABC simply recognises that businesses must understand the factors that drive each major activity, the cost of activities and how activities relate to products.)

Review example – traditional cost allocation versus ABC

To highlight the difference between traditional cost allocation and an ABC allocation system the following illustration is used.

Gamma Products manufacture product A and product B. The following information is available from this company:

	Product A	Product B
Materials ($)	120,000	125,000
Direct labour ($)	60,000	75,000
Units produced	10,000	15,000
Direct labour hours	3,000	5,000
Machine hours	1,200	2,500
Engineering labour hours	125	250
Set-ups	60	70

The overheads have been absorbed on the direct labour cost method: $4 per direct labour hour. The following details are also available:

Machine-related overhead	$350,000
Set-ups	$120,000
Engineering costs	$220,000

Traditional costing system:

Overhead allocation:

Product A: 3,000 direct labour hours × $4.00 per hour = $12,000
Product B: 5,000 direct labour hours × $4.00 per hour = $20,000

$$\frac{12,000}{3,000} = \frac{Overhead\ cost}{direct\ labour\ hours} = \frac{Overhead}{\&\ absorption\ rate}$$

Company's total cost to produce the products:

Product A:
Direct material $120,000 + Direct labour $60,000 + Overhead $120,000 = $300,000

Product B:
Direct material $125,000 + Direct labour $75,000 + Overhead $200,000 = $400,000

ABC system:

Cost pool rates:

Machine-related overhead rate:
Total machine overhead $350,000/(Machine hours for A and B 1,200 + 2,500) = $94.60

Set-ups rate:
Total set-ups costs $120,000/(Set-ups for A and B 60 + 70) = $923.08

Engineering rate:
Total engineering costs $220,000/(Engineering hours for A and B 125 + 250) = $586.67

Costs assigned to products:

	Product A	Product B	Total
Machine-related overhead (Machine hours × $94.60)	$113,520	$236,500	$350,020
Set-ups costs (No. of setups × $923.08)	$55,385	$64,616	$120,001
Engineering costs	$73,334	$146,668	$220,002
Total costs	$242,239	$447,784	$690,023

Limitations of ABC

An ABC system, however, suffers from practical deficiencies. In theory, it should be possible to trace all overheads, but in practice it is quite likely that there will be some costs that cannot be traced, for example the costs of the head office administrative staff. Consequently, arbitrary allocations are likely to remain (Hoque, 2000a). The recent management accounting literature focuses more on the management side of activity-based costing, rather than the technical aspect only. The following section elaborates on this in turn.

Activity-based management: what is it and what does it offer?

Activity-based management (ABM) has been defined (Hansen and Mowen, 1997) as a system-wide, integrated approach that focuses management's attention on activities with the objective of improving customer value and the firm's profit. Therefore, it is not just a system; it is a new way of planning and controlling an organisation to achieve excellence (Digman, 1999). ABM includes ABC and a host of complementary ABC concepts, such as process improvement, modern manufacturing methods (focused, cellular, continuous flow, JIT) and employee empowerment. The ABM philosophy contends that management must focus on the performance criteria that *all* global competitors can use as common denominators – the productivity and efficiency of activities that support value-adding business processes, which must deliver the highest value at the lowest total cost (Digman, 1999). The following paragraphs discuss these in turn.

Process value analysis (PVA) is rooted in the philosophy that management must focus on accountability for activities rather than *only* on costs and emphasise the maximisation of system-wide performance instead of individual performance. PVA's focus is on driver analysis, activity analysis and performance evaluation.

Driver analysis helps identify the root cause of activity costs. The following factors cause activity costs: *activity input* – the resources consumed by the activity in producing its output; and *activity output* – the result or product of an activity.

Activity analysis is concerned with identifying, describing and evaluating an organisation's activities. It assists the organisation in seeking answers to the following major issues:

- what activities are done;

- how many people perform the activities;

- the time and resources required to perform the activities;

- an assessment of the value of the activities to the organisation, including recommendation to select and keep only those that add value.

Value added activities focus on two types of activities: (1) required activities – those are required to comply with legal mandates (e.g. the reporting requirements); and (2) discretionary activities – those that add value. The costs to perform value-added activities with perfect efficiency are classified as value-added cost. Non-value-added activities are unnecessary, that is all activities other than those that are absolutely essential to remain in business, for example scheduling, moving, inspecting, waiting (work-in-progress (WIP) time), rework, storing, etc. Costs that are caused either by non-value-added activities or the inefficient performance of value-added activities are classified as non-valued-added costs.

Activity-based performance evaluation. Measuring performance is critical to strategic management and control. ABM also focuses on measuring and analysing performance based on organisational activities. The recent development of the balanced scorecard philosophy is consistent with the idea of activity-based performance measurement. Additionally, in recent years, a number of approaches have arisen to help strategic managers evaluate and control their organisation's performance. These are discussed in Chapters 10, 11 and 12.

Chapter summary

ABC is simply based on the premise that businesses must understand the factors that drive each major activity, the cost of activities and how activities relate to products in order to run the business efficiently and effectively. The concept originated in management accounting in the early 1980s and continues to dominate the management accounting field. More recently, the philosophy of ABC has been expanded to include the strategic management of the firm by focusing on managing costs for organisational activities. As a result we now have ABM or activity-based management, where emphasis is on not only costs, but also on activity analysis, activity-based budgeting, activity performance management and the like.

Key terms to learn

ABC methodology
Activity-based costing (ABC)

Activity-based management
Cost allocation

Discussion questions

4.1 Describe the changes in the business environment that have reduced the effectiveness of conventional cost systems.

4.2 Conventional costing systems apply overhead using volume-based drivers. List five drivers. Explain why the use of such drivers can be problematic in the new business environment.

4.3 'Conventional costing systems do not suit businesses with high product diversity, overhead-intensive cost structures or where a large proportion of overhead costs are fixed.' Critically evaluate this statement.

4.4 Explain the steps in the ABC methodology. How do these differ from conventional costing systems?

4.5 List possible drivers for the following activities of a DVD player manufacturer:
- process sales orders;
- issue materials;
- assemble player;
- insert motor;
- design player.

4.6 Discuss the relationship between ABM and ABC.

4.7 Classify the following organisational activities into unit level, batch related, product sustaining and facility sustaining:
- manage plant;
- process sales order;
- prepare accounts;
- inspect product;
- operate cutting machine.

4.8 Discuss how an organisation can eliminate non-value-added costs.

4.9 Explain how an organisation can eliminate non-value activities such as inspection and storage, and still maintain high-quality products and productivity levels.

4.10 What are the limitations to activity-based costing?

4.11 Discuss the relationship between firm strategy and ABC and ABM.

Further reading

Anderson, S. W. (1995) 'A framework for assessing cost management system changes: the case of activity-based costing implementation at General Motors, 1986–1993', *Journal of Management Accounting Research*, vol. 7, pp. 1–51.

Cobb, I., Innes, J. and Mitchell, F. (1993) 'Activity-based costing problems: the British experience', *Advances in Management Accounting*, pp. 68–83.

Cokins, G. (1999) 'Using ABC to become ABM', *Journal of Cost Management*, January/February, pp. 29–35.

Ittner, C. D., Larcker, D. F. and Randall, T. (1997) 'The activity-based cost hierarchy, production policies and firm profitability', *Journal of Management Accounting Research*, vol. 9, pp. 143–62.

Shields, M. D. (1995) 'An empirical analysis of firms' implementation experiences with activity-based costing', *Journal of Management Accounting Research*, Fall, pp. 148–66.

CHAPTER 5

Advanced manufacturing technology, JIT, target costing and product life-cycle costing

Key learning objectives

After reading this chapter you should be able to:

- explain the impact of advanced manufacturing technology in today's business environment;
- outline the different types of production management strategies;
- explain the concept 'the just-in-time (JIT) approach';
- describe the differences between traditional manufacturing and JIT;
- demonstrate an understanding of the implications of production management strategies for the design and use of MAS;
- demonstrate an understanding of the relation between JIT production and automation;
- demonstrate an understanding of the relation between JIT production and ABC;
- demonstrate an understanding of the relation between automation and ABC;
- explain the concepts 'target costing' and 'product life-cycle costing'.

Introduction

Management accounting should support the manufacturing goals of an organisation. It is therefore important that management accountants understand the manufacturing systems, production management strategies and advanced manufacturing technology (AMT) used in their organisations. In this chapter I shall focus on manufacturing systems and strategies and consider their implications for the design and use of management accounting systems (MAS).

Advanced manufacturing technology

Today, companies are becoming increasingly aware that excellence in manufacturing can provide a competitive weapon in highly competitive markets. In order to compete effectively, companies must be capable of manufacturing innovative products of high quality at a low cost and also provide first-class customer service. At the same time, they must have the flexibility to cope with short product life-cycles, demands for greater product variety from more discriminating customers and increasing international competition. World-class manufacturing companies have responded to these competitive demands by changing the production process in order to improve quality, reduce set-up times and increase manufacturing flexibility.

World-class companies have invested in AMT such as computer-aided design (CAD), computer-aided manufacturing (CAM), robotics, computer-aided engineering (CAE), computerised numerical control machines (CNC), enterprise resource planning (ERP) systems and flexible manufacturing systems (FMS).

CAD replaces the traditional draftsman or engineer's table with a computer terminal. It helps optimise ideas on new products and manipulates, simplifies and minimises the cost of investment in inventory (Drury, 1992). CAM consists of robotics, numerically controlled machines and computer numerically controlled machines. CNC encompasses a broad range of programmable machine tools. It is often used to denote early numerically controlled machines, which used coded paper tapes to store various set-up and machining instructions for performing operations such as cutting and grinding. Instead of using paper tapes, computer numerically controlled machines entail the use of a computer in or alongside the NC machine and computer programs are used to store the various configurations and to perform the machining operations (Drury, 1992). An FMS is a combination of a computer numerically controlled machine and automated material-handling equipment. It consists of a cluster of machine tools, a robot to change the workpieces and system conveyor belts that shuttle the workpiece from tool to tool, all operating under computer control to produce a variety of parts automatically (Drury, 1992). Computer-integrated manufacturing (CIM) consists of a series of automated subsystems within the factory, which is controlled entirely through a computer network that does not need human beings. It integrates many or all of the elements of AMT into one coherent integrated system (Drury, 1992).

Several others (e.g. Kaplinsky, 1984; Lei and Goldhar, 1991; Meredith, 1987) consider AMT to be multidimensional, which may include computer-assisted design and engineering, computer-controlled manufacturing and computerised accounting, inventory control systems and shop-floor tracking systems (Jonsson, 2000). Some also use the term 'automation' to mean AMT (Hoque, 2000a). AMT helps alter the rules of competition in industries, in effect creating an environment in which the firm has a competitive edge based on its use of AMTs (Jonsson, 2000). Jonsson suggests that greater product variety can be derived from flexible and modular production set-up, but also from the use of group technology and flow-oriented layouts. As a result of AMT, there is less downtime required to shift between families of products or components, which in turn can result in greater productivity.

Production management strategies

The operations and production management literature suggests a number of production management strategies. These are:

1. materials requirement and manufacturing resources planning systems (MRP);

2. optimised production technology (OPT);

3. just-in-time (JIT) manufacturing systems.

An MRP system determines (a) the quantity and timing of finished goods demanded, (b) the requirements for raw materials components and (c) subassemblies prior to each stage of production. To operate an MRP system the organisation must have (a) a master production schedule; (b) a bills of material file; (c) an inventory file; and (d) a master parts file.

OPT philosophy contends that the primary goal of manufacturing is to make money. Three important criteria are identified to evaluate progress towards achieving this goal. These are throughput, inventory and operating expenses. *Throughput* refers to the time from when a product starts along the production line until the time it becomes a finished good (Drury, 1992).

The just-in-time approach

The success of Japanese firms in international markets has generated interest among many western companies as to how this success was achieved. It is claimed that the implementation of JIT production methods has been one of the major factors contributing to this success. The JIT approach involves a continuous commitment to the pursuit of excellence in all phases of manufacturing systems design and operations. The aims of JIT are to produce the required items, at the required quality and in the required quantities, at the precise time they are required.

In particular, JIT seeks to achieve the following primary goals:

* elimination of non-value added activities;

* zero inventory;

* zero defects;

* batch sizes of one;

* zero breakdowns;

* a 100 per cent on-time delivery service.

JIT production is an evolutionary process, which aims to produce the required items, at the required quality and in the required quantities, at the precise time they are required. JIT adoption promotes manufacturing excellence by focusing on quality and on the manufacturing process rather than on products.

JIT versus traditional manufacturing

A JIT production system is different from a traditional manufacturing system in many ways. Table 5.1 illustrates this.

Table 5.1 Demonstrating the main differences between traditional manufacturing and JIT manufacturing, and their impacts on management accounting systems

	Traditional manufacturing	**JIT manufacturing**
Throughput time	Processing time + inspection time + conveyance time + waiting time	Processing time only
Optimum lot size (production)	More than one	One
Set-up time and costs	Long set-up time and therefore high costs	Zero set-up time and thereby no set-up costs
The need for holding inventory	A back-up exists to keep production flowing	Zero inventory
Quality management	Provision for waste, scrap, rework, etc.	Zero-defects; quality environment
Number of suppliers and relationships	Large number of suppliers and short-run relationships	Fewer suppliers and long-term relationships
Factory layout	More space is needed	Reduces the need for space
Management accounting systems	Greater emphasis on costing (short-run strategy)	Greater emphasis on cost management (long-term strategy)
Performance evaluation systems	Greater emphasis on financial indicators (e.g. ROI)	Greater emphasis on non-financial indicators (e.g. customer satisfaction)

The implications of production management strategies for the design and use of cost/management accounting systems

The design of cost and management accounting systems for recording product costs for inventory valuation and periodic profit reporting is influenced by the manufacturing system and the production strategy that has been implemented. In this section I shall examine the implications of AMT and modern production strategies for cost and management accounting systems.

MRP and cost accounting systems. MRP provides the basis for production scheduling and raw materials purchasing. Consequently, it does not influence the design of product costing systems for allocating costs between cost of goods sold and inventories (Drury, 1992).

OPT and cost accounting systems. Overhead should be allocated to products based on throughput time. Management can signal to operating managers that reducing throughput time can reduce product costs. As a result, a 'throughput accounting' system emerges (Drury, 1992).

JIT and the cost accounting system. Installing a JIT system affects:

- the traceability of costs;

- enhances product-costing accuracy;

- diminishes the need for allocation of service-centre costs;

- changes the behaviour and relative importance of direct labour costs;

- impacts job-order and process costing systems (Hansen and Mowen, 1997; Drury, 1992).

In a JIT purchasing environment, the warehouse is no longer needed and thus materials handling costs can be reduced. Many costs formerly classified as indirect labour costs can now be directly traceable to the product line. Table 5.2 illustrates this.

JIT manufacturing, by reducing indirect costs and increasing direct costs, diminishes the need for detailed allocation of costs to various activities. Moreover, costs are directly traceable to each product. These increase the accuracy of product costing.

In a JIT environment, many services are decentralised. These can now be directly traced to a manufacturing cell and consequently to a specific product.

JIT adoption can affect direct labour costs in the following manner:

- Direct labour decreases as a percentage of total manufacturing costs.

- Direct labour changes from a variable to a fixed cost.

In a JIT environment, with zero inventories (or at least insignificant levels), inventory valuation is irrelevant for financial reporting purposes.

Job orders are no longer needed to accumulate product costs as a result of reducing WIP and finished goods inventories. With JIT's zero inventory

Table 5.2 An example of product cost traceability in traditional manufacturing versus JIT manufacturing

Manufacturing cost	Traditional manufacturing	JIT manufacturing
Direct labour	Direct	Direct
Direct materials	Direct	Direct
Materials handling	Indirect	Direct
Repairs and maintenance	Indirect	Direct
Energy	Indirect	Direct
Operating supplies	Indirect	Direct
Supervision	Indirect	Direct
Insurance and taxes	Indirect	Indirect
Building depreciation	Indirect	Indirect
Equipment depreciation	Indirect	Direct
Custodial services	Indirect	Indirect
Cafeteria services	Indirect	Indirect

philosophy, the unit-cost computation is as simple as it sounds: divide the period's costs for a process by the number of units produced. The computation of equivalent unit is no longer needed and there is no equivalent to account for prior period costs.

JIT production and automation: how do they relate?

JIT production is a demand-pull system that ensures that product is not moved from one process step to another until there is a requirement for that product. In contrast, the traditional push-through system of manufacturing produces significantly higher levels of finished goods inventory than a JIT system. The underlying tenet of JIT production is quality. It is argued that implementation of a JIT production system can help managers eliminate waste by compressing time and space and thereby firms are capable of reducing costs of production significantly.

Implicit in the operation management and management accounting literature is the notion that JIT production and automation in the factory should be considered in tandem. Blackburn (1988) suggests that a successful

JIT implementation gives firms the kind of flexible, balanced, yet simple production process that makes automation easier to implement. Blackburn further holds the view that JIT production gives a firm a platform for going in and automating operations. Kaplan and Atkinson (1989) suggest that companies should not undertake major automation until significant progress has been made to the process of moving to JIT. Experiences in the United States have also suggested that if automation is attempted before JIT, the outcome from automation will probably prove highly disappointing (Hronec, 1988; Cooper, 1995a; Brinker, 1995). This view is supported by Hansen and Mowen (1997, p.12), who suggest that the implementation of an automated manufacturing system should typically follow adoption of JIT production and is a response to the increased needs for quality and shorter response time. Young and Selto (1991) suggest that JIT should be a first step to implementing an automated manufacturing process. Thus, as a firm's use of JIT production increases, undertaking automation projects should tend to become more important, as it is directly related to the firm's pursuit of survival in a competitive environment. There is no empirical evidence on this issue, however.

JIT production and ABC: how do they relate?

Traditionally, common costs are attributed to products using measures of volume, frequently based on direct labour, direct material, machine time and energy. Such allocations are needed for, among other things, inventory valuation, especially in the financial accounts. This traditional cost system assumes that products consume all resources in proportion to their production volumes. But many organisational resources exist for activities that are unrelated to the physical volume of units produced. Consequently, traditional volume-based cost allocation practices may report distorted product costs (Cooper and Kaplan, 1988, 1991).

The connection between JIT and ABC in practice is not clear. Some authors argue that JIT is a substitute for short-run cost accounting data and that the physicals are more important (McNair, Mosconi and Morris, 1989; Cooper and Kaplan, 1991; Cobb, 1993). In a JIT production, the ideal batch size is one. This means that all batch-level activities either are converted into unit-level activities or are eliminated. Furthermore, JIT firms are capable of isolating non-value-added costs and can eliminate them, thereby reducing overhead costs. JIT production is oriented toward process and time. Therefore its accounting, reporting and costing methodologies are founded on how long a product is in the process. The ultimate effect is to diminish the need for an ABC system to trace production costs to products. Following these arguments one would expect that firms with a JIT production system are more likely to place less emphasis on an ABC system.[1] Hoque (2000a) has found empirical support for this claim.

Automation and ABC: how do they relate?

Generally, companies operating in an automated manufacturing environment produce a wide range of products and direct labour represents only a small fraction of total manufacturing costs. Overhead labour costs (e.g. computer technicians and operators, maintenance people, software engineers, programmers and process and operations engineers) are of considerable importance. As a result, simplistic overhead allocations using a declining direct labour hour (DLH) base cannot be justified,[2] particularly when information processing costs are no longer a barrier to more sophisticated systems like ABC (Anderson, 1995; Cooper, 1995b; Foster and Swenson, 1997).

The extant literature suggests that the changed manufacturing environment requires a firm to adapt costing systems to its particular circumstances (Gosse, 1993; Johnson, 1990; Cooper, 1996; Brinker, 1995). Today's manufacturing businesses are committed to high-volume, low-cost products with automation, low labour content and high vendor content.

With automation the product is released faster, the manufacturing process is faster and the whole life of the product is shorter. Such a manufacturing environment creates the need for accurate and timely cost data, a better understanding as to where or what is creating the firm's product cost and support costs and a better understanding as to what are the cost drivers by products (Kelder, 1988; Cooper, 1989, 1995b). Hansen and Mowen (1997) suggest that an ABC system provides more than just more accurate product-cost information; it also provides information about the cost and performance of activities and resources. Furthermore, an ABC system allows managers to focus on those activities that might offer opportunities for cost savings – provided they are simplified, performed more efficiently, eliminated and so on. It follows that strategies of cost management and control through implementing an activity-based cost allocation system can be expected when there is an increased use of automation.[3] Hoque (2000a) provides empirical support for this claim.

Target costing

Target costing[4] is a cost-estimation approach which is widely used by Japanese companies. It consists of setting a desired market price for a new product. Market forces drive this market price. A target profit margin is then deducted from the target market price to determine the target cost. The target cost numbers are used in product-pricing decisions and in decisions to introduce the new product. Target costing is also known as a cost reduction tool. The target costs are compared with current estimates, which are almost always higher. The underlying assumption of the target costing philosophy is that market prices determine product costs.

Target costing is based on three premises: (a) orienting products to customer affordability or market-driven pricing, (b) treating product cost as an independent variable during the definition of a product's requirements and (c) proactively working to achieve target cost during product and process development (K. Crow, DRM Associates, 1999).

In summing up, target costs establish what the marketplace says that it will pay and from that comes the target cost that an organisation is going to have to reach. Figures 5.1 and 5.2 illustrate the difference between a traditional cost management approach and a target costing approach.

Product life-cycle costing

The *stage in the product life-cycle* of the organisation's products has been identified in the organisation literature as the most influential factor determining the strategy formulation process (Hofer, 1975; Wasson, 1978; Rink and Swan, 1979). The literature describes the stages of the product life-cycle as (1) emerging, (2) growth, (3) mature and (4) declining. Figure 5.3 illustrates the stages in the product life-cycle.

Figure 5.3 is a perspective from the producer's point of view. The underlying concepts that products pass through are, firstly, that products have limited lives and an arc tracing its sales history can represent a given product's life. Secondly, the stages of the product's life-cycle are identified by the inflection points in the sales history – emerging, growth, maturity and decline, and finally, profit per unit varies as products move through their life-cycles, falling following the growth phase.

The process of tracking and determining the costs of a product through its entire life-cycle, from entry to obsolescence, is termed *product life-cycle costing*.

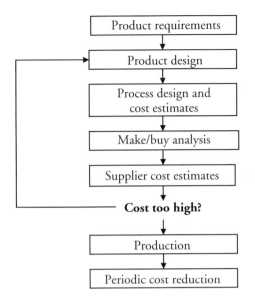

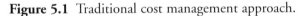

Source: Ken Crow, DRM Association (1999). Reproduced with permission from the author.

Figure 5.1 Traditional cost management approach.

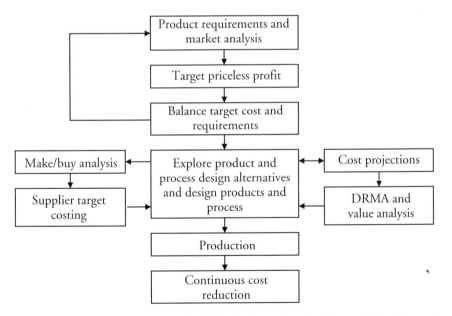

Source: Ken Crow, DRM Association (1999). Reproduced with permission from the author.

Figure 5.2 Target cost concept.

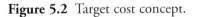

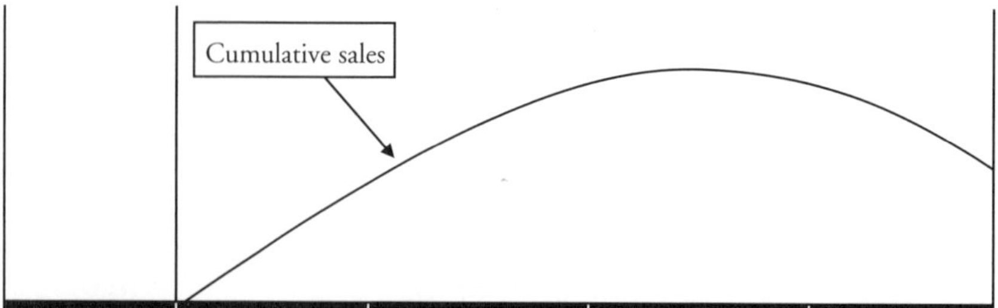

Stage	Emerging	Growth	Mature	Declining
Sales	Low	Rising rapidly	Peak sales	Declining
Prices	High	Falling	Low	Falling
Profit/unit	Negative	High/rising	Average	Declining
Customers	Innovators	Early adopters	Late majority	Laggards
Competitors	Few	Growing numbers	Declining numbers	Further decline

Years after introduction

Source: Adapted from Wilson (1991).

Figure 5.3 Product life-cycle.

Knowing the costs for each stage of the product life-cycle is important because the organisation has to make decisions whether to drop or continue the product(s). Organisations should place emphasis on reporting costs at the each production stage of the life-cycle and monitor the product's performance. Drury (1992, pp. 809–10) suggests that many companies use a life-cycle approach for planning and budgeting new products, but these models are rarely integrated into existing management accounting reporting systems.

From a customer point of view, life-cycle costing is also important (for details, see Burstein, 1988). Life-cycle costs for an automobile customer, for example, include:

- what the car cost the customer upfront;

- how much it would cost to maintain;

- what sort of value it retained.

Committed costs versus actual costs spent

In a life-cycle costing situation, an organisation needs to look at two things. One of them is the relationship of where the organisation commits cash in the development life-cycle to where it spends the cash. How is the timing of those different and why is that relevant in so far as the organisation is concerned? The other is the specific type of decisions made along the way that cascade in their impact (Burstein, 1988). According to Raffish (1991), 85 per cent of the cost of a new product is committed after the design phase and manufacturing can influence only about 10 to 15 per cent or so of the cost. Thus, life-cycle costing is closely associated with the product's life-cycle timing and that timing is important if the producer intends to make reasonable decisions about products, particularly, for example, go/no-go kinds of decisions (Burstein, 1988). The problem, however, here is that an organisation is not capturing and allocating research and development costs so that management can determine the true profitability of a product over its life (Raffish, 1991).

Chapter summary

The adoption of JIT production systems gives managers a much better understanding of a product's full costs, leading to reductions in material losses and the potential for greater improvement in overall factory productivity. For many firms, the increased use of AMT may be necessary for survival. Academics, for example, argue that AMT offers improved quality and reliability for production processes and by virtually eliminating set-up or changeover times permits much greater manufacturing flexibility. By automating manufacturing processes, firms can compete with economies of scope – the ability to efficiently produce a wide variety of products in small batches. The key argument for automation is based on the rationale that competitive advantages lies in the areas of creativity and technology.

In recent years, there have been many commentaries expressing concerns with traditional costing systems which focus on volume-based cost allocations, short-term cost information usage, etc. Such commentaries suggest that rapidly changing manufacturing environments require a concomitant shift from traditional costing systems to a system that captures and reflects the organisation's manufacturing environment. The literature in this area suggests that cost behaviour in an organisation is more complicated and requires additional cost drivers that are unrelated to the volume of product produced. Consequently, more attention has been paid to develop a 'new' cost allocation practice with the result that activity-based costing (ABC) has commanded considerable attention. The literature in this area also suggests that increased automation is likely to create a greater demand for the increased use of cost information in the day-to-day activities of the organisation. In contrast, increased use of JIT reduces the need for detailed and complex costing systems such as ABC. This chapter provides some empirical evidence to this claim.

Key terms to learn

Advanced manufacturing technology (AMT)	Product life-cycle costing
	Production management strategies
Automation and ABC	Target costing
JIT production and ABC	The just-in-time (JIT) approach
JIT production and automation	Traditional manufacturing
Management accounting systems	

Discussion questions

5.1 Describe the importance of AMT in today's manufacturing operations.

5.2 What are the underpinning assumptions of the JIT philosophy?

5.3 Why is a good supplier relationship vital for effective implementation of a JIT system?

5.4 What can companies do to improve their competitive position?

5.5 What are the three criteria used to evaluate progress towards making money?

5.6 In real business practices, companies face many dilemmas. On the one hand they have to have a broad range of products with competitive prices, while on the other hand they have to have new manufacturing technologies and this involves huge investment. If you were the manager of a company faced with this dilemma, what strategy would you take?

5.7 Compare and contrast a traditional manufacturing organisation with a JIT firm.

5.8 How is the design of cost and management accounting systems influenced by the manufacturing system and the production strategy?

5.9   Explain how product cost traceability improves with a JIT system.

5.10   'JIT is a demand-pull system.' Explain what this statement means.

5.11   Is it necessary to have AMT in a JIT manufacturing system? Explain.

5.12   Explain why ABC is important for an automated manufacturing organisation that produces a wide range of products, and direct labour represents a small fraction of the manufacturing costs.

5.13   What is target costing? Explain why target costing is known as a cost reduction tool.

5.14   What is the difference between target costing and product life-cycle costing?

5.15   Referring to the typology of strategies in the previous chapter, explain what is the relationship between product life-cycle and the typology of the strategy. Give examples.

5.16   K & Q Company are considering the introduction of a new product in the market. To determine a target selling price, the company has gathered the following information:

- No. of units to be produced and sold: 50,000 per annum.
- The cost estimates for the product are:
  - Direct materials per unit: $40
  - Direct labour per unit: $20
  - Variable manufacturing overhead per unit: $15
  - Fixed manufacturing overhead per annum: $5,000
  - Variable selling, general and administrative overhead per unit: $7
  - Fixed selling, general and administrative overhead per annum: $3,350
- Estimated investment required by the company $120,000
- Desired ROI 12%
- The company uses the absorption costing approach to cost-plus pricing.

Required:
1. Compute the mark-up the company will have to use to achieve the desired ROI.
2. Compute the target selling price per unit.

Notes

1. It is to be noted that although JIT adoption may diminish the importance of ABC for product costing, it is still very useful for other areas of the company, such as customer-cost analysis.

2. Some Japanese firms use DLH, arguing that taking labour out is the most important issue and full costing promotes this (for details, see Hopper and Kato, 1995; Hopper, 1997).

3. This book does not argue that traditional cost allocation practices should be ignored. For some settings, traditional systems continue to work well and are even cheaper to use (Hansen and Mowen, 1997). The transition from traditional cost allocation practices to an activity-based cost allocation is, however, strongly emphasised for organisations in today's manufacturing environment as it has several benefits, including an improved information base.

4. For a detailed discussion of this tool, see Robert C. Creese (2000) *Cost Management in Lean Manufacturing Enterprises*. AACE International; Robin Cooper and Regine Slagmulder (1997) *Target Costing and Value Engineering*. Portland, OR: Productivity Press.

Further reading

Cooper, R. and Slagmulder, R. (1997) *Target Costing and Value Engineering*. Portland, OR: Productivity Press.

Dutton, J.J. and Ferguson, M. (1996) 'Target costing at Texas Instruments', *Journal of Cost Management*, Fall, pp. 33–8.

Fisher, J. (1995) 'Implementing target costing', *Journal of Cost Management*, Summer, pp. 50–9.

Foster, G. and Horngren, C.T. (1991) 'Flexible manufacturing systems: cost management and cost accounting implications', in Cooper, R. and Kaplan, R.S. (eds), *The Design of Cost Management Systems: Text and Readings*, Englewood Cliffs, NJ: Prentice-Hall, Chapter 1, pp. 84–93.

Hoque, Z. (2000). 'Just-in-Time production, automation, cost allocation practices and importance of cost information: an empirical investigation in New Zealand-based manufacturing organisations', *British Accounting Review*, vol. 32, pp. 133–59.

Kato, Y., Boer, G. and Chow, C.W. (1995) 'Target costing: an integrative management process', *Journal of Cost Management*, Spring, pp. 39–51.

Swenson, D.W. and Cassidy, J. (1993) 'The effect of JIT on management accounting', *Journal of Cost Management*, Spring, pp. 39–47.

Young, S.M. and Selto, F.H. (1991) 'New manufacturing practices and cost management: review of the literature and directions for research', *Journal of Accounting Literature*, vol. 10, pp. 265–98.

CHAPTER 6

Quality costing, total quality management and mangement accounting systems

Key learning objectives

After reading this chapter you should be able to:

- define the term 'quality';
- explain the dimensions of quality;
- demonstrate an understanding of quality costs;
- describe and illustrate hidden quality costs and the Taguchi quality loss function;
- describe quality reporting;
- outline the various dimensions of total quality management (TQM);
- explain the concept of *Kaizen* management;
- demonstrate an understanding of the role management accounting plays in TQM programmes.

Introduction

A quality product or service is one that meets or exceeds customer expectations. The highly competitive, globalised environment that exists today has required businesses to focus upon meeting ever-increasing customer demands in order to survive. Quality is, however, not free. That is, there are costs for quality assurance. Total quality management (TQM) concepts have been implemented by firms interested in enhancing their survival prospects by including quality and continuous improvement into their strategic priorities. Management accounting can play a significant role in the assessment of quality initiatives. This chapter looks into these issues.

What is quality?

In recent years, the concept of quality and its management has received considerable attention as business organisations in countries around the world have sought to remain competitive in both local and international markets. In the dictionary definition, quality is the 'degree or grade of excellence'. In an operational term, quality adopts a customer focus. Some say quality is 'fitness for use', that is the degree to which a product or service satisfies customer wants or the degree to which a product conforms to design specifications and engineering requirement. In essence, all these features involve the customer and continuous improvement. Quality is a term used in this book to denote the provision of goods and services that meet or exceed customer expectations. There are three different issues relating to the quality process:

Quality control. Quality control is the use of techniques and activities to achieve, sustain and improve the quality of a product or service. It involves the following:

- specifications of what is needed;

- design of the product or service to meet the specifications;

- production or installation to meet the full intent of the specification;

- inspection to determine conformance to specifications; and

- review of usage to provide information for the revision of specifications if needed.

Statistical quality control. Statistical quality control is a branch of quality control. It is the collection, analysis and interpretation of data for use in quality control activities.

Quality assurance. Quality assurance is the actions necessary to provide adequate confidence that a product or service will satisfy consumer needs. Quality assurance determines the effectiveness of the quality system, appraises the current quality, determines quality problem areas or potential areas and assists in the correction or minimisation of these problem areas (Besterfield, 1986).

Dimensions of quality

Quality management literature (for details see Hansen and Mowen, 1997) identifies the following dimensions of quality:

- *performance* – how consistently and how well a product or service functions;

- *aesthetics* – concerns the appearance of tangible products;

- *serviceability* – measures the ease of maintaining and/or repairing the product;

- *features* – refer to characteristics of a product that differentiate functionally similar products;

- *reliability* – the probability that the product or service will perform its intended function for a specified length of time;

- *durability* – the length of time a product functions;

- *quality of conformance* – a measure of how a product meets its specifications;

- *fitness of use* – the suitability of the product for carrying out its advertised functions.

Quality costs

The efficiency of any business is measured in terms of dollars. Therefore, like any business activity, the costs of quality must be known. Morse et al. (1987,

p. 19) defines 'quality costs' as costs incurred because poor quality can exist or because poor quality does exist. Albright and Roth (1992, p. 18) view it differently: 'Quality costs are incurred to ensure that quality standards are met or because quality standards are not met.' Quality costs are an essential management tool. They provide:

- a method of assessing the overall effectiveness of the quality programmes;

- a means of establishing programmes to meet overall needs;

- a method of determining problem areas and action priorities;

- a technique to determine the optimum amount of effort between the various quality activities;

- information for pricing products or bidding on jobs (Besterfield, 1986).

A cost of quality programme collects and reports product quality related costs incurred. Four categories of quality costs often used are as follows:

- *Prevention costs* – costs associated with personnel engaged in designing, implementing and maintaining the quality system. Subcategories include quality engineering, design and development of equipment, quality training, quality planning by others, other prevention expenses such as clerical, telecommunications, travel and supply costs, etc.

- *Appraisal costs* – costs associated with measuring, evaluating or auditing products, components and purchased materials to assure conformance with quality standards and performance requirements. Subcategories include inspection and testing of incoming material, inspection and testing at customer's plant prior to product release, product quality audit, materials and services consumed, equipment calibration and maintenance, etc.

- *Internal failure costs* – occur when products, components and materials fail to meet quality requirements prior to transfer of ownership to the customer. Subcategories include scrap, rework, failure analysis, reinspection, faulty supplier, downsizing, etc.

- *External failure costs* – occur when the product does not perform satisfactorily after the transfer of ownership to the customer. Subcategories include complaints, rejects and returns, repairs, warranty charges, errors, liabilities, etc.

Table 6.1 provides some examples of these four categories of costs of quality. Management accounting textbooks suggest that dollars invested in prevention and appraisal activities ultimately reduce internal and external failure costs by an amount that far exceeds the original investment (see also Montgomery, 1991; Albright and Roth, 1992).

Table 6.1 Examples of costs of quality

Quality cost types	Examples
Prevention costs	Quality engineering Quality training programme Quality planning Quality reporting Supplier evaluation and selection Quality audits
Appraisal costs	Inspecting and testing of raw materials Packaging inspection Supervising appraisal activities Product acceptance measurement (inspection and test) equipment
Internal failure costs	Scrap, rework Down time (due to defects) Reinspection Retesting Design changes
External failure costs	Costs of recalls Lost sales Returns and allowances Repair Product liability Customer dissatisfaction Lost market share

Hidden quality costs (the Taguchi quality loss function)

Some quality costs are observable and some are hidden. Observable quality costs are those that are available from an organisation's accounting records. In contrast, hidden quality costs are opportunity costs resulting from poor quality

(Albright and Roth, 1992). Note that the hidden costs are all in the external failure category (Hansen and Mowen, 1997). How are hidden quality costs estimated?

Albright and Roth (1992) have outlined three methods for estimating hidden quality costs. These are presented below.

The multiplier effect – One method for estimating hidden quality costs is to determine the known quality costs and then multiply that number by a constant. An organisation can use its experience to determine this constant number. For example, Westinghouse Electric Corporation reported that its 'experience indicates that a multiplier effect of at least three or four is directly related to such hidden effects of quality failure'.

Market research – A second method for estimating hidden quality costs is to use market research. It assesses how poor quality and variability in products may affect market share. Heagy (1991, p. 67) describes this method as follows:

> For example, a firm's salesforce knows its customers and the effects of losing customers because of poor quality. Also, trends in a firm's market share lost to competitors can be analysed. Based on the findings of market research, a projection can be made of future loss of contribution margin. This amount can then be discounted to its present value. Making estimates like this is not so radical. After all, future cash flows are estimated in evaluating capital budgeting decisions.

Taguchi's quality loss function – Another method for estimating hidden quality costs is to use the 'Taguchi quality loss function (QLF)'. According to this method, the QLF measures the loss to society from a product that does not perform satisfactorily. In this model, costs increase quadratically as actual product characteristics deviate from a target value. For example, if a $0.50 loss occurs when a product's actual weight deviates 0.1 grams from the target weight, then a $2 loss occurs when the product's weight deviates by 0.2 grams. The quadratic function means that when the deviation from target doubles, the loss becomes quadrupled.

Thus the Taguchi QLF estimates the loss that occurs from producing products that vary from a target value, regardless of whether they fall inside or outside the specification limits. This differs from the traditional view of losses from poor quality (Albright and Roth, 1992). This method defines the QLF in terms of the deviation between the actual value and the target value of the characteristic. If y represents an actual value and T represents the target value, then the unit loss function L (y) is

$$L(y) = k (y - T)^2$$

where: y = actual value of characteristic;
           T = target value of characteristic; and
           k = proportionality constant which is dependent upon the
              cost structure of the process or organisation;

$$k = \frac{c}{d^2}$$

where: c = loss associated with a unit produced at the limit, assuming
           the loss at target is zero; and
           d = distance from target value to specification limit.

Thus, the value of k depends on the loss associated with the product at the upper or lower specification limit of the quality characteristic and on the size of the specification limit.

An illustration

Alpha Company manufactures a product that has a target weight of 15 grams with specification limits equal to the target weight plus or minus 0.15 grams. If a unit of the product is produced at the upper specification limit of 15.15 grams it loses $15. During last month, 4,500 units were produced. Eight of these units were weighed as a sample representing the population. The weights of these eight units are shown in column 2 of Table 6.2.

Table 6.2 Hidden quality costs data

Unit No.	Measured weight (y)	Measured – target weight (y–T)	Measured – target weight squared (y–T)²	k (y–T)² ($)
1	15.10	0.10	0.0100	6.67
2	15.25	0.25	0.0625	41.67
3	15.15	0.15	0.0225	15.00
4	15.05	0.05	0.0025	1.67
5	14.90	−0.10	0.0100	6.67
6	15.06	0.06	0.0036	2.40
7	15.24	0.24	0.0576	38.40
8	15.07	0.07	0.0049	3.27
Total hidden loss			0.1736	$115.75
The average loss			0.0248	$16.54

Using the Taguchi QLF the values of the variables are calculated as follows:

T = 15 grams
y = actual value (e.g. 15.10 for the first unit)
c = $15.00
d = 0.15 grams

$$k = \frac{c}{d^2} = \frac{\$15}{0.15^2} = \frac{\$15}{0.0225} = \$666.67$$

Quality reporting

An organisation can use the following tools to identify and reporting quality-related problems:

Quality cost report. A quality cost report shows various categories of quality costs that are expressed as a percentage of sales.

Trend analysis. A trend analysis provides information for long-range planning. It also provides information for the instigation and assessment of quality improvement programmes. Trend analysis can be accomplished by cost category, by subcategory, by product, by measurement base, by plant within a corporation, by department, by work centre and by combinations thereof. Data for trend analysis come from the monthly quality cost report.

Pareto analysis. A pareto distribution has a few items that represent a substantial amount of the total. These items are refereed to as the 'vital few'. Also, a pareto distribution has many items that represent a small amount of the total. They are refereed to as the 'trivial many'. Pareto distribution can be established for quality costs by operation, by machine, by department, by type of defect or by product line.

Total quality management defined

The journey to quality has a long history going back to early craftsmanship. With the development of large industrial organisations, the search for quality continued through 'scientific management' and statistical approaches to 'quality control' during the first quarter of the nineteenth century. Today, the term 'quality' is widely used in business firms to describe a much broader focus on quality. The quality idea has now broadened to incorporate every aspect of business operations. The literature has labelled this 'total quality management' or TQM in short.

TQM concepts are broad and are related to a paradigm shift in management thinking from business-as-usual to continuous improvement. TQM in essence reflects a massive change effort that began in the mid-1970s, due to competitive and cost pressures and to rising customer and employee expectations. That is, the emphasis is on customer satisfaction and speedier response at every stage of the company–customer relationship. Johnson (1994) presents the view that TQM focuses attention on the competitive power that resides in building relationships and empowering people to solve problems – specifically problems that impede the profitable satisfaction of customers' wants.[1] TQM is one of the most important issues of today due to the high costs associated with quality – 15–20% in many organisations.

There are numerous TQM gurus; chief among these are Philip Crosby, W. Edwards Deming, Armand Fiegenbaum, Kaoru Ishikawa, Joseph Juran and Genechi Taguchi. Although each has his distinctive approach to quality improvement, here is what they say in common:

- Producing a quality product or service costs less because there is less waste.

- Preventing quality problems is better than detecting and correcting them.

- Statistical data should be used to measure quality.

- Managers need to take leadership in improving quality.

- Managers and employees need training in quality improvement.

- Companies need to develop a quality management system.[2]

Dimensions of TQM culture

TQM is both a philosophy and a way of doing business in the 1990s. Organisations have to reflect about what, how and why they do what they do, and they have to take appropriate actions continuously in order to listen to their customers and consequently improve their business performance (Kermally, 1997). Thus a TQM culture may vary along a number of dimensions. Powell (1995) highlights the following:

- a top executive commitment to initiatives on quality-related activities;

- the adoption of a quality philosophy that is included in the organisation's mission statement;

- close customer relationships and seeking customer inputs to their requirements;

- working closely with suppliers and requiring suppliers to meet quality specifications;

- assessing performance compared with best practices, both internally and externally;

- educating management and staff through training in quality principles and processes;

- adopting an open, trusting, less bureaucratic culture;

- increased employee empowerment in decision-making and planning, and increased interaction between employees and suppliers;

- programmes for a goal of zero defects and continuous improvement in the manufacturing process;

- implementing contemporary manufacturing systems, e.g. just-in-time, flexible manufacturing systems, etc.;

- a programme to improve internal business processes, e.g. cycle time, quality, process value analysis, non-value-added activities, etc.;

- a programme to monitor and measure quality management related activities.

Advocates of TQM claim that these principles are all very important because they have to support each other to enable the organisation to be innovative, competitive and profitable (Albright and Roth, 1992). In order to become successful TQM companies, all these factors must be present in the organisational culture. TQM to successful companies is not a destination, but a journey. Gilmour and Hunt (1995) perhaps best describe the impact of TQM on the firm as 'unlike anything since the industrial revolution'. Yamin and Gunasekaran (1999) liken the influence of the quality movement to 'evangelical fundamentalism' suggesting that TQM is the most pervasive and influential initiative of worldwide management practices undertaken in the past 20 years. Saunders and Preston (1995) also note that TQM is of value in what it can achieve to satisfy customers' needs, to improve productivity, to maintain the value of the organisation and to remain in business, thus satisfying the needs of all stakeholders. Essentially TQM within a firm can only be assessed after understanding the firm's customer needs (and what constitutes an improvement) and the firm's processes (so changes can be evaluated). This, more significantly, requires an understanding of the relationships with customers and suppliers, as well as an understanding of the processes and techniques of the firm, such that potential improvements may be assessed.

In broad terms, improvements come from asking what is required by those being served, then analysing how far activities or products meet these requirements. The check question is: 'Are they fit for purpose?' If there is a discrepancy, appropriate corrections and improvements are sought and implemented (Codling, 1996).

So far in this section, I have examined some basic themes of development and some key practices of TQM, especially in relation to the effectiveness of TQM efforts. Throughout I have offered a managerial perspective, highlighting the potential strengths of the TQM initiative. I now turn my attention to the problems associated with the development and practices of TQM initiatives from a critical perspective. It is suggested that the theoretical promise of TQM is not necessarily matched with the experience of its implementation and outcomes. Ezzamel (1994) argues that there are inherent problems with TQM because it encompasses both a 'hard' and a 'soft' face. TQM promises to achieve the 'best' results while creating and maintaining a supportive culture. The 'hard' side of TQM focuses on zero defects and the prevention of errors. These two sides of TQM are contradictory as they seek to involve employees in the process of creating a quality programme but then implement a top-down measurement, monitoring and control approach to ensure that quality is achieved. The suggestion is that when implementing TQM there is a tendency for management to overemphasise the use of detailed written rules and procedures, which separate the individuals from their work.

There is the view that while much about the concept of TQM remains ambiguous, the longer-term effects upon employees' work experience, organisational change processes and outcomes are unclear. Morgan and Murgatroyd (1994) have identified three common points of resistance to TQM: the resistance components; the resentment components; and the technical objections. From a resistance point of view, it is suggested that TQM is a source of discomfort and fear. The most common fears identified are as follows: (a) a fear that the widespread adoption of TQM will reduce the number of jobs available or the opportunities for promotion; (b) a fear that their own sphere of influence and control may be affected as empowerment develops; (c) a fear that the work they undertake will become more complex; (d) a fear that the risks of TQM will not be compensated for through the reward and recognition structure; (e) a fear of skill inadequacy; and (f) concerns about teamwork arising from either a feeling that this depersonalises their work or a feeling that they are unable to accept shared responsibility for their own work and that of others. The common forms of resentment are: (a) TQM is another 'management fad' and we are the victims of management in this latest experiment; (b) it's a fine mess you got us into; (c) TQM is a cover for me being asked to solve the problems created by others – the big burden problem; (d) TQM tasks are not my job, this is not what I was hired to do; etc. Some of the technical objections are: (a) TQM requires me to give up some professional independence to the team; (b) we cannot start until everyone in the organisation starts; (c) only senior managers can determine strategy; (d) TQM only works for management procedures (finance, payroll, human resources (HR)); etc. (Morgan and Murgatroyd, 1994).

Thus the role of employees and workers in the development of TQM is critical. It is suggested that using 'management rights' as the basis for introducing TQM is not a substitute for effective dialogue and joint approaches for what will be, after all, significant cultural change for an organisation. The literature suggests that often TQM philosophy may lead to more work with a higher level of responsibility with no adjustments in pay. Morgan and Murgatroyd (1994) suggest that significant cultural change, which TQM represents, requires significant strategic analysis and planning before implementation for it to be successful. Workers at all levels are engaged in the whole process, so TQM should not simply focus on financial performance, but also should pay attention to workers and their welfare and satisfaction (Wilkinson and Witcher, 1993; Tuckman, 1994; Wilkinson and Willmot, 1995).

Kaizen management

Kaizen is a Japanese term, which means 'continuous improvement'. *Kaizen* involves everyone – both managers and workers – and entails relatively little expense (Imai, 1986). Toyota Motor Company uses this phrase to describe its commitment to progress. In general, *Kaizen* management captures the following themes:

- 'A journey with no end.'

- 'We are running harder just to stand still.'

- 'If you're not going forward, you're going backwards.'

Major *Kaizen* systems include the following:

- *TQC/TQM* – emphasises control/management of the quality process.

- *A JIT production system* – aims at eliminating non-value-adding activities of all kinds and achieving a lean production system to accommodate fluctuations in customer orders

- *Total productive maintenance (TPM)* – while TQM emphasises improving overall management performance and quality, TPM focuses on improving equipment quality. TPM seeks to maximise equipment efficiency through a total system of preventive maintenance spanning the lifetime of the equipment.

- *Policy development* – management should establish clear targets to guide everyone and make certain to provide leadership for all *kaizen* activities directed towards achieving the target.

- *A suggestion system* – this system functions as an integral part of individual-oriented *kaizen* and emphasises the morale-boosting benefits of positive employee participation.

- *Small-group activities* – this strategy includes small-group activities – informal, voluntary, intracompany group – organised to carry out specific tasks in a workshop environment. An example of this would be 'quality circles' to address, not only quality issues, but also such issues as cost, safety and productivity (Imai, 1986).

Management accountants can play a significant role by providing managers with high-quality information to achieve an organisation's strategic goals.

Management accounting data for TQM programmes

It has been suggested (Albright and Roth, 1992) that quality is an important cost-management topic, because quality management can help organisations lower costs and improve profits. They suggest that most accounting systems do not provide data for helping companies evaluate quality, although accounting data can play a vital role in quality management if the system has a cost-management focus. According to Shank and Govindarajan (1994), whichever approach a firm chooses, quality is such an important strategic variable that management accounting can no longer ignore it; one way or another, a strategically effective management reporting system must deal explicitly with the issue of quality. Other writers in the accounting area also emphasised the importance of quality cost management in an organisation (see Kaplan, 1983; Albright and Roth, 1992; Johnson, 1994; Ezzamel, 1994; Hoque and Alam, 1999).

Thus, to achieve effective TQM, changes are required in management accounting systems. Ittner and Larcker (1995) describe these changes as the gathering of new information, the dissemination of information across the organisational hierarchy and changes in reward systems. Hoque and Alam's (1999) case study suggests that TQM firms should have a different sort of management accounting system (MAS). Table 6.3 summarises the difference between pre-TQM MAS and post-TQM MAS, as suggested by Hoque and Alam (1999).

Table 6.3 Comparison of pre- and post-TQM adoption MAS in the company studied

Pre-TQM MAS	Post-TQM MAS
Financial accounting orientation (e.g. costs, profit, ROI, revenue growth, etc.)	Orientation encompassing both financial and non-financial measures (e.g. innovation, customer satisfaction, process efficiency)
Focuses on aggregated cost data	Focuses on activity-based costing
No quality costing	Provision for quality costing
No linkage to strategy and short-term orientation	Linkage to strategy and long-run focus
Accountants are mainly bean counters	Accountants are part of the management
Annual feedback on performance	Continuous feedback

Source: Hoque and Alam (1999).

In describing the costing system that TQM organisations need to adopt, Albright and Roth (1992) note:

If the cost-management system is to provide relevant data for managing companies in the current environment, quality measurement must be considered. Although non-financial measures of quality, such as number of customer complaints and number of defects, are important quality measures, financial data may be just as important. Quality costs are one type of financial data that cost-management systems need to provide.

Chenhall (1997) argues that the potential for TQM to improve firms' profitability is enhanced when managers are evaluated using direct measures of manufacturing. He suggests that traditional performance measurement involving budgetary control and financial indicators (e.g. ROI) is inappropriate for TQM, which requires a more precise measure to ensure that the quality of processes is under control and can be continuously improved. Sim and Killough (1998) suggest that in a TQM environment, workers are responsible for improving manufacturing capabilities and performing a variety of activities. Given the importance of the workers' role in TQM practices, MAS are often used as mechanisms to motivate and influence workers' behaviour in ways that will maximise the welfare of both the organisation and the workers. As such, the MAS that an organisation should focus on are those that are directly linked to control issues on the manufacturing or service shopfloor.

Chapter summary

Total quality management (TQM) is concerned with continuous improvement. Companies adopt this concept in order to satisfy their customers so that they remain competitive. 'Quality is everyone's business' and it is designed to send the message that all business processes, systems, all levels of management and all employees must be concerned with customer, quality and continuous improvement. TQM philosophy means employees are expected to promote and use 'leadership through quality' tools personally. The emphasis is also on employee behaviour and performance.

TQM requires a different sort of management accounting information system, which is broad in scope and nature. Apart from data on internal management TQM firms also need information on customers, competitors, suppliers and their own employees. TQM firms need a multidimensional performance measurement system in order to assess the effectiveness of TQM. This issue is further explored in Chapter 11.

Key terms to learn

Dimensions of quality

Dimensions of TQM culture

Kaizen management

Management accounting data

Quality

Quality costs

Quality reporting

Total quality management (TQM)

Discussion questions

6.1 What are the dimensions of quality?

6.2 List the quality costs and provide examples.

6.3 Why is it important that quality costs are incurred as prevention and appraisal failure costs rather than internal or external failure costs?

6.4 What is meant by hidden quality costs? If you were a manager explain how you can estimate and control these hidden costs.

6.5 Compare and contrast Albright and Roth's (1992) methods for hidden quality costs. How do these differ?

6.6 What is TQM? Explain how this has changed the culture of organisations.

6.7 Critically evaluate TQM. What are some of the problems associated with the development and practices of TQM initiatives?

6.8 Explain the relationships between *Kaizen* systems.

6.9 What are the implications for the MAS of a TQM programme?

6.10 What type of strategy would a company have if they implemented a TQM?

6.11 What is the relationship between JIT and TQM? Explain why TQM is important in JIT manufacturing systems.

6.12 Is there a relationship between organisation structure and TQM? Explain.

Notes

1. For critical commentaries on TQM, see the 1994 issue (Volume 5) of *Critical Perspectives on Accounting*.

2. For details on these issues, see the Sixth Anniversary Issue of *Commitment Plus*, a publication of the Quality and Productivity Management Association in the USA (Volume 7, Number 1, November 1991).

Further reading

Chenhall, R.H. (1997) 'Reliance on manufacturing performance measures, total quality management and organizational performance', *Management Accounting Research*, vol. 8, pp. 187–206.

Ezzamel, M. (1994) 'From problem solving to problematization, relevance revisited', *Critical Perspectives on Accounting*, vol. 5, pp. 269–80.

Hoque, Z. and Alam, M. (1999) 'TQM adoption, institutionalism and changes in management accounting systems: a case study', *Accounting and Business Research*, vol. 29 no. 3, Summer, pp. 199–210.

Johnson, H.T. (1994) 'Relevance regained, total quality management and the role of management accounting', *Critical Perspectives on Accounting*, vol. 5, pp. 259–67.

CHAPTER 7

Value-chain analysis and accounting

Key learning objectives

After reading this chapter you should be able to:

- explain the concept 'value-chain analysis';
- describe differences between value-added analysis and value-chain analysis;
- demonstrate an understanding of how Porter's value-chain framework can be applied to the business for excellence;
- outline the strategic cost classifications in the value-chain framework;
- describe the differences between the corporate value chain and an individual product's value chain;
- demonstrate an understanding of how management accounting systems play a vital role in value-chain analysis;
- understand the application of a value-chain framework in a manufacturing setting.

Introduction

As companies enter a new millennium, they should remain committed to enhancing their long-term competitiveness by providing high-quality products and services at a reasonable, competitive price. To achieve this aim, companies need to analyse their cost structure and identify strategies for building long-term growth. Managing costs and monitoring effectiveness requires a broad focus that Michael Porter calls the 'value chain'. A good way to achieve this aim is to ascertain where a firm's products are located in the value chain. Value-chain analysis is a method for decomposing the firm into strategically important activities and understanding their impact on cost behaviour and differentiation, the generic strategies proposed by Porter. How management accounting tools can be usefully accommodated within the value-chain concept has received limited attention. This chapter looks at this contemporary issue.

Value-chain concept: what is it and what does it offer?

A value chain describes the linked set of value-creating functions that are required to bring a product or service to the customer. It begins with basic raw materials from suppliers, moving to a series of value-added activities involved in producing and marketing a product or service and ending with distributors getting the final products or services into the hands of the ultimate customers. Michael Porter (1980, 1985) has developed this value-chain concept as a tool to help businesses analyse their cost structures and identify competitive strategies.

A value-chain analysis emphasises that costs occur, not merely in manufacturing, but across the business. It provides a useful perspective for understanding non-manufacturing cost classifications. Supplying and manufacturing activities are described as 'upstream' segments of a value chain, while marketing and distribution activities are 'downstream' segments of a value chain.

Value-added analysis and value-chain analysis: how do they differ?

Value-added analysis involves classifying activities as value-added or non-value-added. This concept is adopted to identify which activities to keep and which to eliminate. The following activities in organisations tend not to add value to the core activities: preparation time; waiting time; unnecessary process steps; overproduction; rejects; set-up times; transportation/distribution; process waste; materials waste; communications; administration/decision-making; untidiness; bottlenecks; and timing (Morgan and Murgatroyd, 1994).

Value-chain analysis places emphasis on understanding the total value of all operations across the business, as well as the industry. By considering the value chain organisations, can determine areas where cost can be minimised (for cost-leadership strategy) and areas where customer value can be enhanced (for product differentiation strategy). The value chain of a business focuses on the set of value-creating activities that range from the receipt of raw materials from suppliers and research and development of products and processes, to the sale of the product to the customer and the provision of after-sales customer support. Customer value refers to the characteristics of a product or service that a customer perceives as valuable.

Porter's value-chain framework: applying it to the business for excellence

Porter proposes to extend value-chain analysis beyond the value chain of the business to consider a linkage with suppliers and customers, as well as the value chains of competitors.

Porter proposes that a firm's value chain is composed of nine categories of interrelated activities. These activities are, in part, *primary activities* and, in part, *support activities*. The latter exist to facilitate the former.

Primary activities
Primary activities include:

- *Inbound logistics* activities involve managing inbound items such as raw materials handling and warehousing.

- *Operations* activities involve the transformation of inbound items into products suitable for resale, for example research and development, product design and manufacturing.

- *Outbound logistics* activities involve carrying the product from the point of manufacturing to the buyer such as warehousing and distribution.

- *Marketing and sales* activities involve informing buyers about products and services with a reason to purchase, such as distribution strategy and promotional activities, including advertising.

- *Service* includes all activities required to keep the product or service working effectively for the buyer, after it is sold and delivered. Examples of such activities include installation, repair, after-sales service, warranty claims and answering customer inquiries.

Support activities

In support of the above primary activities of the value chain, Porter proposes four support activities: (1) procurement (purchasing), (2) human resource management (HRM), (3) technology development (R&D) and (4) the firm's infrastructure (accounting, finance, strategic planning, etc.). These activities feed into each stage of the primary activities.

Markets develop and evolve in response to changing customer expectations and the continuous improvement of offerings by the organisation and its competitors. It becomes necessary to look constantly for newer, more effective ways of targeting or changing the organisation's offerings, formally done by implementing a strategic plan. Before setting the strategic plan, the corporate capabilities, market opportunities and threats and the key success factors in the industry, all need to be identified. The business is then able to set reasonable objectives for itself, for example to be a market leader or to increase market share by a certain percentage. As discussed in Chapter 2, Porter sees competitive advantage as being created in two main ways – through cost leadership or differentiation.

As discussed in Chapter 2, Porter has identified five forces that can affect the profitability of the firm: (1) the threat of new entrants; (2) the threat of substitute products and services; (3) the rivalry among existing organisations within the industry; (4) the bargaining power of suppliers; and (5) the bargaining power of consumers. He puts all these concepts into a framework, which he labels as the *value chain*. Porter suggests that the initial step for a firm's strategic analysis is to define its value chain. It is suggested that competitive advantage, irrespective of whether the firm adopts a cost leader or differential strategy, be achieved in the marketplace by giving value for money, that is competitive advantage comes from carrying out the value-creating activities more cost-effectively than one's competitors. According to Porter, 'The value chain desegregates a firm into its strategically relevant activities in order to understand the behaviour of costs, and the existing and potential sources of differentiation. A firm gains competitive advantage by performing these activities more cheaply or better than its competitors.'

Porter's value-chain analysis has several distinctive characteristics. One of these attributes of value-chain analysis insists on the complex linkages and interrelationships both between the strategic business unit and its customers and suppliers as well as those found internally. If these linkages are exploited, a firm is more likely to gain a competitive advantage. This necessitates management having to refocus, looking not only at the activities internal to the firm, but also at those activities external to the firm. This in turn highlights opportunities for the firm to work with suppliers and end-customers, which in turn should lead to increased competitive advantage. Value-chain analysis also recognises that activities internal to the firm are interdependent rather than independent. A firm's history, its strategy, its approach to implementing its strategy and the underlying economics of its situation are reflected in the Porter value-chain framework.

Corporate value chain: what is it and how does it differ from an individual product's value chain?

The systematic examination of individual value activities can lead to a better understanding of a corporation's strengths and weaknesses. Porter (1985, p. 36) suggests that differences among competitor value chains are a key source of competitive advantage. Wheelen and Hunger (1998) propose the following steps in a corporate value-chain analysis:

- Examine each product line's value chain and consider its strengths and weaknesses.

- Examine the 'linkage' within each product line's value chain. Linkages are connections between the way one value-added activity (e.g. marketing) is performed and the cost of performance of another activity (e.g. quality control).

- Examine the potential synergies among the value chains of different product lines or business units. Each value element (e.g. advertising or manufacturing) has an inherent economy of scale in which activities are conducted at the lowest possible cost per unit of output (i.e. sharing resources by two separate products in the corporate value chain).

A case study of the Porter value-chain framework

Alpha is a subsidiary of a large New Zealand multinational corporation. Alpha produces and markets plastic packaging for eggs, ice cream and pet food and other disposable packaging. Alpha has four main functional departments: accounting, sales and marketing, manufacturing and technical. The manufacturing department has four divisions: human resources, quality, purchasing and process engineering. The financial accountant, sales and marketing manager and technical manager form the company's management team responsible for strategic decision-making.

Alpha operates in an intensely competitive environment. Competition is intense due to the limited number of customers. Alpha concentrates on selling to the major manufacturers of margarine, ice cream and butter products in New Zealand which are able to purchase goods in large quantities. The main priority of Alpha's target customers is to receive quality packaging delivered on time. Since price is not their customers' primary concern, Alpha is able to charge a premium. According to the chief executive, 'The source of the company's competitive advantage is the hygienic and clean manufacturing conditions the company has and a production method not yet used by any other New Zealand competitors.'

Australian manufacturers are constantly approaching Alpha's customers seeking new business. At the time of the study, the favourable New Zealand exchange rate allowed the company to keep its existing customers, although Australian plastic food-packaging companies were a constant threat. Risk and uncertainty are prevalent throughout the organisation's environment. The chief executive reports that a number of New Zealand food producers are currently considering building megasites in Australia. These proposed plants would be large enough to cater to the whole Australasian market. Goods would be manufactured and packaged in Australia and then supplied to New Zealand. If this becomes a trend, Alpha would need to make some major strategic decisions concerning its operations.

The main risk the company faces is in the manufacturing environment. There is a constant danger that large technologically-driven multinational organisations with immense resources in the plastics field will develop a better and cheaper end-user product than is currently available from Alpha.

Alpha's sales and profitability have been steadily increasing with a growth in sales of 37 per cent over the last three years. At the time of the study, the company's gross turnover was $30 million. The company places emphasis on the strategy of increasing sales and market share. The emphasis on quality through ISO 9000 certification and total quality management (TQM) practices has been a positive influence on profitability. The ability of the company's technical staff to form liaisons with the customer's markets is seen as one of the key success factors of the company.

The Alpha strategy:

> To build a long-term profitable future for Alpha Food Packaging employees and stakeholders by striving to be the 'highest value supplier' of packaging solutions to domestic and international markets.

Alpha adopted a differential value-chain strategy to improve its competitive advantage. The company continuously searches for market opportunities and regularly experiments with possible new trends and product innovations. Figure 7.1 illustrates Alpha's overall position in the value-chain of the plastic food-packaging industry. Oil refiners, plastic granule manufacturers and die manufacturers supply basic raw materials. Alpha has two different groups of customers: food companies and distributors/retailers. Alpha's strategy focuses on producing products of high quality. In order to achieve this strategic goal, the company attempts to be 'creators of change' by working on product innovation. The company's regular experiments with product innovation are founded on the basic question: 'What does the customer want?' This helps Alpha identify ways to exploit linkages with both their suppliers and customers, and to enhance differentiation.

To achieve competitive advantage, Alpha also introduced *partnership plans* with its customers in late 1993. Alpha works with its customer groups to better understand their needs and to negotiate their customer requirements. Customers are invited to visit the factory site to examine the production process. Technical and design staff advise customers on various aspects of the production process. Alpha management believes that such 'partnership with customers' policy helps the company to 'lock' customers into the business.

Management at Alpha places emphasis on continuous improvement programmess and TQM principles across the organisation. Alpha's ability to meet and pre-empt customer needs enables it to focus, not only on the activities internal to the firm, but also on those activities that are external to the firm. This highlights opportunities for the firm to work with suppliers and end-customers, which in turn leads to increased competitive advantage. Alpha enhances competitive advantage by understanding (1) the linkage between suppliers' value chains and the company value chain and (2) the linkage

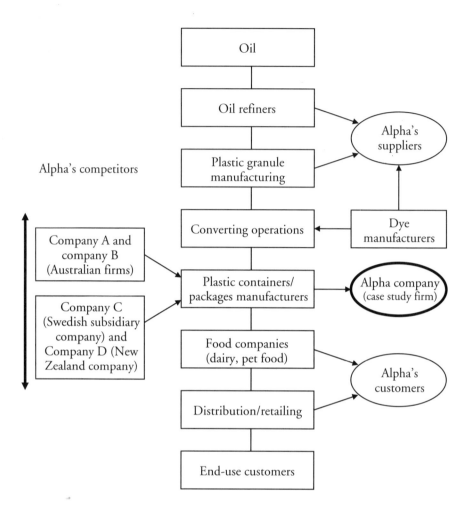

Figure 7.1 Alpha's value chain framework.

between the buyers' value chains and the company value chain. In general, most managers believe that such an exercise provides opportunities for the firm to increase its profitability.

The value-adding activities at Alpha are summarised in Figure 7.2. These activities are managed and organised in line with the company's strategic choice and business-like principles, such as customer focus and continuous improvement, change in management/organisational culture and 'partnerships' with customers and suppliers.

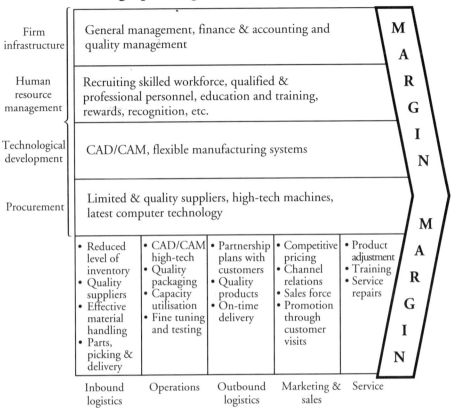

Strategic planning and decision-making team

							M
Firm infrastructure	General management, finance & accounting and quality management						A R G I N
Human resource management	Recruiting skilled workforce, qualified & professional personnel, education and training, rewards, recognition, etc.						
Technological development	CAD/CAM, flexible manufacturing systems						
Procurement	Limited & quality suppliers, high-tech machines, latest computer technology						M A R G I N

• Reduced level of inventory • Quality suppliers • Effective material handling • Parts, picking & delivery	• CAD/CAM high-tech • Quality packaging • Capacity utilisation • Fine tuning and testing	• Partnership plans with customers • Quality products • On-time delivery	• Competitive pricing • Channel relations • Sales force • Promotion through customer visits	• Product adjustment • Training • Service repairs
Inbound logistics	Operations	Outbound logistics	Marketing & sales	Service

Source: Hoque (2001).

Figure 7.2 Value-chain elements of Alpha Packaging Company.

Management accounting systems in the value-chain framework

When organisational philosophies move to an external orientation involving customer satisfaction in order to gain a competitive advantage, accounting too needs to change its focus and become more strategically oriented. Traditional management accounting systems have been criticised for a greater internal focus within which a key theme is to maximise the difference (that is, the value added) between purchases and sales. There is the view that traditional management accounting does not give adequate information on non-financial and external factors crucial to the long-term survival of the firm. The challenge, therefore, involves management accounting moving away from a traditional 'managerial cost analysis' to a forward thinking 'strategic cost analysis' or 'strategic management accounting' (Shank and Govindarajan, 1992a, 1992b, 1993; Hoque, 2001).

According to Porter (1985), a value-chain cost management methodology involves the following steps:

- Identify the value chain, then assign costs, revenues and assets to value activities.

- Diagnose the cost drivers regulating each activity.

- Develop sustainable competitive advantage, either through controlling cost drivers better than competitors, or by reconfiguring the value chain.

Within the value-chain framework, costs are classified into structural and executional. Structural cost drivers derive from a company's choices about its underlying economic structure. These choices drive cost positions for any given product group. There are at least five strategic choices that a firm must make about its underlying economic structure:

1. *Scale* – the size of the investment in manufacturing, R&D and marketing resources.

2. *Scope* – the degree of vertical integration.

3. *Experience* – how many items in the past has the firm already created and what is it doing again?

4. *Technology* – what process technologies are used in each step of the firm's value chain?

5. *Complexity* – how wide a line of products or services is being offered to customers?

Executional cost drivers are the determinants of a firm's cost position that hinges on its ability to 'execute' them successfully. These cost drivers may include:

- workforce involvement;

- total quality management;

- capacity utilisation;

- plant layout efficiency;

- product configuration;

- linkage with suppliers and customers.

The process of costing the value chain has caught the attention of many management accounting researchers. Shank and Govindarajan's (1988) study of the Baldwin Bicycle Company shows that a change from a traditional accounting system (such as standard costing) to one that better fits with the organisation's strategy can be advantageous. Costs are assigned to each value activity comprising the chain in an organisation and cost drivers are identified for each activity. The final step is to build a sustainable competitive advantage either operating on the cost drivers to reduce costs or by rearranging the value chain, focusing on those activities in which the firm has a competitive advantage.

Accounting in the value chain covers more than the conventional concept of value added which ignores important linkages with both suppliers and customers by focusing only on value added within the firm. From a strategic approach value added has problems because it starts too late and finishes too soon. Starting cost analysis with purchases misses all the opportunities for taking advantage of the firm's suppliers. That is, firms need to develop good relations with suppliers and investigate how costs can be reduced for both the firm and its suppliers, e.g. through ordering, freight and quality.

Porter's value-chain analysis provides the better basis for strategic management accounting design. For example, Shank and Govindarajan (1988) suggest that life-cycle costing relies on value-chain analysis as explicit attention to post-purchase costs by the customer can lead to more effective market segmentation and product positioning. Similarly, JIT relies on value-chain analysis as it considers supplier relationships. In light of Porter's value-chain framework, Shank and Govindarajan (1992a) suggest that a strategic-focused management accounting is required to provide managers with information to support decisions relating to each activity and process of an organisation. Others suggest that management accounting information can assist managers in: establishing new competitive strategies; evaluating existing competitive strategies; and monitoring and assessing progress towards particular strategies.

Strategic management accounting literature suggests that companies choosing a cost leadership strategy would put heavy emphasis on conventional costing and control systems, such as standard costing and variance reporting, structural cost driver analysis (e.g. scale, scope, experience, technology and complexity) and flexible budgeting. Conversely, firms pursuing a differentiation strategy largely focus upon non-conventional information and control systems such as executional cost driver analysis (e.g. workforce involvement, TQM, capacity utilisation, product configuration, linkage with suppliers or customers), marketing cost analysis and non-financial performance measures. There is the view that strategic management accounting moves from structural drivers to executional drivers because the insights from analyses based on structural drivers are too often obsolete and hence ineffective.

As the value-chain concept is radical and no longer uses many conventional measures of achievement such as contribution margin analysis, strategic management accounting needs to be adopted. Management accountants will need to identify appropriate cost drivers and activities which are able to provide information about what activities are performed, why they are performed and how well they are performed. This suggests a system-wide, integrated approach – *activity-based management* – that focuses management's attention on all activities of the organisation and maps the complete length of processes (Hansen and Mowen, 1997). Thus through activity-based management accurate cost and performance information can be routinely used as the basis for decision-making, thereby enabling a firm to be better able to identify opportunities for improvements and to understand the relationships between drivers and resources/activities volume and performance measures. The immediate advantage of value-chain analysis will be the result of the process itself as well as the enhanced quantitative awareness of the external competitive arena and the firm's part in it.

Simmonds (1981) suggests that strategic management accounting can enable a firm to study competitors' pricing, costs, strategies and volume, which is essential to assess its position relative to its competitors. Management accountants must understand that each component is interdependent in each value chain in order to analyse whether or not an activity is value-added. The suggestion is for the greater use of non-financial measures in order to assess the firm's strategic initiatives (Hoque, 2000b). Recently, researchers have advocated for an 'integrated' or 'balanced' performance measurement system that combines both financial and non-financial measures of performance (Kaplan and Norton, 1996; Hoque and James, 2000).

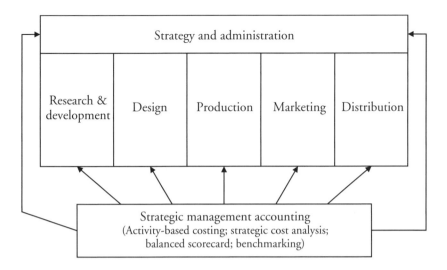

Figure 7.3 The value-chain framework and strategic management accounting.

Figure 7.3 shows the relationship between an organisation's value-chain framework and management accounting systems. The figure shows that the value chain is the sequence of business functions in which utility (usefulness) is added to the products or services of an organisation. It also shows a strategy and administration function, which spans all individual functions. This category includes senior executives charged with the overall responsibility for the organisation.

Strategic management accounting is a major means of helping managers (a) to administer each of the business functions presented in Figure 7.3 and (b) to coordinate their activities within the framework of the organisation as a whole.

Chapter summary

Value-chain analysis is a way of breaking down a firm's strategically relevant activities in order to understand the behaviour of costs. According to Porter, competitive advantage comes from carrying out these activities more cost-effectively than one's competitors. Any enterprise seeking a sustainable competitive advantage must select a generic strategy rather than attempting to be 'all things to all people' or 'stuck in the middle'.

In recent years, traditional management accounting has been criticised by several academics for its inability to provide adequate information for strategic planning purposes. Few conventional MASs go beyond spotlighting the cost of production within firms and to monitor these internal costs relative to plan. Information traditionally supplied to senior executives limits them to a narrow view of the business. It does not give sufficient information on non-financial and external factors crucial to strategic planning and control. Traditional management accounting cannot be an appropriate vehicle for assessing the economic value of a given strategy or for choosing between competing strategies. Strategic management accounting, on the other hand, has the ability to provide accounting information to guide decisions in the strategic arena. If strategic objectives cannot be monitored and controlled through the accounting system, the overall impact of the decision will not be known until after it has been implemented.

Key terms to learn

Corporate value-chain   Strategic cost classifications
Management accounting systems   Value-added analysis
Porter's value-chain framework   Value chain

Discussion questions

7.1 Explain the value chain concept. How can the value chain help businesses?

7.2 Categorise the following processes as value adding or non-value adding:
- transportation/distribution;
- materials waste;
- rework;
- quality inspection;
- set-up;
- assembly;
- painting.

7.3 What is the difference between primary activities and support activities in the value chain?

7.4 What are the steps in a corporate value chain analysis?

7.5 What are the differences between the corporate and an individual product's value chain?

7.6 Describe the relationship between the value-chain framework and the MAS.

7.7 Compare the differences between structural cost drivers and executional cost drivers.

7.8 What are the problems with using traditional accounting methods in the value added chain? Explain how strategic management accounting can be used to overcome these problems.

7.9 If a company has 'cost leadership' as its strategy, how can accounting contribute to meeting this goal?

7.10 Why is strategic management accounting necessary for the value-chain concept to be successful?

7.11 Explain the relationship between the value chain, strategic planning and decision-making. Give examples.

Further reading

Lord, B. (1996) 'Strategic management accounting: the emperor's new clothes?', *Management Accounting Research*, vol. 7, pp. 347–66.

Partridge, M. and Perren, L. (1994) 'Cost analysis of the value-chain: another role for strategic management accounting', *Management Accounting* (UK), pp. 22–6.

CHAPTER 8

Customer profitablility analysis/customer accounting

Key learning objectives

After reading this chapter you should be able to:

- explain the concept 'customer profitability analysis' (CPA);
- outline the relationship between CPA and activity-based management (ABM);
- describe the implementation processes of CPA;
- illustrate how a customer profile is maintained by using sales revenue, order size and age group;
- illustrate the preparation of an income statement by customer.

Introduction

Customers are the main players in a business. Keeping customers happy is one of the difficult tasks facing the firm and it is the best defence against competition. The marketing management team plays an important part in this matter. However, the marketing planner needs to know the relative profitability of a customer/group of customers. One of the ways in which this can be done is through customer profitability analysis (CPA). Although the idea originates in the marketing literature, recently there is growing recognition in the academic community that CPA has so much to offer in the management accounting literature. This chapter focuses on this new direction of management accounting.

Keeping customers happy: a key to success

How an organisation achieves this is a matter that has received increasing recognition in the marketing literature. Keeping customers happy is the best defence against competition. The firm that keeps its customers happy is virtually unbeatable (Lele and Sheth, 1987). There is growing recognition that companies that adopt the strategy of maximising customer satisfaction obtain several competitive advantages. Their long-term profitability is normally higher than their competitors', they have more protection against shifts in technology and customers' needs and if they should slip up, their chances of regaining lost customers and markets are better.

Organisations can keep customers happy in one of two ways (Lele and Sheth, 1987):

- Work to make certain that the performance of their products exceeds customer expectations.

- Alternatively, they can lower the expectations of customers about their products so that they are satisfied whatever the organisations provide.

Customer profitability analysis: what is it and what does it offer?

Anandarajan and Christopher (1986, p. 86) define customer profitability analysis (CPA) as follows:

(...the evaluation, analysis and isolation of all the significant costs associated with servicing a specific customer/group of customers from the point an order is received through manufacture to ultimate delivery and the revenues associated with doing business with those specific customers/customer groups.)

The marketing planner needs to know the relative profitability of the customer/group of customers. One of the ways in which this can be done is through CPA. CPA is the only way to identify the strong (or profitable) and weak (or non-profitable) customers.

What makes a profitable customer? A profitable customer has been defined (Kotler, Leong and Tan, 1999, p. 53) as follows:

> A PROFITABLE CUSTOMER is a person, household, or company that over time yields a revenue stream that exceeds by an acceptable amount the company's cost stream of attracting, selling and servicing that customer.

The primary focus of CPA is on the lifetime stream of revenue and cost, not on the profit from a particular transaction (Kotler et al., 1999).

Organisational managers need specific information about a product or customer in terms of both sales revenues generated and the costs associated with a given level of revenue. Traditional management accounting fails to provide this sort of information as it mainly collects information on individual products/group of products. Foster et al. (1996) have described the role of CPA in an organisation as follows:

> The 'why?' of customer profitability analysis can be reduced to the simple statement that each dollar of revenue does not contribute equally to profit.

The relation between CPA and ABM

From a strategic management accounting perspective, two of the fundamental purposes of CPA are to identify both the cost of dealing with customers (e.g. ordering and purchasing behaviour patterns of different segments) and the non-value-added activities that may be used to reduce costs (cost leadership strategy) or to distinguish the firm's product (differentiation strategy). This suggests that CPA is related to ABM. Using Guilding et al. (2001), it can be suggested that ABM illustrates how activities might serve as an appropriate unit of analysis in a costing management exercise and highlights the benefits that may be derived from considering a variety of cost objects. It is in this context, as Guilding et al. (2001, p. 175) maintain, '...that the potential differential cost allocation to customers (i.e. treating customers as cost objects) has commanded renewed interest'. Considerable research demonstrates how the ABC or ABM framework can be applied when customers are the unit of accounting analysis (for references, see Guilding et al. 2001).

The implementation of CPA

The implementation of CPA can be achieved (Wilson and Gilligan, 1998) in a series of steps as shown in Figure 8.1.

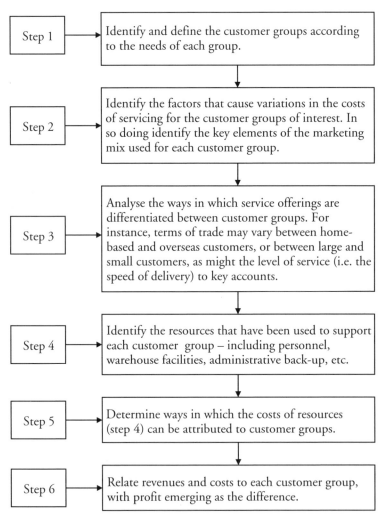

Step 1	→	Identify and define the customer groups according to the needs of each group.
Step 2	→	Identify the factors that cause variations in the costs of servicing for the customer groups of interest. In so doing identify the key elements of the marketing mix used for each customer group.
Step 3	→	Analyse the ways in which service offerings are differentiated between customer groups. For instance, terms of trade may vary between home-based and overseas customers, or between large and small customers, as might the level of service (i.e. the speed of delivery) to key accounts.
Step 4	→	Identify the resources that have been used to support each customer group – including personnel, warehouse facilities, administrative back-up, etc.
Step 5	→	Determine ways in which the costs of resources (step 4) can be attributed to customer groups.
Step 6	→	Relate revenues and costs to each customer group, with profit emerging as the difference.

Figure 8.1 Step-by-step process to the implementation of CPA.

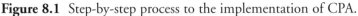

Profile of customers by sales revenues

An organisation can analyse its customers by sales revenues. Table 8.1 presents data on customers by sales revenues generated for four different types of products.

Table 8.1 Sales ($) analysis by customers

Products	Sales by customers ($000)			
	Total	Saikat	Simul	Bappi
A	15,000	5,000	4,500	5,500
B	57,000	10,000	12,500	34,500
C	63,630	23,450	20,500	19,680
D	23,090	6,700	7,600	8,790

Profile of customers by order size

Another type of CPA is shown in Table 8.2. The company's customers are categorised according to their order size. Using this sort of information, the company can achieve profit control. As can be seen in the data presented in Table 8.2, many of the customers were placing small orders, which actually resulted in losses. Organisations can take corrective actions that could improve their order size and permit them to continue to deal with them (Stevens et al., 1997).

Table 8.2 Number of customers by order size

No. of customers	Order size ($)
60	Over 2,000
75	1,600 – 1,999
50	1,200 – 1,599
75	800 – 1,199
90	400 – 799
85	200 – 399
55	Less than 200

Profile of customers by age group

An organisation can also benefit from a customer profile analysis by customer age group. For example, in the case of mobile phones, an organisation should know who the users of their mobile phones are or which age group (young, middle or old) contributes significantly to their sales revenues. With this sort of analysis, an organisation can initiate a strategy change to increase their market share. Table 8.3 provides an example of customer profile analysis by age group. This table shows that the majority of the company's customers are in the younger age groups. The company can now find out through a mail-out survey to this group what makes them buy the company's products or services. This analytical technique helps the organisation to make long-term business decisions regarding its customer or market portfolio.

Table 8.3 Customer profile by age group

No. of customers	Age group
60	Under 18
105	18 – 21
160	22 – 25
120	26 – 30
90	31 – 35
85	36 – 40
60	41 – 50
30	Over 50

Income statement by customer

Table 8.4 shows an income statement by customer. It uses a contribution margin approach. By using this income statement, an organisation can measure an individual customer's profitability and take corrective actions. This statement can further analyse customers by age group. It may be found that although the company has more customers in the 22–25 group, it is the 26–30 age group that is more profitable. Further analysis into usage of service type or product by age group would be appropriate.

Table 8.4 ABC Ltd: income statement by customer (amounts in $000)

	Total	Shehab	Adnan	Sharmi
(a) Net sales	2,000	1,000	500	500
(b) Cost of goods sold	1,200	600	300	300
(c) Gross margin (a – b)	800	400	200	200
Direct operating expenses:				
Direct selling	40	20	15	5
Advertising	8	5	2	1
Transportation	6	4	1	1
Storage	2	1	0.5	0.5
Credits & collections	1	0.5	0.2	0.3
Financial & clerical	1.9	1	0.5	0.4
(d) Total direct expenses	58.9	31.5	19.2	8.2
(e) Contribution margin (c – d)	741.1	368.5	180.8	191.8
Indirect expenses:				
Direct selling	10	5	2	3
Advertising	13	6	4	3
Transportation	8	4	2	2
Storage	5	3	1	1
Credits & collections	4	2	1	1
Financial & clerical	6	3	2	1
(f) Total indirect expenses	46	23	12	11
(g) Net profit before tax (e – f)	695.1	345.5	168.8	180.8

Chapter summary

The ultimate emphasis of CPA is on the lifetime stream of revenue and cost, not on the profit from a particular transaction. CPA focuses on multiple transactions of a customer, rather than any single transaction: it captures costs for a customer/group of customers not specific to products or services, and it can be done at the aggregate level or at the individual level.

Key terms to learn

Customer accounting   Customer profitability analysis
Customer profile   Customers

Discussion questions

8.1   Chapter 8 suggests there are two ways to keep customers happy. List
       these and provide examples.

8.2   What is a customer profitability analysis (CPA)? Explain.

8.3   Why is a CPA important for management?

8.4   What are the strengths and weaknesses of CPA?

8.5   Referring to target pricing, what is the role of a CPA in this matter?

8.6   Referring to MAS, what MAS is needed for CPA? Give examples.

8.7   What is the role of accountants in CPA? Explain and give examples.

8.8   What is the relationship between CPA and ABM?

8.9   Why does the traditional management accounting system fail to provide
       relevant information for a customer-focused organisation?

8.10   What are the steps required to implement a CPA?

Further reading

Bellis-Jones, R. (1989) 'Customer profitability analysis', *Management
    Accounting* (UK), February, pp. 26–8.

Cannolly, T. and Ashworth, G. (1994) 'Managing customers for profit',
    Management Accounting (UK), April, pp. 34–9.

Foster, G., Gupta, M. and Sjoblom, L. (1996) 'Customer profitability analysis:
    challenges and new directions', *Journal of Cost Management*, Spring, pp.
    5–17.

McNair, C.J. (1996) 'To serve the customer within', *Journal of Cost
    Management*, Winter, pp. 40–3.

CHAPTER 9

Competitor analysis/ competitor accounting

Key learning objectives

After reading this chapter you should be able to:

- state the importance of competitor accounting;
- outline the basic steps for competitor accounting;
- illustrate the ingredients of competitor accounting;
- describe various sources of information for competitor accounting;
- identify the problems with competitor accounting;
- demonstrate an understanding of the management accountant's role in competitor accounting;
- explain the contingency view of competitor accounting.

Introduction

Competition is the life-blood of a business. This chapter is concerned with accounting for the competition. The central focus here is to describe how an organisation can create and recreate its business via competitor accounting (or competitor analysis). Originating in strategic management literature, competitor analysis has now become a central issue in strategic management accounting literature. The accounting academic community labels this 'competitor-focused accounting' or 'accounting for the competition'.

Importance of competitor accounting

The competition and market structure are essential parts of the organisation's business environment. 'Where will we compete?' 'What value will we create?' 'How can we be superior?' 'How can our strategy be successfully implemented?' These are four generic strategic issues faced by any business organisation. As was discussed in Chapter 2, an organisation must set a strategic goal as to how it will compete in the market. There is the view in the strategic management literature that the competitive or industry environment affects those businesses of a company that compete within a particular industry. Therefore competitor analysis is critical for the identification of potential opportunities and threats.

As competitors partly determine the organisation's success, an organisation must address the following questions in its strategic business decisions:

- Who are our main competitors?

- What are their objectives?

- What are their major strengths and weaknesses?

- How well are they doing?

- Can we predict their future moves?

Wilson (1994) suggests that competitor analysis[1] should be a central element in management planning and control, with detailed attention being paid to each competitor's objectives, resources and competitive stance, as well as to individual elements of its strategy. Others (e.g. Flavel and Williams, 1996) claim that competitor analysis helps the organisation avoid the element of surprise. If the organisation knows a lot about its competitors there is less chance they will make a surprise move that will be detrimental to the organisation. Through competitor analysis, an organisation can identify its competitors' strengths and weaknesses and in this way it can counter its competitors to its competitive advantage (Wilson, 1994; Flavel and Williams, 1996). Francis (1994) identifies the following four key benefits of competitor analysis:

1. industry benchmarking (comparing yourself, in detail, with similar firms so that you can identify your strengths and weaknesses);

2. learning competitors are excellent teachers (they are performing experiments for you in similar market segments);

3. positioning (knowing competitors' strengths help you to choose how to compete);

4. identifying opportunities and threats (competitors' actions threaten you and you create opportunities: being forewarned enables you to be forearmed).

Competitor accounting helps the organisation identify its competitors' make or sell strategy. It can also focus on understanding competitors' behaviour by reading their mission statements or annual reports. Wilson (1994, p. 24) suggests competitor analysis helps decision-makers to understand their organisation's competitive situation and the associated problems.

Basic steps of competitor analysis

No clear-cut blueprint exits for competitor analysis. Dorhan and O'Connor (1998), however, suggest the following basic steps for competitor analysis:

1. Determine what you do for whom (customers and services).

2. Identify your current and potential competitors.

3. Gather basic information on each competitor.

4. Conduct in-depth research on each competitor.

5. Conduct a comparative analysis of your competitors.

Ingredients of competitor accounting

Recently there has been considerable interest regarding the issue of competitor accounting. A number of accounting academics and practitioners have argued that competitor accounting puts an organisation in the position of identifying opportunities as well as threats, and arms the organisation with the knowledge that the organisation needs to make effective long-term decisions. Contemporary management accounting literature has recognised competitor accounting as one of the key components of management accounting and control systems in organisations. Top US companies are now spending hundreds of million of dollars on competitor accounting or competitor analysis (Jones, 1988; Guilding, 1999).

The key ingredients of competitor accounting are: (1) competitor cost analysis, (2) competitor quality and price analysis, (3) best-practice benchmarking, (4) value-chain analysis, (5) competitive profiling (or competitive position monitoring) and (6) industry profitability analysis.

Comparison of competitors' relative costs

A strategic cost management approach can be applied in competitor analysis. As discussed in Chapter 2, Porter (1985) suggests that an organisation can compete in the market through either a low-cost strategy or a differentiation strategy. To successfully compete in the market based on cost, the organisation must analyse its competitors in terms of their cost structures: are competitors A and B high-cost/low-share competitors? You can rank competitors based on cost, either against each other or, more likely, against your company. Then you can achieve competitive advantage by carefully analysing those rankings. There is the view that competition is where strategies really come to life (Digman, 1999).

Competitor accounting for competitors' relative quality and price

Another method of competitor accounting is to compare the position of the business with that of its competitors with regard to quality and price, in other words relative value (Digman, 1999). If the industry is mature, the basis of competition is frequently based on selling prices, as the products become a well-understood commodity. Consequently, the key success factor is to achieve a comparative cost advantage and this is where competitor accounting should be concentrated (Ward et al., 1992).

Best-practice benchmarking

As will be discussed in Chapter 12, a recommended approach for those seeking to better the competition is to 'benchmark' one's activities against the best – firms known to be excellent in a particular functional area, regardless of their industry (Digman, 1999). Benchmarking analysis helps the organisation to further increase its productivity growth and to 'break through' to a higher standard of performance.

Value-chain analysis

As discussed in Chapter 6, value-chain analysis helps in the understanding of where and how a firm adds value. Within such an exercise the amount of value added, rather than costs, are assigned to each activity. The value chain is the basic tool for systematically examining the activities a business performs, how they interact and how they are necessary in order to determine its sources of competitive advantage. This suggests that one cannot understand competitive advantage by studying a business as a whole; it must be dissected into its 'strategically relevant activities' to understand the sources of competitive advantage through either cost leadership or differentiation (Digman, 1999).

Competitive position monitoring

Competitive position monitoring is the analysis of competitor positions within the industry by assessing and monitoring trends in competitor sales, market share, volume, unit costs and return on sales (Guilding, 1999, p. 584). Such an exercise serves a useful introduction to understanding whether a competitor's product positioning is sustainable in the future and indicates any alternative strategies that could prove successful, given its relative cost structure (Ward et al., 1992; Simmonds, 1981; Guilding, 2000).

Industry profitability analysis

Industry profitability analysis provides a structure to gauge the nature and intensity of competition. Michael Porter (1980) has advocated this framework, which is essentially a structured means of examining the competitive environment of an organisation so as to provide a clear understanding of the market forces at work. As was discussed in Chapter 6, there are five key forces affecting industry competition: (1) entry barriers – how easy is it for a new firm to enter the industry? (2) competitive rivalry – how intense is competition in the industry? (3) substitute products – what substitutes pose a threat to industry profitability? (4) the power of buyers – how much bargaining power do buyers possess? (5) the power of suppliers – how much bargaining power do buyers possess? These forces determine industry profitability because they influence the elements of return on investment – prices, costs and required level of investment. To sum up, industry profitability is a function of industry structure – the five forces – not product, process or technological characteristics per se (Digman, 1999).

Sources of information for competitor analysis

But where does one obtain the information for conducting competitor analysis? Information can be gathered from the following sources:

- personal observation and experience;

- customer contacts;

- in-house sources;

- accounting documents;

- competitive intelligence;

- management and accounting consultants;

- public information (websites, books, magazines, newspapers, etc.).

Problems with competitor accounting

The main challenge in analysing competitors is the gathering of information on them. Today's market is highly volatile; therefore, organisations are reluctant to share information among themselves. This makes it almost impossible for a firm to implement a competitor analysis approach in the organisation. Another challenge is to quantify the direct financial benefits of a competitor analysis. However, the competitor analysis approach simply assumes that the company with high emphasis on competitor analysis will perform better than the company with no emphasis on competitor analysis. Competitor analysis can be limited to large organisations, due to resource constraints. Smaller organisations cannot afford to put any money into such a complex system.

The management accountant's role in competitor analysis

Management accountants can play a vital part in competitor analysis. The key roles management accountants can play in this process are (a) collecting, analysing and comparing competitors' relative costs and investments; (b) assessing the quality of the information; and (c) predicting the future costs of competitors' products. The whole idea is to bring together many ideas into one whole – strategic management accounting. The ultimate goal is to manage costs for improved financial performance in the long term.

Contingency view of competitor accounting: empirical evidence

Guilding (1999) documented the frequency and perceived usefulness of competitor accounting in light of the insights taken from contingency theory literature using a mail-out survey in New Zealand's 230 largest companies. His survey focused on five competitor accounting practices: competitor cost assessment, competitor position monitoring, competitor appraisal based on published financial statements, strategic costing and strategic pricing. To assess the extent to which the sampled firms used these practices, his survey instrument asked this question, on a seven-point scale ranging from 1 (not at all) to 7 (to a great extent): 'To what extent does your organisation use the following (listed) practices?' His survey used a similar method to measure the perceived usefulness of the above practices: 'To what extent do you consider the following (listed) practices could be helpful to your organisation?' Table 9.1 summarises his results (mean) on these two issues.

Table 9.1 Competitor accounting practices in New Zealand firms

Competitor accounting practices	Usage rate (mean)[*]	Perceived usefulness (mean)[*]
Competitive position monitoring	4.95	5.69
Strategic pricing	4.63	5.32
Competitor appraisal based on published financial statements	4.17	5.16
Competitor cost assessment	3.91	5.05
Strategic costing	3.41	4.86

[*] Theoretical range 1–7: 1 = not at all, 7 = to a great extent.
Source: Guilding (1999).

To explore these issues further, Guilding's study examined the extent to which four contingent factors – strategic mission, competitive strategy, company size and industry – might affect the relative use and perceived usefulness of each competitor accounting practice appraised. His study found significant relationships between competitor accounting practices and competitive strategy, strategic mission and company size. In his study, 'prospector' firms made greater use of and perceived greater usefulness in competitor accounting practices. Further, his study found that firms pursuing a 'build' strategic mission had a greater propensity to use strategic pricing and strategic costing, and perceived greater helpfulness in four of the five competitor accounting practices. Size was also positively associated with greater use of and greater perceived usefulness in competitor accounting practices.

Chapter summary

Competitor accounting (or competitor analysis) has received increasing attention in the accounting community. Competitor accounting is about generating and monitoring competitor cost and strategic information. The simple step for competitor accounting is to divide a competitor's costs from the published financial statements by the units produced and determine an average product cost. In a complex, multiproduct environment, however, it would not yield very useful information. The ideal technique in this situation would be the development of very specific product cost estimates based on detailed information about the competitor's cost structure, products and the product's costs in the production process (Jones, 1988).

Key terms to learn

Competitive position   Competitor analysis
Competitor accounting   Industry profitability

Discussion questions

9.1   Explain why it is important for an organisation to set a strategic goal for how it plans to compete in the market.

9.2. Why is competitor analysis critical for identifying opportunities and threats? What questions should an organisation ask to identify these?

9.3 What particular factors should a company pay attention to when it is carrying out a competitor analysis?

9.4 What is competitor accounting?

9.5 Assume you work for the Hilton chain of hotels. What factors would you consider when making an analysis of your competitors?

9.6 What strategies can the organisation use to compete with competitors?

9.7 What is relative value?

9.8 Assume you work for a water company. What benchmarks would be useful to you? Explain why you chose each benchmark.

9.9 There are five key forces affecting industry competition; describe and provide examples of each of these.

9.10 If you were the company accountant for Coles/Myer supermarket chain, where would you go for information on competitors?

9.11 What role does management accounting play in competitor analysis?

9.12 What are the basic steps for competitor analysis?

9.13 What are the ingredients of the competitor analysis?

9.14 What is the relationship between value chain and competitor analysis?

9.15 What is the advantage of industry profitability analysis?

9.16 Referring to strategy typology, competitor analysis is likely to be important for which strategy? Explain.

Note

1. This textbook uses used the terms 'competitor analysis' and 'competitor accounting' interchangeably to refer to the accounting, or analysis, of competitors based on key factors and criteria. This form can be used to assess relative strength, as well as to compare the strengths and weaknesses of competitors with those of your firm.

Further reading

Guilding, C. (1999) 'Competitor-focused accounting: an exploratory note', *Accounting, Organizations and Society*, vol. 24, pp. 583–95.

CHAPTER 10

Responsibility accounting, financial performance measures and transfer prices

Key learning objectives

After reading this chapter you should be able to:

- describe the role of performance measurement systems in organisational effectiveness;
- illustrate the different types of responsibility centres;
- demonstrate an understanding of key financial performance measures: return on investment (ROI) and residual income (RI);
- explain the concept 'economic valued added' (EVA);
- explain the concept 'market value added' (MVA);
- identify the problems with conventional financial measures;
- illustrate and demonstrate an understanding of the transfer pricing policy of firms.

Introduction

Organisations use a series of performance measures to evaluate the performance of their business units and their managers. These measures allow managers to keep them focused on the organisation's goals. Financial measures such as return on investment (ROI) or net earnings are important performance evaluation tools. In this chapter, I will discuss the various financial measures that managers can use in performance evaluation. Over the past decade these measures have become very popular in many organisations. Recently, these practices, however, have been criticised for their shortcomings, such as ignorance of non-financial measures of performance. This chapter also critically discusses this issue.

The role of a performance measurement system

The role of performance evaluation (or measurement) is not merely to monitor managers' performance and the firm's progress in achieving desired goals, but also to assist managers in the monitoring of the firm's strategic position. Through performance measures, an organisation communicates how it wishes the manager to behave and how this behaviour will be judged and evaluated.

Performance measurement is an essential part of the organisation's planning and control, because it shows if organisations are achieving their targets set at strategic (or unit) and operational levels. Organisations must measure their business outcomes regularly. Performance measures or performance evaluation systems should be emphasised to measure specific characteristics of the business that will help provide the business with a competitive advantage. Lynch and Cross (1991) suggest that one purpose of a performance evaluation system is to assess the performance of the particular manufacturing process or the progress of improvement; if the measure is not related to either of these concepts then it will not be able to convey to management the actual performance of the particular process. According to them performance indicators must be made to fit to the process flow and focus attention on causal relationships and teamwork, which enables any non-value activities or faults to be recognised.

Performance can be focused on products, processes and people (employees and customers). Managers use performance measures to track their performance against the targets set. This allows managers at all levels of the business to assess progress in achieving targets and to take corrective actions if necessary. It may also indicate the need to amend plans and targets when there have been changes in the internal (micro) or external (macro) environment of the business.

Performance measurement is of greater value if the actual performance is compared with some benchmark, which may be a budgeted target or an external benchmark. Corporate management may use performance measures to evaluate their unit managers' performance as the basis for rewards.

Organisations have to move fast in order to remain competitive. Thus it is essential for organisations to use a range of performance measures that reflect their competitive environment and strategies to ensure that managers are motivated and rewarded for achieving the things that matter. Performance measures should not just inform managers of the outcomes of past decisions and operations; they should give an indication of the capability of the firm to compete effectively in the future and point to areas of future growth.

Responsibility centres/responsibility reporting

A responsibility centre can be defined as follows: any organisational or functional unit headed by a manager who is responsible for the activities of that unit. All responsibility centres have their own budgets and use resources (inputs or costs) to produce outputs (products/services). Literature identifies four types of responsibility centre.

Revenue centres are those organisational units in which outputs are measured in monetary terms, but are not directly compared to input costs. A sales department is an example of such a unit.

Expense or cost centres are those organisational units in which inputs, but not outputs, are measured in monetary terms. Budgets are devised only for the input portion of these centres' operations. Administrative, service and research departments are examples of such centres. We can see two types of expense centres: engineered and discretionary. Engineered expenses are those for which costs can be calculated or estimated with high reliability – for example the costs of direct labour or raw material. Discretionary expenses are those for which costs cannot be reliably estimated beforehand (e.g. research and development costs) and must depend to a large extent on the manager's judgment (or discretion). At review time, actual input expenses will be measured against budgeted input expenses (Stoner, 1982).

Profit centres are responsible for earning a profit. In a divisionalised organisation, in which each of a number of divisions is completely responsible for its own product line, the separate divisions are considered profit centres. The expenditures of all of a division's subunits are totalled and then subtracted from the revenues derived from that division's products or services. The net result is the measure of that division's profitability.

Investment centres are decentralised units or divisions for which the manager is given maximum discretion for making short-run operating decisions on product mix, pricing and production methods, as well as the level and type of assets to be used (Kaplan and Atkinson, 1989). In addition to inputs and outputs, in an investment centre, a control system also assesses how those outputs compare with the assets employed in producing them. For example, a company requires a capital investment of $40 million in property, buildings and equipment and working capital. In its first year, the company has $4 million in labour and other input expenses, and $8 million in revenue. The company would not be able to earn a $4 million profit for two reasons: a deduction from revenues would have to be made to allow for depreciation of buildings and equipment; and the cost of that investment, in terms of what could have been earned if the funds had been invested elsewhere, would have to be taken into account. In this way, a much more accurate picture of profitability would be obtained. Any profit centre can be considered an investment centre as well, because its activities will require some form of capital investment. However, if a centre's capital investment is minor or if its managers have no control over capital investment, it may be more appropriately treated as a profit centre (Stoner, 1982).

Key financial performance measures

Financial performance measures focus on the financial aspects of the organisation. They are also called accounting-based measures, because as they are based on financial statements such as income statements and balance sheets.

Accounting-based measures generally include measures such as return on investment (ROI), residual income (RI), net earnings or profits, earnings per share (EPS), revenue growth, cash flows, economic value added (EVA) and market value added (MVA). These methods are used to evaluate an organisation's performance in dimensions that are crucial to its health and survival. Some of these financial measures of performance are discussed below in turn.

Return on investment (ROI)

An approach to financial performance measurement that has received considerable attention and study is the Du Pont system of financial measurement. The key rationale of the Du Pont system is *return on investment*

(ROI), which is expressed as follows:

$$ROI = \frac{Sales}{Investment} \times \frac{Profit}{Sales}$$

The first line determines the total asset turnover ratio. It is arrived at by adding current assets to fixed assets, which equals total capital employed and then dividing this total into the total sales revenue. The second line determines the profit margin on sales. As shown above, dividing the net profit by total sales yields the profit margin on sales. For both of these measures, the intent is to capture the firm's rate of return per dollar of investment (Gordon, 1998).

An ROI encourages management to adopt an integrated approach to assessing organisational efficiency. For instance, if the ROI is low (relative to that of competitors or the organisation in the past), managers can backtrack to find possible sources of the problem – say a low turnover ratio. ROI also discourages excessive investment in assets.

The ROI system has two major limitations. First, a satisfactory ROI may actually conceal weaknesses. An efficient use of manufacturing assets, for example, might be offset by a particularly effective sales campaign and still result in a satisfactory ROI. If sales return to normal, the continued efficient use of manufacturing assets will cause a marked decline in the ROI to appear. Once managers are aware of these possibilities, they can establish additional standards and control at each point in the system. The other problem is that concentration on ROI, with its emphasis on current sales and capital utilisation, may tend to overshadow the company's long-term goals. Current return on capital, for example, may sometimes need to be sacrificed in order to build a firm foundation for future expansion. Such pitfalls can be overcome by establishing additional standards and controls for the firm's other activities and goals (Stoner, 1982).

Residual income (RI)

Residual income (RI) is expressed by the following formula:

Residual income (RI) = Net income before tax (NIBT) – CC (capital charge)

Capital charge is the firm's cost of capital multiplied by capital employed.

The RI corresponds closely to the economist's (but not the accountant's) measure of income, discussion of which follows. Measuring a subunit's

---

performance based on RI is equivalent to establishing the subunit somewhere between a profit and investment centre (Gordon, 1998).

Like ROI, RI also focuses on short-term benefits and cannot be used to evaluate the relative performance of different-sized subunits (for details, see Kaplan and Atkinson, 1989; Gordon, 1998). In spite of this weakness, RI has many positive uses. RI takes account of the subunit's required rate of return in assessing performance and it maximises the economic wealth of the subunit. So, it is usually accurate enough to justify its use as a decision-making aid and as a control device.

Information for financial measures comes from three financial statements – the profit and loss account (or the income statement), the balance sheet and the sources and application of funds – and the budget. That is why financial measures are sometimes referred to as *accounting-based performance measures*.

Economic value added (EVA)

Strategic management literature suggests that management should strive to increase the value of the company. Management can, in fact, be operating a business at a profit and increasing its net worth, but could be reducing the value of the company in relation to what could be earned elsewhere on the capital employed in the business (Digman, 1999). Economic value added (EVA) provides this kind of information. It indicates whether a business is creating wealth or, in fact, destroying capital. EVA can be expressed as follows:

EVA = After-tax operating profit (r) – Cost of capital (c)

If the EVA figure is positive, wealth is being created, i.e. the firm is adding more capital than it is costing. If negative, the reverse is true; this implies the firm would get a better return on its capital by investing it elsewhere.

EVA is the best measure of periodic performance, setting suitable targets for monopoly or competitive behaviour and enabling direct comparison with other similar companies.

Digman (1999) suggests three ways for management to improve EVA: (1) using less capital (i.e. by cutting invested capital perhaps by outsourcing, leasing, etc.); (2) increasing profits without increasing capital invested – this implies cost cutting; and (3) investing in high-return projects (earning more than the total cost of capital required).

An illustration

To compute EVA, I shall use the following as an illustration:

Alpha Products uses economic value added (EVA) analysis in its performance management system. The following information is available:

	1997	1998	1999	2000	2001
Net operating profit after tax ($m)	–	1,350	1,260	972	1,292
Total capital employed ($m)	8,919	9,123	9,068	9,082	9,995
Cash flow from operation ($m)	–	1,078	1,334	(80)	900
Cost of capital	12.5%	12.7%	11.6%	11.5%	9.3%

Required:

(a) Calculate the required rate of return on investment for the corporation for each of the years 1998, 1999, 2000 and 2001.

(b) Calculate the EVA in total dollars for the corporation for each of the years 1998, 1999, 2000 and 2001.

(c) Based on your calculations conducted for part (b) of this question, do you believe the corporation has performed well in the period 1998–2001?

Solution:

(a) r = the required rate of ROI = Net profit after tax/Total capital employed (beginning)

1998 = $1,350 /$8,919 = 0.1514 or 15.14%
1999 = $1,260/$9,123 = 0.1381 or 13.81%
2000 = $972/$9,068 = 0.1071 or 10.71%
2001 = $1,292/$9,082 = 0.1423 or 14.23%

(b) EVA (%) = r – c (cost of capital)   EVA ($) = EVA% × Total capital

1998 = 15.14 – 12.7 = 2.44%   2.44% × 9,123   = $222.60
1999 = 13.81 – 11.6 = 2.21%   2.21% × 9,068   = $200.40
2000 = 10.71 – 11.5 = (0.79%)   (0.79%) × 9,082 = ($71.75)
2000 = 14.23 – 9.3 = 4.93%   4.93% × 9,995   = $492.75

(c) Overall performance for 1998–2001:

$$\text{Average } r = [15.14\% + 13.81\% + 10.71\% + 14.23\%]/4 = 13.47\%$$
$$\text{Average } c = [12.7\% + 11.6\% + 11.5\% + 9.3\%]/4 = 11.28\%$$
$$\text{Total EVA} = [222.60 + 200.40 + (71.75) + 492.75]/4 = \$211m$$

Based on the above information, the company has performed well for the 1998–2001 period except for the financial year 2000, on average for four years having a positive figure of $211m from 1999–2001.

Market value added (MVA)

A related concept to EVA, market value added (MVA) focuses on the total value of a company at a given point in time – a sort of a value-added balance sheet. MVA can be expressed as follows:

MVA = Total market value of the company – Capital tied up in the company

where the total capital tied up equals all profits the company has reinvested in the business plus all money contributed by stockholders and lenders, and the company's market value is the current value of all the company's equity and debt. If the MVA figure is positive, the company (since its inception) has created capital; if negative, it has destroyed capital (Digman, 1999).

Table 10.1 shows the computation of a range of financial measures.

Problems with conventional financial measures

ROI and RI are important accounting-based measures of conventional responsibility reporting and performance evaluation. In today's competitive environment, one that encompasses fierce global competition, advancing technology and increased customer awareness, these measures of performance reporting can be inadequate for a business unit. Kaplan (1994), in his book *Measures for Manufacturing Excellence*, states that although many companies had made enormous strides during the 1980s to embrace total quality management (TQM), just-in-time (JIT) manufacturing and distribution processes, design for manufacturability (DFM) and flexible manufacturing systems (FMS) into their operations, they were much slower to adjust their managerial accounting and control systems to the new operating environment and, as a result, operating improvements, which were significant, were not being tracked well by traditional financial performance measurement systems.

Table 10.1 Typical financial performance measures

Performance measurement focus	Performance measures or indicators	Computational techniques
Profitability	Return on capital employed	Operating profit or profit before interest and tax/Capital employed (fixed and current assets)
	Return on net assets	Profit before interest and tax/Net assets
	Return on investment	(Profit after tax/Total revenues) × (Total revenues/Investment)
	Return on equity	Profit after tax/Ordinary shareholders' funds
	Profit margin	Operating profit/Sales × 100
	Economic value added	After-tax operating profit – Cost of capital
	Market value added	Total market value – Total capital tied up (all profits + all money contributed by stockholders and lenders)
	Profit per employee	Operating profit/Number of employees
Solvency	Acid ratio	Debtors + Cash/Current liabilities
	Current ratio	Current assets/Current liabilities
Financial structure	Gearing ratio	Total debt/Shareholders' funds × 100

ROI, though, can aid in detecting weakness with respect to the use or non-use of individual assets – particularly in connection with inventories – and focus management's attention upon earning the best profit possible on the capital available and avoid isolating individual business units, in that it may not be reasonable to expect the same ROI for each unit. If the unit sells their respective products in markets that differ widely with respect to product development, competition and consumer demand, lack of agreement on the optimum rate of return might discourage managers who believe the rate is set at an unfair level.

For the sake of making the current period performance measure look good, be it ROI, RI, operating income or EPS, managers may be influenced to make decisions that are not in the best long-term interests of the firm. Research in the United States has shown that these measures produced irrelevant and misleading information and also 'provoked behaviour that undermined the achievements of strategic objectives' (Kaplan and Norton, 1996). A major concern with accounting-based performance measures is that these performance measures focus on results largely internal to the firm.

During the last decade there has been an overemphasis on the use of financial criteria to measure firm performance. This has resulted in the organisation losing sight of important indicators that measure levels of customer satisfaction, process flexibility or adaptation in response to changing needs. A strategy which concentrates on financial criteria is too closely related to short-term profit maximisation. Broader measures, such as customer-based measures, product and process measures, and continual improvement and innovation measures, enable the organisation to establish longer-term improvements which further effective competition. This issue is taken up in the following chapter.

Transfer pricing systems

Transfer pricing issues remain at the heart of decentralised firms. Much of the early empirical research on transfer pricing was based on a traditional economic theory that suggests that the role of transfer prices is to allocate resources within the firm to determine the optimal product mix. This is based on the assumption that managers are motivated to maximise their division's profits, because at least some of their rewards are tied to divisional financial performance (Eccles, 1985; Ezzamel, 1991). Organisations can determine optimal transfer prices that may lead both the selling and buying divisions to choose output levels that maximise the total profits of the firm. Theorists argue optimal transfer prices can be derived under different market conditions ranging from perfect competition, through imperfect competition and discriminating monopoly to complete absence of external markets. What is a transfer price? How is a transfer price set? These are discussed in turn.

What is a transfer price?

A transfer price is the price one responsibility centre (or segment) of an organisation charges for a product or service supplied to another segment of the same organisation (Kaplan and Atkinson, 1989). A transfer pricing system facilitates cost determination and control and performance accountability. Goods transferred from one unit to another are called *intermediate products*. The division providing an intermediate product is the *supplying division* and the division receiving it is the *buying division*. An intermediate product becomes the *final product* at the buying division.

Strategic issues involved in a transfer pricing decision are as follows. Should units be free to decide whether to sell/buy from other units? Should units be able to source externally when internal goods are available? At what price will the transfer be made? Which type of transfer pricing method will be used (market, cost or negotiated)? How is the exact transfer pricing determined, once the method is selected? How are disputes resolved (negotiation, arbitration or directives)? These are practical issues required for an effective transfer pricing system in an organisation.

An opportunity cost approach is adopted when setting a transfer price. The opportunity cost approach identifies the minimum price that a selling division would be willing to accept and the maximum price that the buying division would be willing to pay. They are defined for each division as follows. The minimum transfer price is the transfer price that would leave the selling division no worse off if the good is sold to an internal division. The maximum transfer price is the transfer price that would leave the buying division no worse off if an input is purchased from an internal division.

Transfer pricing methods

There are two broad classes of transfer pricing: (1) market-based transfer pricing and (2) cost-based transfer pricing.

Market-based transfer prices. If a perfectly competitive market for the product exists, then the market price is recommended as the correct transfer price. A perfectly competitive market exists when there is a homogeneous product with equivalent buying and selling prices, and no individual buyers and sellers can affect those prices by their own actions.

Cost-based transfer prices. If a market price does not exist, use cost-based transfer prices. The simple rules for constructing such a price must be prescribed by top management to avoid conflict between the buying and supplying divisions. There are two subclasses of cost-based prices: *marginal-cost transfer prices* and *full-cost transfer prices*. In the absence of a market price, economic theory indicates that the theoretically correct transfer price is the marginal cost of production. Full-cost transfer pricing includes all production costs as well as costs from other business functions, such as R&D, design, marketing, distribution and customer service. There are two subclasses of full-cost prices: *full cost plus mark-up* and *incremental (marginal or variable) cost plus fixed fee*. Full cost plus mark-up includes full production costs plus mark-up; the mark-up can be negotiated. On the other hand, full cost plus variable cost plus fixed fee can be a viable transfer pricing approach, provided that the fixed fee is negotiable.

Negotiated transfer pricing. When imperfections exist in the market for the intermediate product, negotiated transfer prices may be a practical alternative. Using such a pricing method, the supplying division is free to negotiate the transfer price with the buying division. The negotiated transfer price is the outcome of a bargaining process between the 'selling' and the 'buying' divisions (Kaplan and Atkinson, 1989). Negotiated transfer pricing has limitations. First, it is time-consuming. Second, it may lead to conflict between divisions. Third, it may make the divisional measurement sensitive to the negotiating skills of managers. Fourth, it requires the time of top management to oversee the negotiating process and to mediate disputes. Finally, it may lead to a sub-optimal (too low) level of output if the negotiated price is above the opportunity cost of supplying the transferred goods (Kaplan and Atkinson, 1989).

Limitations/issues of transfer pricing systems

Ezzamel (1991) notes three limitations of the traditional economic model of transfer pricing. First, the traditional view of transfer pricing overemphasises the attainment of corporate optimality at the expense of maintaining divisional autonomy and this is likely to result in adverse behavioural implications. Second, marginal cost-based transfer prices reasonably reflect opportunity cost only when the market for the intermediate product is highly competitive, or if there exists one demanding division, the opportunity cost will be the highest of the marginal cost and the revenue forgone by diverting resources from alternative uses. Third, the traditional model assumes that company divisions are independent of each other with regard to both production technology and demand. However, the prevalence of technological and demand interdependence in practice restricts the applicability of the model significantly. In general, economic transfer pricing models are of limited value because of their simplifying assumptions. Academic research continued through the lines of mathematical programming models to deal with complexities of multiple products, divisions and goals. However, this research is based on purely technical and analytical elaboration, rather than seeing transfer pricing in organisational contexts.

When transfer pricing is viewed from an organisational perspective, different questions are asked on the nature of transfer pricing along with the process through which such prices are established. How did a particular transfer price come to be established? What are the behavioural influences of various transfer pricing methods? And more recently, following a contingency perspective, how can various contextual factors influence the internal functioning of a particular transfer pricing method? The emphasis on such behavioural aspects arises out of organisational attempts to establish internal pricing systems, which motivate, coordinate and control the allocation of economic resources and factors of production so that the overall organisational goals can be achieved (Abdel-Khalik and Lusk, 1974).

Behavioural research paid due importance to organisational decentralisation and integration issues (Watson and Baumler, 1975). Transfer pricing was seen as an integration device in a decentralised firm. While a decentralised environment gives more autonomy, conflict can arise over the settlement of transfer pricing disputes. Transfer pricing conflicts can be resolved through negotiation. Even though behavioural research addresses some important implications of transfer pricing on organisational members, they do not address wider organisational issues such as the influence of contextual factors, e.g. divisional size, managerial autonomy, market factors, product diversity and strategy.

Borkowski (1990), for example, investigated the environmental and organisational factors influencing a firm's choice of transfer pricing method. Her findings, based on a sample of 452 US manufacturing firms, indicate that the presence of certain variables – particularly market price – does not imply the use of the market price method. Firms are using cost-based methods, even though a market price for the transferred good is available. Her results support the contingency theory of management accounting choice, in which firms choose a method based on what is perceived as optimal in their particular situation.

Chapter summary

A performance measurement system guides the day-to-day activities of managers and assesses the performance of organisations and their managers. The system also facilitates the coordination of managerial and business unit goals with overall corporate goals. Through performance, a firm can communicate how it wishes its business units and managers to behave and how this behaviour will be judged and evaluated.

Managers may be instructed to maximise operating income, return on investment (ROI), return on assets (ROA) or residual income (RI). For the sake of making the current period performance measure look good, be it ROI, ROA, RI, operating income or earnings per share (EPS), managers may be influenced to make decisions that are not in the best interests of the firm. This behaviour results in the organisation losing sight of important indicators that relate to the firm's success, such as customer satisfaction, process flexibility or adaptation in response to changing needs. Empirical research on transfer pricing has found a substantial difference between the actual methods used in practice and the methods discussed above in this chapter.

Key terms to learn

Economic valued added	Performance measurement systems
Financial performance	Residual income
Market value added	Responsibility centres
Performance evaluation	Return on investment

Discussion questions

10.1 What is responsibility accounting and why is it important for performance measurement systems?

10.2 What is the role of a performance measurement system in organisations?

10.3 Categorise the following responsibility centres as either a profit centre, a revenue centre, an expense centre or an investment centre:
   (a) a conference sales division of a hotel company;
   (b) the accounting and finance department of your university;
   (c) the geology division of a mining company;
   (d) a commercialised business unit of a local government;
   (e) the refund department of a Coles/Myers supermarket;
   (f) a winery operated by a large vineyard.

10.4 The ROI has two limitations. What are they?

10.5 Is the ROI or the RI a better measure of profitability?

10.6   What are the strengths and the weaknesses of financial performance measures?

10.7   There is an argument that financial performance measures may only give short-term benefit. Explain this statement with examples.

10.8   EVA is used to indicate what?

10.9   Why is the traditional MAS not sufficient for effective performance measurement?

10.10 Define transfer pricing. Why is transfer pricing used in organisations? What are its limitations?

10.11 Explain three methods of transfer pricing. Explain which one you think is the best method from an organisational performance point of view.

10.12 What is the relationship between transfer pricing and performance measures? Give examples.

Further reading

Broadbent, M. and Cullen, J. (1995) 'Divisional control', in Berry, A.J., Broadbent, J. and Otley, D. (eds), *Management Control: Theories, Issues and Practices*, London: Macmillan Press, chapter 7.

CHAPTER 11

Measuring non-financial performance

Key learning objectives

After reading this chapter you should be able to:

- understand the importance of non-financial measures in performance evaluation;
- identify key non-financial performance indicators or measures;
- build a strategic performance measurement system for an organisation;
- understand the operation of a performance measurement system in an uncertain environment.

Introduction

'If you are relying on traditional performance measures, you are probably not getting the answers you need to help you become more competitive. Even highly successful organisations have the sense of succeeding in spite of – rather than because of – performance measures' (Lynch and Cross, 1991, pp. 4–5). This chapter addresses what needs to be done to overcome this problem and how to do it.

The importance of non-financial performance measures

Traditional financial performance measures such as return on investment (ROI) or net earnings do not consistently support the intended strategy. In recent years, numerous authors have expressed discontent with traditional measures of organisational performance, which mainly focus on financial criteria (Lynch and Cross, 1991; Kaplan and Norton, 1996). The suggestion is that in today's fierce competitive environment, markets are changing swiftly and innovation is considered paramount. Consequently, the past overemphasis on such financial criteria as operating income, sales growth, ROI and earnings per share (EPS) to measure firm performance has resulted in the organisation losing sight of important indicators which measure levels of customer satisfaction, process flexibility or adaptation in response to changing needs.

There is also the view that non-financial measures should reflect the drivers of future financial performance (Kaplan and Norton, 1996). The bottom line is that the traditional performance measures should be replaced with more flexible, dynamic measures. Broader criteria such as customer-based measures, product and process measures and continual improvement and innovation measures enable the organisation to establish longer-term improvements that are likely to lead to increased productivity and competitiveness (Simons, 1995; Kaplan and Norton, 1996). The argument put forward in the relevant literature is that the use of non-financial measures for performance evaluation enables managers to understand those factors that are most critical to the firm's long-term success (Lynch and Cross, 1991; Maisel, 1992; Newing, 1995; Thorne, 1995). Nevertheless, the importance of non-financial measures to the system of performance evaluation has been recognised in the literature; for example, the National Association of Accountants (NAA) in its monograph *Measuring Entity Performance* (1986) observed:

> Non-financial performance measures provide a rich opportunity for managers to improve entity evaluations and operations. Such measures direct

management's attention to the entity's operations and, in the long-term, may better reflect the financial returns generated by an entity than do the short-term historical financial measures. (Cited in Lothian, 1987, p. 6)

Note, the performance measures do not merely monitor managers' performance and the firm's progress in achieving desired goals, but also assist managers in monitoring the firm's strategic positions. Several writers (e.g. Kaplan and Norton, 1996; Simons, 1995) suggest that the appropriate performance measures to include in a performance reporting system depend on the business strategy. Ittner et al. (1997, p. 233) suggest one potential determinant of the relative information content of alternative performance measures is the firm's business strategy. Thus performance measures, if devised strategically, will profoundly influence business performance.

Key non-financial performance measures

Performance measurement literature identifies the following common measures of non-financial performance of a business. Note these measures are by no means all-inclusive, but they are cited mostly in the literature.

- *Efficiency measures* are those used for tracking intra-organisational indicators to determine whether the business units are effectively using internal processes and resources. They focus on quality, time and efficiency such as direct materials efficiency variances, effect yield, manufacturing lead time, head count and inventory, together with manufacturing geometry versus competition and actual introduction schedule versus plan.

- *Innovation measures* assess an organisation's innovative capacity, and measure such things as number of new patents, number of new product launches, process time to market and time taken to develop 'next-generation' products.

- *Learning and growth measures* assess organisational learning capacity to enhance organisational long-term growth, and measure such things as employee intellectual capacity, employee training and development, the employee incentive system, employee turnover, etc.

- *Customer measures* trace performance leading to relationships with customers and encompass such measures as market share, customer response time, on-time performance, product reliability, share of key accounts purchases, ranking of key accounts and number of cooperative engineering efforts.

Table 11.1 provides an example of the use of non-financial performance measures in 71 New Zealand manufacturing firms (Hoque, Mia and Alam, 2001).

Table 11.1 The use of (mean) non-financial performance measures by New Zealand manufacturing firms

Non-financial measures	Mean use[*]
Internal business perspective	
Materials efficiency variance	3.90
Ratio of good output to total output at each production process	3.49
Manufacturing lead time	3.68
Rate of material scrap loss	3.50
Labour efficiency variance	4.27
Innovation and learning perspective	
Number of new patents	2.47
Number of new product launches	3.06
Time-to-market new products	3.41
Employee satisfaction	3.93
Customer perspective	
Market share	3.84
Customer response time	3.74
On-time delivery	3.37
Number of customer complaints	3.04
Number of warranty claims	4.16
Survey of customer satisfaction	3.41
Percentage of shipments returned due to poor quality	2.83
Number of overdue deliveries	3.82

[*]Theoretical range 1–5: 1 not at all; 5 to a very great extent. N = 71.
Source: Hoque et al. (2001).

Building a strategic performance measurement system

The role of performance evaluation is not merely to monitor managers' performance and the firm's progress in achieving desired goals, but also to assist managers in the monitoring of the firm's strategic position. Through performance measures, the organisation communicates how it wishes the manager to behave and how this behaviour will be judged and evaluated. During the last decade or so there has been an overemphasis on the use of financial criteria such as ROI or net earnings to evaluate organisational effectiveness. This has resulted in the organisation losing sight of important indicators that assess levels of customer satisfaction, process flexibility or adaptation in response to changing needs (Lynch and Cross, 1991; Kaplan and Norton, 1996).

As illustrated in Chapters 2 and 3, strategy plays an important role in the organisation's planning and control. An increasing body of literature suggests that performance measures used by the organisation should reflect its competitive strategy. Empirical evidence demonstrates the relationship between non-financial measures and organisational strategy, classified into defenders and prospectors (James and Hoque, 1999). Defender organisations have narrow product-market territories. Top managers within this type of organisation are highly expert in their organisation's limited area of operation, but do not tend to search outside their territories for new opportunities. As a result of this narrow focus, these organisations seldom need to make major adjustments in their technology, structure or methods of operation. Instead, they devote attention to improving the efficiency of their existing operations. Companies emphasising a defender-type strategy thus operate in a stable business environment. These organisations tend to focus on the efficiency of operations, to emphasise stability, to defend the company's position in the market and to earn the best profit possible, given its external environment. As a result, it is suggested that short-term, retrospective financial measures such as cost control, operating profit, cash flow from operations or ROI are relatively informative measures of performance in a defender-type organisation (Miles and Snow, 1978; Simons, 1987; Ittner et al., 1997).

The second type of organisation identified by Miles and Snow is the prospector. This type of organisation seeks new market opportunities. Prospectors regularly experiment with potential responses to emerging environmental trends. Thus the level of uncertainty is high in organisations pursuing a prospector-type strategy. These organisations are the creators of change and uncertainty to which their competitors must respond. They generally focus on product innovation and market opportunities, emphasising creativity over efficiency and maintaining flexibility rather than monitoring purely their financial position (Miles and Snow, 1978; Simons, 1987). Measures for focuses such as these would necessarily come from knowing what the customer wants, the level of staff involvement in creativity and the ability of the organisation to produce and market new products. Hence a greater usage of non-financial indicators as opposed to financial indicators would be prominent in this type of organisation.

Miles and Snow identify analysers as a third group, which is, in fact, the mixed strategy.[1] It combines the strongest characteristics of defenders and prospectors. They are organisations that operate in two types of product-market territories, one relatively stable and the other changing. In their stable areas, these organisations operate routinely and efficiently using formalised structures and processes. In their more turbulent areas, top managers watch their competitors closely for new ideas and then they quickly implement the new ideas that appear to be the most promising to maintain a competitive advantage, for example the pizza war between Domino's, Eagle Boys and Pizza Hut. The mixed strategy firms are more likely to place emphasis on a combination of both financial and non-financial performance measures than defenders or prospectors.

Performance measures in an uncertain environment

Financial measures such as ROI or net earnings are good for the measuring of past performance and for firms with no need to succeed in investment in long-term 'capabilities' etc. However, the business environment is changing rapidly and that introduces uncertainty. Uncertainty is defined as the organisation's inability to predict accurately the effects of various sources of uncertainty such as competition, production technologies, customer tastes and preferences, deregulation and globalisation, government regulation and policies, and industrial relations. Non-financial measures are better suited for the measuring of performance under uncertainty, because they will make managers consider them and act accordingly.

Contingency research in accounting suggests that effective organisations place less reliance on financial performance measures under conditions of high environmental uncertainty when evaluating subunit performance (see, for example, Govindarajan 1984; Hirst 1983; Brownell 1985; for a review see

Chapman, 1997). This is usually explained in terms of conventional performance measurement systems being unable to satisfactorily capture important dimensions of performance and information under such circumstances. The recent performance measurement literature indicates that in uncertain situations, measuring firm performance requires management's greater reliance on non-financial measures such as market share, customer satisfaction, efficient use of R&D dollars, efficiency and quality. Kaplan and Norton (1996) suggest that without such measures, no longer can a firm gain sustainable competitive advantage. These observations resemble the insights from several other studies – see, for example, Govindarajan and Shank (1992), Ittner and Larcker (1998), Chenhall (1997), Perera et al. (1997), Banker et al. (2000) and Hoque and James (2000).

Kaplan and Norton (1996) suggest that in today's competitive environment companies must be masters at anticipating customers' future needs, devising radical new product and service offerings and rapidly deploying new product and production technologies into operating and service delivery processes. They further suggest that such environmental uncertainty for companies requires new capabilities for organisational success; managers must have the ability to better understand their uncertain environments and to cope with varying degrees of uncertainty. According to Kaplan and Norton (1996, p. 6), 'Breakthrough in performance requires major change and that includes changes in the measurement and management systems used by an organisation … Navigating to a more competitive, technological and capability-driven future cannot be accomplished merely by monitoring and controlling financial measures of past performance.' Ideally, financial measures assess the effectiveness of past events and they are adequate for companies for which investments in long-term capabilities and customer relationships are not critical for success. These measures are inadequate for evaluating and guiding the journey that a business unit must take to create future value through investment in customers, suppliers, employees, processes, technology and innovation.

High environmental uncertainty may induce managers to use non-financial measures to a greater extent than financial measures when evaluating subunit performance. Non-financial measures would encourage managers to attend to more than just financial measures, because the pertinent notion of performance is broader in today's uncertain environment. Additionally, when non-financial performance measures are linked to the organisation's external environment, managers will be motivated to pay attention to those things that affect organisational performance and, subsequently, their own performance.

Chapter summary

A performance measurement system should be able to help top management assess their strategic initiatives. The past emphasis on traditional performance metrics such as ROI or net earnings distracted from due concern for non-financial factors such as market share, customer satisfaction, efficiency and productivity, product quality and employee satisfaction. This chapter suggests that non-financial measures are required to recognise changes in the market environment, to determine and assess progress towards business objectives and to affirm achievement of performance goals. Strategically driven measures of performance evaluation provide both management and employees with the means to identify with the success of the strategy and track their own contributions to its achievement. However, strategy implementation does not occur in a vacuum – the level of uncertainty the firm is operating in is critical. Companies with different operating environments will have different strategic initiatives and hence will require different management information systems designed to enhance organisational performance. Higher levels of environmental uncertainty affecting the performance of firms are associated with greater emphasis on non-financial measures in performance evaluation.

Key terms to learn

Customer satisfaction
Innovation
Internal business processes
Learning and growth

Non-financial performance
Uncertainty
Strategy

Discussion questions

11.1 Why are non-financial performance measures important? Explain.

11.2 List five non-financial performance measures.

11.3 Why are non-financial performance measures critical to a firm's long-term success?

11.4 There are four types of non-financial performance measures. Explain what each of these is.

11.5 Why are non-financial performance measures important for not-for-profit organisations?

11.6 How are non-financial performance measures designed?

11.7 Why do performance measurement systems help management to monitor the firm's strategic initiatives?

11.8 Referring to the strategy typology, what is the relationship between the type of strategy and the performance measurement system? Explain.

11.9 The theory suggests that the more uncertain the business environment, the greater the extent of the application of the multiple performance measurement. Do you agree with this statement? Explain.

11.10 What is the difficulty in combining financial with non-financial performance measures?

11.11 Is there any relationship between multiple performance measures and TQM? Explain.

11.12 Is there any relationship between multiple performance measurement and JIT? Explain.

Note

1. In today's competitive environments, it would be wrong to assume that an organisation chooses either a defender-type strategy or a prospector-type strategy to compete in the marketplace. It is now increasingly recognised in the extant literature that some firms are likely to display characteristics of both defender and prospector archetypes, which is the mixed strategy, in order to enhance their competitiveness (Shank and Govindarajan, 1993; Abernethy and Guthrie, 1994; Langfield-Smith, 1997; Chenhall and Langfield-Smith, 1998).

Further reading

Fisher I. (1995) 'Use of non-financial performance measures', in Young, S.M. (ed.), *Readings in Management Accounting*. Englewood Cliffs, NJ: Prentice Hall, pp. 329–35.

Ittner, C.D., Larcker, D.F. and Rajan, M.V. (1997) 'The choice of performance measures in annual bonus contract', *Accounting Review*, vol. 2, no. 2, April, pp. 231–56.

Perera, S., Harrison, G. and Poole, M. (1997) 'Customer-focused manufacturing strategy and the use of operations-based non-financial performance measures: a research note', *Accounting, Organizations and Society*, vol. 22, no. 6, pp. 557–72.

CHAPTER 12

The balanced scorecard

Key learning objectives

After reading this chapter you should be able to:

- describe the balanced scorecard evolution;
- discuss Kaplan and Norton's four balanced scorecard dimensions;
- identify arguments for the adoption of balanced scorecards;
- understand the relationship between contextual factors and the balanced scorecard;
- understand the relationship between total quality management and the balanced scorecard;
- review balanced scorecard practices in the public sector.

Introduction

'The Balanced Scorecard provides managers with the instrumentation they need to navigate to future competitive success …The Balanced Scorecard translates an organisation's mission and strategy into a comprehensive set of performance measures that provides the framework for strategic measurement and management systems' (Kaplan and Norton, 1996, p. 2). This chapter discusses this revolutionary performance measurement philosophy, which has gained prominence in management, accounting and operations management literature.

Balanced scorecard evolution

The imperative for improved performance measures cannot be ignored with today's worldwide competition and advancing technologies. Once new technologies are introduced, major organisation changes are required, as the interaction between people and technology is essential to ensure business processes become more and more effective and, therefore, performance measures that focus on only financial criteria will not reflect the new technological environment. New performance measures, if devised strategically, will profoundly influence business performance. Scholars, for example, suggest that more attention needs to be placed on generating suitable performance measures to be a successful competitor, given today's environment.

Research has revealed that for many companies, the difficulty is that there are 'too many performance measures', ones that are outmoded and that are not harmonious. Performance measures should observe changes in the market environment, determine and assess progress towards business unit objectives and affirm achievement of performance goals (Kaplan and Norton, 1996).

The literature suggests that any fresh, competent combination of measures must look to four essential focuses that are missing in traditional measures. Firstly, a method to trace customer satisfaction – in a competitive environment, customers must be content, or market share will drop. Customers care more about price, faster and reliable deliveries, design, quality and level of service. Secondly, a method to trace appropriate financial performance – that is, is the company profitable? The third area is that firms need a plan to ascertain competitive performance. Finally, there must be a method for tracking inter-organisational indicators to determine whether the business units are effectively using materials and resources.

As a result of the focus on these factors, top management must be aware that if they are to fulfil their strategic plans, they should adopt a more 'balanced approach' to gauge performance by considering financial and non-financial performance measures. Significant attention is now being given by academics and managers to building a more extensive and linked set of measures for appraising and directing corporate and divisional performance, influenced largely by Kaplan and Norton's (1992, 1993, 1996) notion of the 'balanced scorecard'.

The balanced scorecard philosophy

The balanced scorecard (BSC) approach focuses on both financial and non-financial measures. The financial measures indicate if improvements in financial performance resulted from sacrificing investments in new products or on-time delivery. The BSC includes financial measures that tell the 'results of actions already taken'. Kaplan and Norton suggest that financial measures should not be eliminated altogether, as a well-designed financial control system can actually enhance rather than inhibit an organisation's management programme. The 'balanced scorecard' supplements the financial measures with operational measures on customer satisfaction, internal processes and the firm's innovation and improvement activities. Kaplan and Norton suggest that operational measures are the drivers of future financial performance.

The components of the balanced scorecard are, firstly, the financial perspective, which includes profitability measures such as cash flow, quarterly sales growth and operating income by division, increased market share and return on equity. Secondly, the customer perspective encompasses such measures as market share, customer response time, on-time performance, product reliability, percentage of sales from new products, percentage of sales from established products, on-time delivery, share of key accounts purchases, ranking by key accounts and number of cooperative engineering efforts. Thirdly, the internal business processes include such measures as number of new patents, number of new product launches, process time to market, time to develop next-generation, quality, time and efficiency measures (such as direct materials efficiency variances, effect yield, manufacturing lead time, head count and inventory). The learning and growth perspective identifies the infrastructure that the organisation must build to create long-term growth and improvement. The objects in the learning and growth perspective are the drivers for achieving excellent output in the initial three scorecard perspectives.

Three essential principles for this perspective identified by Kaplan and Norton are employee capabilities, information system capabilities and motivation. Table 12.1 summarises the four BSC dimensions.

Table 12.1 Balanced scorecard dimensions and their measures

Balanced scorecard dimensions	Key indicators (or measures)
Financial	Operating income, return on investment, net earnings, earnings per share, sales growth, generation of cash flow and economic value-added
Internal business processes	Product design, product development, post-sale service, manufacturing efficiency and quality
Learning and growth	The intellectual ability of employees, information systems, organisational procedures to manage the business and adapt to change, employee training and development, and employee satisfaction
Customer	Customer satisfaction survey, customer retention, new customer acquisition, customer response time, market share and customer profitability

Arguments for the adoption of the balanced scorecard

Several companies, especially in the United States, have already adopted the 'balanced scorecard'; as Kaplan and Norton observed, 'their early experiences using the scorecard have demonstrated that it meets several managerial needs'. Firstly, the scorecard brings together in one report many miscellaneous elements of a company's competitive plan, e.g. customer orientation, improvement in response time, quality, promotion of teamwork and encouragement of shorter product launch times as well as looking to the long-term. Secondly, the scorecard guards against sub-optimisation. By forcing top management to think about all the important operational measures together, the 'balanced scorecard' enables them to see if improvement in one area has been achieved at the expense of another area.

Kaplan and Norton's 'balanced scorecard' has been put forth, presumably, because traditional measurement systems have developed from, as they suggest, the finance role and because traditional systems have a control bias. That is, traditional performance measurement systems stipulate the type of behaviour that employees should take and are then used to determine whether the employees have in fact behaved in the particular manner. As such, traditional systems attempt to control behaviour as opposed to the 'balanced scorecard' which is used to encourage behaviour directed at improving the key indicators.

The 'balanced scorecard' focuses on strategy and vision, not control; this focus is the kind of focus that many organisations are trying to accomplish, that is 'cross-functional integration, customer supplier partnerships, global scale, continuous improvement and teams rather than individual accountability'. By utilising the 'balanced scorecard' firms can establish management goals and managers can take whatever actions are necessary and adapt their behaviour as appropriate to accomplish those goals.

In their 1993 paper, Kaplan and Norton suggest that different market situations, product strategies and competitive environments require different scorecards and that business units will create their scorecard to match their strategy, mission, technology and culture. Kaplan and Norton identify a number of firms who have implemented the 'balanced scorecard'. Some examples are: Apple Computers, which use the scorecard as a device to plan long-term performance, not as a device to drive operating changes; Advance Micro Devices, a semiconductor company, which wanted to consolidate their strategic information; and Rockwater, a global engineering and construction company, which is a worldwide leader in underwater engineering and construction, whose executives wanted a metric that would communicate the importance of building relationships with customers.

Research has found that many companies that are now implementing local improvement programmes, such as process redevelopment, total quality management and employee involvement, are moving to the 'balanced scorecard' as a means of measuring the success of these endeavours (Hoque et al., 2001; Hoque and James, 2000). Furthermore, the 'balance scorecard' communicates priorities to management, employees, investors and even customers. It is used as the focal point for the firm's efforts in achieving its goals. Firms using the 'balanced scorecard' do not have to rely on short-term financial measures as the sole indicators of the company's performance; the scorecard contributes to linking long-term strategic objectives with short-term processes. Creating a 'balanced scorecard' has forced companies to unite their strategic planning and budgeting, which has helped ensure that their budgets support their strategies.

The academic community has recognised that the BSC advances the management literature by specifying a range of measures stated above that managers should attend to in order to build long-term, sustainable competitive advantage. Atkinson et al. (1997) suggest that the BSC has the potential to provide planners with a way of expressing and testing a sophisticated model of cause-and-effect in the organisation, a model that provides managers with a basis to manage desired and actual results.

The use of a BSC *does not* mean just 'using more measures': it means putting a handful of strategically critical measures together in a single report in a way that makes cause-and-effect relations transparent and keeps managers from sub-optimising by improving one measure at the expense of others. To achieve a *balance* among the four dimensions of the BSC, a company should pay attention to all of them, according to Kaplan and Norton (1996). In other words, one can achieve this by putting equal emphasis on both the financial and non-financial measures of the BSC. Atkinson et al. (1997, p. 93) suggest that the name 'scorecard' is misleading, because BSC is not a scorecard in the conventional sense. Rather, it is a sophisticated information system and management approach that links effects (also called organisational objectives, such as profit levels) with causes, such as customer or employee satisfaction. This argument makes sense because one should not take the BSC as a *blueprint*; it's a *philosophy*. It has the potential to provide managers with a linked set of measures that specifies how the four perspectives of measures stated above can be aligned with overall company strategy, how managers should attend to both financial and non-financial measures of performance and how they can integrate them.

No doubt, Kaplan and Norton's BSC philosophy is extremely useful as one of the 'new' theories that can be applied (with positive effect) to many organisations. It is a logical conclusion to a complex problem and after studying it, there are a number of points that make straightforward common sense. It has been put forward with clarity, articulation and rationality, which itself contributes to its worth as a sound and reasonable theory. The biggest criticism that can be made is that the BSC attempts, in my opinion, to convey that an all-encompassing solution to performance evaluation problems has been found. Deriving useful results from its application is dependent on a number of factors, namely industry concentrations, the operating environment and the management systems of the organisation.

Linking balanced scorecard measures to size and market factors: the Hoque and James (2000) study

Hoque and James (2000) consider the size of organisations, product life-cycle stage and market position as potential contextual factors of BSC usage, and explore how organisational performance is affected by different uses of BSC in different settings. Each of the potentially contingent factors will now be considered in turn.

Organisation size and the balanced scorecard

Contingency theories of organisations developed by Burns and Stalker (1961), Lawrence and Lorsch (1967) and Woodward (1965) suggest that size may affect the way organisations design and use management systems. Merchant (1981, 1984) claims that organisational growth poses increased communication and control problems. As the size of the firm increases, accounting and control processes tend to become more specialised and sophisticated. The contingency theory literature suggests that size is related to greater decentralisation and structuring of activities, due to information processing constraints upon senior management. Furthermore, the need to stimulate effective communication flows becomes more apparent in larger organisations, as in such organisations the behavioural orientation characterising management controls in small organisations becomes unworkable. As a consequence, in large business enterprises, a broader set of information and measurement issues arises. Small companies frequently do not require elaborate performance evaluation techniques as the strategy setters, usually the owners, are close to the 'action'. Organisations that have sole customer arrangements, unless faced with the prospect of competition further down the track, are usually best off focusing on internal processes and financials. Hoque and James (2000) found support for this view.

Product life-cycle stage and the balanced scorecard

One potential determinant of the use of BSC measures is the firm's product life-cycle. Product life-cycle stage relates to the evolution of the product in terms of the widely accepted product life-cycle model. A product's stage in this life-cycle has been defined as an organisational characteristic that will determine production and firm output. Merchant (1984) sees product life-cycle stage as a market factor and suggests a relationship with budgeting for planning and control. There is the suggestion that, if companies are to survive and prosper in today's complex business environment, they must use measurement and management systems derived from their strategies and capabilities (Kaplan and Norton, 1996). As a consequence, it is anticipated that product life-cycle stage has a major influence on the organisational arrangements adopted in order to attain strategic objectives, for example the structure, systems and management style.

The organisational strategy literature classifies product life-cycle stage into four categories: emerging, growing, maturing and declining. At the emerging stage, the product is launched and sales are low with high prices. Sales begin to rise rapidly at the growth stage because of the introductory promotions and growing customer awareness. At the mature stage, there is no more sales growth as the potential for new customers is exhausted. At this point sales have peaked, while prices remain low. Sales reduce at the declining stage as the product is gradually replaced with either innovations or an enhanced version (Wilson, 1991).

Each of these stages also provides for the number of competitors facing the firm. In the early stage of a product's life there are few competitors. However, as the product becomes popular, competition increases as other firms see advantages to entering the market. At the mature stage, firms are beginning to recognise the product's limited life and subsequently depart from the market; this departure continues through to the declining stage.

Merchant (1984) suggests that organisations with products in the early product life-cycle stages tend to make less use of traditional financial control tools, such as budgeting, compared to organisations with products in the later stages. This rationale can be extended by considering the potential relationship between product life-cycle and BSC usage.

As noted earlier, the primary focus of an organisation with products in the early stages is to seek new market opportunities by creating something that has a perceived uniqueness in the market. This type of organisation stresses effectiveness in innovation and the development of successful relationships with customers. Kaplan and Norton (1996) suggest that the BSC retains financial measurement as a critical summary of managerial and business performance, but that it also highlights a more general and integrated set of measurements that link current customer, internal process, employee and system performance to long-term financial success. It follows that businesses with products at the growth stage would be more prone to incorporate a broad-based performance evaluation system such as that required by the BSC philosophy, which incorporates not only financial information, but also information pertaining to strategic factors such as efficiency, innovation and customer relations. At the later product life-cycle stage, firms can be expected to be less concerned with the future effects of current sales and therefore financial measures would adequately serve measurement and management needs. It is to be expected, therefore, that this type of organisation is likely to place less emphasis on BSC usage.

Hoque and James's (2000) study shows the positive association between early product life-cycle stage and a greater reliance on BSC. They found that firms that have a higher proportion of new products have a greater tendency to make use of measures related to new products. While this may be true, it is noted that decline-stage firms may also have a greater need to make use of a BSC to rebuild their competitive positions in the market.

Market position and the balanced scorecard

Market position refers to the organisation's market share in relation to its competitors in a particular market. Merchant (1984) included this variable in his study and suggests that when an organisation has a strong market position, the use of budgets for controls would be more prominent than in a firm in a weak market position. This is because greater control may be needed for firms with a strong market position. In a strong market position there is the need to have the entire organisation committed to a group of pragmatic, feasible goals that can be conveyed to every area of the organisation to ameliorate the systematisation of activities. Furthermore, Merchant, following Galbraith (1977), suggests that there is a greater need for increased communication in firms holding a strong market position.

The effect of market position on firms' use of the BSC may be highly significant. This is because today's competitive environment demands greater communication across all organisational areas in order to maintain awareness of market developments (Kaplan and Norton, 1996; Libby and Waterhouse, 1996). MacArthur (1996) suggests that to be world-class competitors, companies need performance measures that count. He further suggests managers must need meaningful performance measures about each process and its output which support decision-making. It seems likely that a BSC can satisfy this greater need, as it facilitates decisions and actions that support strategies based on the needs of stakeholders, internal and external customers, regulatory bodies, managers and employees, and requires involvement by all levels of the organisation. In their study, Hoque and James (2000) propose that organisations with a strong market position are likely to place greater emphasis on the use of a BSC, as it will assist maintenance of an already strong position. Conversely, a weak position in a particular market creates a lesser demand for sophistication in management systems. A lesser demand for sophistication suggests a lower deployment of sophisticated management systems, such as the BSC. Thus, organisations with a weak market position can be expected to place greater emphasis on traditional, financial oriented, performance evaluation systems for assessing performance. They found some support for this proposition.

Balanced scorecard practices in the public sector

Many public sector organisations have implemented BSC. Table 12.2 and Figure 12.1 provide evidence of BSC usage in two public sector organisations. Table 12.2 illustrates the implementation of the BSC indicators in an Australian water authority and Figure 12.1 outlines the BSC of the housing authority of Fiji.

Total quality management and balanced scorecard linkage

According to the performance measurement literature, a performance measurement system should encourage actions that are congruent with organisational strategy (Lynch and Cross, 1991; Kaplan and Norton, 1996; Simons, 2000). More specifically, Lynch and Cross (1991) demonstrate how a business unit strategy directly translates into how it plans to reach its strategic goals and what performance measures are truly critical to the unit's success. Strategically driven measures provide both management and employees with the means to identify with the success of the strategy and track their own contributions to its achievement.

Table 12.3 illustrates how all four BSC dimensions (or categories) can contribute to the effectiveness of TQM programmes. The figure outlines key TQM activities (or factors), key TQM-related performance metrics and critical BSC categories for each TQM factor. It lists eight key TQM-related activities. Note that in the light of the TQM literature, these eight factors are considered to be critical to organisational effectiveness. From TQM and performance measurement literature, key performance metrics are chosen (the second column) and these metrics are then linked to the BSC category (the final column).

Table 12.2 Balanced scorecard measures at Elsewhere Water

BSC dimensions	Key performance indicators
Customer focus	% customer satisfaction % compliance with verbal service request response times Number of water supply interruptions per 1,000 properties Number of planned water supply interruptions per 1,000 properties Number of unplanned water supply interruptions per 1,000 properties % of water and wastewater service interruptions within 5 hours Number of customer complaints per 1,000 properties Number of water quality complaints per 1,000 properties Number of odour complaints per 1,000 properties % of meters installed within 14 days from date of payment
Chosen employer	% lost working days Training expenditure versus total operating expenditure (%)
Environmental sustainability	% tests meeting WWTP EPA licence criteria Quantity of treated water supplied per property (kL) – not seasonally adjusted Number of uncontained wastewater spills % of wastewater spilt per wastewater treated % effluent reused
Commercial sustainability	Combined operating costs per property % expended off revenue funded capital expenditure Water & wastewater renewals expenditure as a percentage of current replacement cost of system assets % unaccounted water Operating profit (EBITD and abnormals) Return on turnover (net profit after tax/sales) Return on net operating assets (EBIT/total net assets) Debt-equity ratio (total interest bearing debt/total equity) Total financial distribution to council (as a % of post-tax profits)
Quality water service provision	% tests meeting NHMRC (1996) bacteria criteria % tests meeting NHMRC (1996) chemical criteria Water main breaks per 100 km of water main Sewer chokes per 100 km of wastewater main Wastewater main (gravity & pressure) breaks per 100 km of main
Accountability	% compliance to waste water spillage procedure (ensures spillages are properly reported and remediated) Maintenance of ISO 9000 & 14000 third-party certification

Source: Moll and Hoque (2000).

Financial perspective	
Goals	**Measures**
Survive	Profit & loss Cash flow
Financially viable	Loans approved Collection effficiency Sales of houses/plots

Customer perspective	
Goals	**Measures**
Responsive supply	Average loan processing time FNPF* receipts
Customer satisfaction	Customer queries/problems/ complaints to be attended and resolved to customer satisfaction within 5 working days

Internal business perspective	
Goals	**Measures**
Technology capacity	Payroll reconciliation Bank reconciliation General ledger closure

Innovation and learning perspective	
Goals	**Measures**
Training	Training taken up
Product focus	Production equals sales

*FNPF refers to the Fiji National Provident Fund. Both the employer and employee contribute 8% of the basic salary of the employee. The FNPF provides its members with two-thirds of their savings towards home deposits at the Housing Authority. The FNPF receipts refer to the collection of these two-third savings from each of their homebuyers.

Source: Sharma and Hoque (2001).

Figure 12.1 Key performance indicators within the BSC at a housing authority.

Table 12.3 TQM – BSC linkages

Key TQM success factors	TQM-related performance metrics	BSC dimension
Executive commitment and management competence	• Employee opinion survey • Employee satisfaction • New techniques introduced compared with competitors	• Learning and growth • Internal business processes
Customer relationships	• Customer satisfaction survey • Customer acquisition rate • Customer retention (or loyalty rate) • % of the industry market share • Number of customer complaints • Warranty repair cost	• Customer • Financial (or shareholders)
Supplier relationships	• Supplier satisfaction survey • Supplier retention rate	• Internal business processes
Benchmarking	• Labour efficiency compared with competitors • Rework/scrap rate • Cost of quality (% of sales) • Return on investment • Market share	• Internal business processes • Financial (or shareholders)
Employee training	• Employee satisfaction survey • Employee capabilities • Spending levels in dollars for employee development and training	• Learning and growth
Open, less bureaucratic culture and employee empowerment	• Customer satisfaction survey • Employee satisfaction survey • The degree of decentralisation in corporate governance	• Customer • Learning and growth
Monitoring quality programmes (zero defects culture)	• Incidence of product defects • Material and labour efficiency variances • % shipments returned due to poor quality • Warranty repair cost	• Internal business processes • Customer
Internal business process improvement and manufacturing innovation	• Investment in high technology • Introduction of new management system (e.g. JIT) • Sales growth	• Internal business processes • Financial (or shareholders)

As discussed earlier, a BSC system incorporates a wide range of performance indicators, financial as well as non-financial, which together can provide managers with continuous signals as to what is most important in their day-to-day work and where efforts must be directed. Therefore, to achieve TQM goals, TQM firms should implement a BSC-like performance measurement system that identifies appropriate non-financial and financial indicators, so that employees are motivated and rewarded for achieving desired outcomes and also encouraged and rewarded to provide feedback on areas where improvements can be made. It is the feedback mechanism that is the success ingredient. It is by empowering employees to contribute towards achieving continuous performance improvement that TQM success is achieved.

Table 12.3 shows that there are a number of dimensions for which TQM and BSC converge. Firstly, strategic management accounting literature suggests that traditional accounting systems do not support the drivers of quality and the evaluation of drivers of quality and that management control systems should change to support TQM. Traditional accounting supports cost and production analysis well, but does not support quality analysis and problem-solving well. This is because quality is driven by non-financial factors such as product design, process design, rework and on-time delivery.

There is also the view that non-financial performance measures are better indicators of management effort and reflect the causal reasons for future financial performance (Ittner and Larcker, 1995, 1997; Ittner et al., 1997; Banker et al., 2000). Therefore, non-financial measures must supplement financial measures in providing support for TQM. Goals and objectives for non-financial factors can be set and measures used to provide feedback and rewards. BSC, with its emphasis on supplementing financial information with non-financial information, then, supports TQM.

According to Kaplan and Norton (1996), a BSC approach focuses on strategy and provides a broader control focus that thereby contributes to manager orientation towards longer-term objectives. As shown in Figure 12.1, TQM programmes promote this broader focus – the type of focus that many organisations are now working to accomplish, that is cross-functional integration, customer supplier partnerships, global scale, continuous improvement and teams rather than individual accountability (i.e. TQM philosophy). By using BSC dimensions, firms can assess these goals and success factors, and managers will take whatever actions are necessary, together with adapting their behaviour to accomplish those goals and success factors. The BSC measures can also be designed to pull people towards the firm's overall TQM programme, along with its other organisational strategic priorities.

Table 12.3 further demonstrates that for successful TQM implementations and effectiveness, the firm should use performance measures that align the interests of employees with those of the firm (i.e. learning and growth). The use of traditional financial measures are not likely to present indicators that direct employees to take a holistic view; instead they encourage employees to take a narrow view of what actions are required to achieve targets. That is, employees traditionally focus on their own immediate targets often to the exclusion of what may benefit the firm.

Traditionally, hierarchical firms developed strategies and budgets at the organisational or divisional level which were imposed upon employees at the business unit level. Management at business unit level had little, if any, input into the design of the budget or its respective targets. Financial performance indicators provided little incentive for employees to do anything other than meet or exceed budget. The 'success ingredient' for TQM firms adopting BSC, apart from identifying the necessary indicators, lies in the fact that it is the employee at the shop-floor level that can impact most positively on performance and profitability. It is not the CEO, nor other senior management, that sees first-hand how the customer 'feels' or how 'red tape' hinders meeting customer service. Only by having employees contribute to the identification of all processes that can impact on profitability can the firm embrace continuous improvement. It is only through developing a BSC-like performance measurement system that encourages employees to embrace continuous improvement that firms can direct action towards achieving TQM objectives.

To sum up, firms wishing to be competitively successful through TQM practice (combined with the firm's other strategic priorities) should develop a BSC that will provide indicators of how the firm is viewed by shareholders (financial perspective), how customers see the firm (customer perspective), in which areas the firm must excel (internal business processes perspective) and how and where the firm can learn and create value (learning and growth perspective).

Chapter summary

Each firm is unique and so directs its own course for building a balanced scorecard (BSC). As a result of this process, an entirely new information system that links top management objectives down through to the plant floor and particular site operational measures could be developed. Its primary benefit is its ability to join together manufacturing capabilities in a strategic environment and financial control. It could be seen to be a bridge between financial and manufacturing goals.

The exercise of creating a BSC forces companies to integrate their vision and strategic objectives into measures that will support short- and long-term goals. A BSC creates a framework for managing an organisation's operations to gain competitive advantage. Before jumping onto this 'bandwagon', management should ask one key question. Do we need a BSC?

Key terms to learn

Contextual factors
Market factors
Product life-cycle strategy
Public sector performance
management

Size
The balanced scorecard
TQM

Discussion questions

12.1 What is the balanced scorecard? Explain the concept.

12.2 How does the balanced scorecard relate to performance measurement?

12.3 Why is the balanced scorecard very important for an organisation? How can the balanced scorecard help a company improve its ability to meet its strategies?

12.4 What are the four perspectives covered by the balanced scorecard?

12.5 What does it mean by 'balanced' in the balanced scorecard approach? Should it be in the same amount or weight? How can such a balance be achieved? Explain.

12.6 Explain how to develop critical measures for each dimension of the balanced scorecard. Give examples.

12.7 Should the balanced scorecard be used in a public sector organisation?

12.8 Critically evaluate the advantages of using the balanced scorecard in a public sector environment.

12.9 Why would a company adopt the balanced scorecard?

12.10 What are the limitations to using the balanced scorecard?

12.11 Explain the relationships between the balanced scorecard, size and market factors.

12.12 Explain how the balanced scorecard can be used to achieve TQM.

12.13 Discuss the relationship between the balanced scorecard and the other management accounting system in an organisation.

12.14 Why should a company with a stronger market position place greater emphasis on the use of the balanced scorecard than one with a weak market position? Explain.

12.15 Does organisation size have any effect on the implementation of the balanced scorecard? Explain.

12.16 Referring to ABM, what is the relationship between ABM and the balanced scorecard? Explain with examples.

12.17 Is there any relationship between TQM and the balanced scorecard? Explain.

12.18 What is the role of MAS in the implementation of the balanced scorecard?

12.19 Is the balanced scorecard more useful in a JIT environment? Explain.

Further reading

Hoque, Z. and James, W. (2000) 'Linking balanced scorecard with size and market factors: impact on organizational performance', *Journal of Management Accounting Research*. In press.

Kaplan, R.S. and Norton, D.P. (1992) 'The balanced scorecard – measures that drive performance', *Harvard Business Review*, January–February, pp. 71–9.

Kaplan, R.S. and Norton, D.P. (1996) 'Using the balanced scorecard as a strategic management system', *Harvard Business Review*, January–February, pp. 75–85.

Maisel, L.S. (1992) 'Performance measurement: the balanced scorecard approach', *Journal of Cost Management*, vol. 6, no. 2, pp. 47–52.

Otley, D. (1999) 'Performance management: a framework for management control systems research', *Management Accounting Research*, vol. 10, pp. 363–82.

CHAPTER 13

Benchmarking analysis and management accounting

Key learning objectives

After reading this chapter you should be able to:

- define what is benchmarking;
- identify what benchmarking analysis has to offer;
- discuss various types of benchmarking;
- illustrate the benchmarking process;
- understand the relation between TQM and benchmarking;
- understand the role of management accounting in benchmarking.

Introduction

In a complex, dynamic, fast-changing environment, companies must strive for superiority in order to survive. Competitive edge cannot be achieved or maintained by setting goals based on past or even present performance. Benchmarking is a management practice that can be used to pursue excellence. It does this by identifying, comparing and emulating best practice wherever it occurs. Management accounting data play an important role in this analysis that managers conduct and this chapter illustrates how. What is this new approach? Why do you need benchmarking? How do you carry it out? Exactly what management accounting systems do you need to do it? The chapter addresses these questions.

What is benchmarking?

In recent years benchmarking has become increasingly popular in many organisations worldwide. The concept of benchmarking originated in Rank Xerox in 1979 and it became a company-wide effort in 1981. Rank Xerox defined benchmarking as 'a continuous systematic process of evaluating companies recognised as industry leaders, to determine business and work processes that represent best practices and establish rational performance goals'. It is a search for industry best practices that lead to superior performance. It illustrates how good a company currently is in comparison to its competitors, that is benchmarking analysis demonstrates what others are doing as well as what others are achieving.

What does benchmarking analysis offer?

Benchmarking is an integral part of the organisational improvement process and it looks for ideas to borrow from those who are doing better, perhaps in one very specific aspect (Bendell, Boutler and Goodstadt, 1998). At Rank Xerox, benchmarking has become a lifestyle and is applied across all aspects of the organisation – from environment, purchasing, human resources through to software design, the audit function and so on.

Traditional competitive analysis focuses on performance indicators, strategic choices and products or services within a given industry sector. This indicates the company's performance in relation to its peers and how much it deviates from the standards.

Benchmarking is broad and focuses on an ongoing process of measuring and improving products, services and practices against the best that can be identified worldwide. Performances are evaluated, based on the performance of the best organisations in the world.

The benchmarking technique has now been applied to many world-class companies like AT&T, DuPont, American Express, General Electric (GE), General Motors, Honda Motors, Proctor and Gamble, Apple Computer, IBM and Motorola. Benchmarking is also spreading as a direct result of its inclusion in the assessment criteria for the quality award.

Benchmarking is the cornerstone of total quality management (TQM), business process re-engineering and time-based management. Benchmarking literature identifies numerous advantages. For instance it:

- provides direction and impetus for continuous improvement;

- indicates early warning of competitive disadvantage;

- promotes competitive awareness;

- becomes the stepping stone to 'breakthrough' thinking;

- identifies the 'best practice';

- provides an objective attainment standard for key areas of business operation;

- links operational tactics to corporate vision and strategy;

- exposes performance gaps;

- triggers major step changes in business performance;

- helps companies redefine their objectives;

- challenges the 'status quo';

- allows realistic stretch goals.

Types of benchmarking

Benchmarking activities may be divided into three major groups: internal benchmarking, external benchmarking and best-practice benchmarking.

- *Internal benchmarking* is a process of comparing performance within the company or division, that is it looks for internal comparisons (comparing yourself to the best). A comparison is made across internal operations and parameters, such as purchasing, marketing, research and development, administration and so on.

- *External benchmarking* focuses on external comparisons, that is performance is compared with a spread of 'look-alike' businesses in similar positions experiencing similar market growth, fluctuations and circumstances.

- *Best-practice benchmarking* requires seeking out the undisputed leader in a particular process that is critical to the entire business process – regardless of sector, industry or location – and comparing it with your own.

The benchmarking process

The benchmarking process may be divided into the following stages (Codling, 1996):

- *Stage 1: Planning.* (a) Select the broad functional or procedural area to be benchmarked – manufacturing, warehousing, marketing, etc. (b) Identify comparative companies or activity centres. (c) Determine data collection method and collect data.

- *Stage 2: Benchmark partners.* Identify potential benchmarking partners from three locations, internally, externally and global best practice.

- *Stage 3: Data analysis.* Collect the data and from these confirm the most likely benchmark partners to contact. Determine current performance gap and project future performance levels.

- *Stage 4: Action.* Develop action plans, communicate benchmark objectives and results throughout the organisation and other companies; implement specific actions and monitor progress.

- *Stage 5: Review and recycle.* Monitor performance, review and analyse progress and calibrate performance improvements and targets.

Rank Xerox devised a ten-step benchmarking process:

Phase 1: Planning
1. Identify benchmark outputs
2. Identify best competitors
3. Determine data collection method.

Phase 2: Analysis
4. Determine current competitive gap
5. Project future performance levels
6. Establish functional goals
7. Develop functional action plans.

Phase 3: Action
8. Implement specifications
9. Monitor results/report progress
10. Recalibrate benchmarks.

The relation between TQM and benchmarking

The TQM culture influences the way in which benchmarking develops in the organisation (Codling, 1996). So benchmarking is a natural evolution from quality measurement and TQM concepts. TQM firms have a clear mission with a better understanding of their customers' needs and they are more confident in their activities. TQM firms devote considerable time and resources to employee training and development in the area of the company–customer relationship.

With these understandings, TQM firms encounter less of a struggle in focusing their efforts to produce usable results or actionable recommendations. Emphasis on these factors grows as organisations progress along the benchmarking learning curve. Although in theory any company can implement benchmarking, whether going down the TQM path or not, in practice the more that quality is ingrained, the easier it is for people to relate to benchmarking (Codling, 1996). In a TQM environment top-level commitment is essential for an effective TQM philosophy. This is also central to best-practice benchmarking.

TQM has limited ability to monitor developments outside a specific industry sector. Taking some of the tools of quality improvement and problem-solving and developing them into the rigorous benchmarking process adds the external dimension that, over time, provides a cutting edge to achieve competitive superiority (Codling, 1996).

Benchmarking literature (Swift, Gallwey and Swift, 1996) reveals that in one form or another, the following elements are common to both TQM and benchmarking tools:

- continuous improvement;

- meeting customer requirements;

- certain performance standards;

- understanding industry's best practices;

- concurrent engineering;

- measuring of elements (targets).

It has been suggested in the literature that benchmarking could be incorporated directly into the TQM model. The biggest obstacle would be the idea of getting used to using dissimilar companies as benchmarks. Just as managers had to be educated in achieving customer satisfaction to yield a high-quality product, they will need to be educated in the principles of 'competitive benchmarking' and will have to be shown its benefits (Swift, Gallwey and Swift, 1996).

Management accounting for benchmarking

Management accounting can supply useful data for benchmarking analysis. In benchmarking it is not sufficient to look only at traditional cost and budget data. It is necessary to look at a wide range of external information on the company's customers, suppliers and competitors. As discussed in Chapter 1, management accounting literature labels this 'broad-scope' management accounting systems (MAS) information. This means that organisations adopting benchmarking practice need an MAS that has such a broad focus.

A typical benchmarking team is comprised of a leader and other members with analytical skills, work process documentation skills and information search and analysis capability, together with customer representatives (internal and/or external). This indicates that management accountants can play a significant role in the benchmarking process from data collection through to data analyses and presentation. When collecting and analysing information it must be remembered that irrelevant and 'nice to know' data should be ruthlessly discarded, because more does not necessarily help to provide a clearer picture. A benchmarking-oriented MAS focuses more on non-financial information, for example measuring good working atmosphere, and collects the following information:

- labour turnover over a fixed period;

- reward and recognition systems (levels/frequency/reviews);

- off-site or on-the-job training per person per year (days/spend);

- number/variety of shared social events;

- employee well-being initiatives (canteen/health care, etc.)

Likewise satisfied customers can be established by measuring:

- number/type of complaints;

- number of repeat orders;

- technical back-up (team/specific initiatives);

- average 'age' of customer relationships;

- special promotion packages (number/type).

It has been suggested that good benchmarking combines a measurement of quantitative and qualitative data and management accounting can play an important role in this process. Note that it is best to collect as much data as possible and gradually draw out and emphasise that which is most meaningful.

Chapter summary

As discussed above, benchmarking supports companies in their efforts to improve their competitive situation. Benchmarking should not be thought of as a one-time event; it's a continuous performance assessment process in at least two different environments – the company's own and the reference object. Most of the activities discussed above involve organisational change and a benchmarking process benefits from dynamic cross-functional organisational structures (Hansen and Riis, 1996).

Benchmarking is an important element of the company's total quality management programme. Benchmarking helps a company to be competitive with the 'best of the best' and it needs to be understood that this is a dynamic and continuous process (Swift, Gallwey and Swift, 1996).

When benchmarking is used as a performance improvement tool, it is important to process a wide range of both financial and non-financial information to assess the effectiveness of benchmarking and to understand that management accountants can play a significant role in this matter. Thus benchmarking companies benefit from a dynamic management accounting system. Probably the most significant focus in the management accounting system should be the redirection of the reference point from an internal focus to an external one.

Key terms to learn

Benchmarking	Continuous improvement
Best practice	External benchmarking
Competition	Internal benchmarking

Discussion questions

13.1 What is benchmarking? Why is benchmarking important for an organisation? Explain.

13.2 What are the relations between benchmarking and performance measurement?

13.3 Identify the three types of benchmarking and provide examples.

13.4 What is the relationship between TQM and benchmarking?

13.5 Describe how management accounting relates to the benchmarking process.

13.6 Explain the statement: 'Benchmarking requires a non-financially-based management accounting system.'

13.7 What is the relationship between benchmarking and competitor analysis?

13.8 Why is benchmarking a natural evolution from the TQM concept? Explain.

13.9   What is the role of benchmarking in developing an organisation's MAS?

13.10 Explain how organisations can use benchmarking as a weapon to survive in today's competitive business environments.

Further reading

Coburn, S., Grove, H. and Fukami, C. (1995) 'Benchmarking with ABCM', *Management Accounting* (USA), January, pp. 56–60.

Elenathan, D., Lin, T.W. and Young, M.S. (1996) 'Benchmarking and management accounting', *Journal of Management Accounting Research*, vol. 8, p. 37–54.

Kharbanda, M. (1993) 'Benchmarking: making it work', *CMA Magazine*, March, pp. 30–3.

Malcolm, I. (1995) 'Benchmarking finance function activities', *Management Accounting* (UK), February, p. 22.

CHAPTER 14

Incentive plans

Key learning objectives

After reading this chapter you should be able to:

- identify the key objectives of an organisational incentive plan;
- describe the characteristics of executive compensation plans;
- identify what are the ideal conditions for an effective incentive system;
- discuss different types of incentives;
- illustrate forms of monetary compensation plans;
- understand the concept of 'gainsharing';
- understand the performance-related pay scheme;
- demonstrate the agency view of incentive systems.

Introduction

Management compensation frequently includes incentives tied to performance. Its aim is to encourage employees to act in the best interests of the firm. This chapter is concerned with this issue.

Objectives of an incentive plan

There are two components to an incentive compensation scheme: first the bonus pools from which the funds will be obtained for bonuses; and second the allocation methods, that is the actual scheme utilised.

In determining the magnitude of the bonus pool, compensation scheme designers must decide what items to include in defining the pool. The simplest method of computing the bonus pool is as a fixed percentage of the profit earned by the organisation as a whole. A variation to this rule includes a residual income component where the bonus pool is only activated when the organisation has received some return on investment (ROI). These methods are generally associated with profit-sharing incentive schemes. One other method also utilised is that where the pool is based on the organisation's profit improvement, in other words only when there is an increase in profit from the previous year is an amount set aside for the bonus pool (generally associated with gain-sharing incentive schemes). As with the previous method, this plan is focused at the organisational level and, subsequently, is volatile in the face of environmental factors not in the control of the individual, such as economic downturn or industry-specific factors.

Pools based on overall organisation performance rather than divisional or departmental performance work best for vertically integrated firms producing a single major product rather than multiple products. In these types of firms there is a high degree of interaction and coordination among divisions. In contrast, pools based on divisional level performance would be most appropriate when the firm is highly decentralised, that is where there are separate responsibility centres.

Management accounting literature (Kaplan and Atkinson, 1989) identifies three aims for an incentive plan:

- to attract and retain high-quality managers;

- to encourage profit-maximising decisions;

- to stimulate individuals to higher levels of performance.

What are the ideal conditions for an effective incentive system?

Patton (1972, cited in Kaplan and Atkinson, 1989, p. 725) suggests the following conditions as ideal for an effective incentive system:

- Profits are affected by numerous short-term decisions.

- The managers have the authority to make the decisions.

- The control system is well-defined and performance is evaluated on a systematic basis, either by comparison with a plan or by comparison with the performance of similar firms.

- The managers are expected to be entrepreneurial and ambitious.

Types of executive compensation schemes

Executive compensation schemes can take various forms. Kaplan and Atkinson (1989, p. 728) categorise executive compensation schemes as follows:

- *Immediate versus long-term.* Immediate incentives include cash or equity based on current performance, whereas long-term incentives include stock options whose value is tied to the long-term performance of the company's common equity.

- *Cash versus equity.* Awards in the form of cash or in the form of equity.

- *Monetary versus non-monetary.* Monetary awards include cash awards (e.g. salary increments, bonus, etc.). Non-monetary awards include, for example, vacation trips, executive parking privileges, the provision of a company car, life insurance, club memberships and specialised healthcare, as well as informal recognition in the form of social invitations from more senior executives and participation in personnel development programmemes that are reserved for top management.

Forms of monetary compensation plans

Kaplan and Atkinson (1989) discussed several forms of compensation plans:

- *Cash bonus or profit sharing and the stock bonus.* Cash or stock bonuses are awarded at the end of an accounting period.

- *Deferred bonus and compensation awards.* Cash or stock deferred until a future period, e.g. bonuses are not paid until the executive retires.

- *Stock options.* Employees have the right to purchase company stock at a future date at a price established when the options were granted (usually the current market price or 95% of the market price).

- *Performance shares or units.* These are awarded in the form of company stock for achieving a specified, usually long-term, performance target. The common target is to achieve a growth in earnings per share over a three-to-five-year period.

- *Stock appreciation rights.* Stock appreciation rights are deferred cash payments based on the increase of the stock price from the time of award to the time of payment.

- *Phantom stock plans.* These are awards in units of stock. After qualifying for receipt of the vested units, the executive receives in cash the number of units multiplied by the current market price of the stock.

- *Participating units.* These awards are similar to stock appreciation rights except that payment is dependent on operating results (pre-tax income, ROI, sales, etc.) rather than stock price.

Gainsharing – a group bonus plan

The literature has discussed another form of bonus plan, which is commonly known as *gainsharing*. Imberman (1995) explains gainsharing as follows:

> Gainsharing is not an incentive or bonus plan for individuals exceeding a standard or quota. That's the old piecework system. Gainsharing is a group bonus plan. The entire factory workforce is involved in an effort to exceed past performance and achieve target gains. If successful, the gain is translated into cash and shared. Usually the workforce receives 50% of the gain in bonuses and the company receives an equal share in savings. That's gainsharing in its simplest from.

Imberman (1995) has discussed the following three sample gainsharing formulas:

- *The Scanlon Plan.* This plan involves the ratio of payroll costs to sales, as expressed below:

$$\frac{\text{Cost of work and non-work time paid} + \text{Pension} + \text{Insurance}}{\text{Sales dollars} - \text{Returned goods} + \text{Inventory changes}}$$

- *The Rucker Plan.* This plan involves the value added by manufacturing. It provides an incentive to save material and labour costs. It can be expressed as follows:

$$\frac{\text{Cost of wages, benefits}}{\text{Sales dollar value of product} - \text{Goods returned} - \text{Supplies, services, materials}}$$

- *ImproShare Plan.* This measures only labour costs and uses time standards and past production records to set a production criterion. Its bonus formula is given below:

$$\frac{\text{Standard value hours earned (current period)} \times \dfrac{\text{Total actual hours worked (base period)}}{\text{Total standard value hours earned (base period)}}}{\text{Total hours worked (current period)}}$$

Performance-related pay schemes

Performance-related pay (PRP) schemes are of two types: long-run PRP schemes and short-run PRP schemes. Under long-run PRP schemes, incentive benefits depend upon the long-run performance of the firm while under short-run PRP schemes the benefits depend upon the short-run performance of the firm.

Profit-sharing is considered as a short-run PRP scheme. Profit-sharing schemes are a means by which employees receive a share of the profits of the company in which they work. The essence of a profit-sharing scheme is the creation of a distributable pool based on the profits of the company.

Profit-sharing schemes encompass a number of different computational formats with entitlement and payment varying with the profit level at which payment is triggered (Ogden, 1995). Commonly, 5 to 10 per cent of the corporate profit before tax is set aside and managed by a trust for the benefit of the employees. The amount is distributed according to some agreed formula.

There are alternative methods for calculating the employees' share of profit. One alternative is to take a certain percentage of profit before tax after deducting a minimum return necessary for the investment. The minimum return is called the cost of capital. This method is consistent with the assumption that the incentive bonus is paid for performance beyond normal performance. Another method sets aside a specified percentage of profit before tax, subject to a maximum limit. Under this method, there is an upper bound on the total amount the employees can share. The objectives of the upper bound are (a) retaining sufficient funds for investment (ploughing back profit) and (b) discouraging income manipulation behaviour by managers. Another alternative is to employ both a lower and upper bound. The lower bound is the minimum amount of profit that must be earned before a bonus will be paid and the upper bound is the maximum limit to which employees share in profits. The latter model satisfies the objectives of the previous two models, that is providing for employees' abnormal performance, maintaining sufficient funds for reinvestment and mitigating income manipulation behaviour. However, this model is not free from limitations. Referring to this model, Healy (1985) showed that managers manipulate profit not only by increasing the amount of reported profit, but also by reducing it. He observed that managers use income decreasing accounting accruals (big bath) instead of income increasing accruals (smoothing) when earnings fall below the lower bound of a bonus scheme with a view to maximising their own future bonuses.

Profit-sharing as a financial incentive applied to all employees in a company has been found to be of limited usefulness (Ogden, 1992, 1993, 1995). Ogden, in his study of profit-sharing and organisational change in the newly privatised water industry in England and Wales (1995), argues that profit-sharing is principally valued not for any immediately discernible impact on employee motivation, or as an incentive to efficient working, but rather as a rhetorical device to reinforce and support the singular importance of profit as a measure of organisational performance. From this perspective it can be argued that profit-sharing is more concerned with persuading employees of the legitimacy of contributing to company performance (Reed, 1989; Fox, 1985) than as a direct employee incentive. Support for this view can be found in Smith (1986), Baddon et al. (1989), Bell and Hansen (1987), Dewe et al. (1988) and Ogden (1995). Reed (1989) viewed profit-sharing as aimed at mobilising employees' consent to increased company income performance. Smith (1986) has shown that employers typically referred to profit-sharing as an attempt to make employees feel more involved and interested in the company, to increase employees' sense of commitment to the company and to increase the sense of cooperation between management and staff.

In the UK, the government's introduction of tax incentives encouraged companies to introduce profit-sharing schemes (see Poole, 1988; Schuller, 1989; Smith, 1986). Procter et al. (1993) suggest that profit-sharing becomes a fundamental part of the process by which management can exercise control over efforts and rewards and, ultimately, affects the profitability of the organisation. Thompson (1990) suggests that management cannot rely on coercion as the sole means of control, but must engage the cooperation and consent of employees in order to improve employee as well as company performance. The above suggests several rationales for the introduction of profit-sharing. First, an organisation's profit-sharing scheme can change employee attitudes about cooperation with management on issues such as work practices and productivity improvements, and more generally their attitudes towards involvement with, and commitment to, the company (Ogden, 1995). Second, a profit-sharing scheme can be viewed as the successful result of collective bargaining between employees and the employer. Third, adoption of a profit-sharing scheme may be a response to government regulation.

Considerable effort has gone into researching profit-sharing schemes used by employers to secure employee involvement (e.g. Procter et al., 1993; Smith, 1993; Ogden, 1992; Kennedy, 1995; Marks, 1995; Wood, 1996; Poland, 1996; Thomas, 1996). These studies suggest that profit-sharing ensures high financial benefits for high performance and establishes the workers' claim on 'residuals', thus causing them to be more involved with their business and more motivated to ensure its success (for a review, see Ogden, 1995). In the UK, securing greater employee involvement has been the major justification offered by employers introducing profit-sharing schemes. It is also the principal argument in the government's promotion of its profit-related pay scheme (Ogden, 1992, 1995).

Agency view of incentive schemes

As discussed in Chapter 1, there can exist a relationship in the organisation where the principal hires another party (the agent) to perform some service.

Management accounting literature (Kaplan and Atkinson, 1989) highlights two types of principal–agent relationship. First, the firm's owners or shareholders acting as the principal hire the CEO to be their agent in managing the firm in their best interests and second the firm's top management group acts as the principal and hires division managers as agents to manage the units or divisions.

Kaplan and Atkinson suggest that all individuals – principals and agents – care not only about financial compensation and wealth, but also about perquisites of the job, such as attractive working conditions and flexibility in hours worked. If a straight salary is the only compensation for the top executives of the firm, they may not be sufficiently motivated to take actions that maximise the value of the firm to the shareholders.

Agency costs in the owner–manager relationship

Agency costs in the owner–manager relationship are the sum of:

- the costs of the incentive compensation plans (bonus, rewards, etc.);

- the costs of monitoring the managers' actions (audited financial statements);

- the remaining costs of actions taken by managers that diverge from the preferences of the owners.

Chapter summary

To improve organisational performance and effectiveness, businesses over the past few years have embarked upon various incentive schemes. This chapter has shown that incentive plans provide motivation for organisational managers and executives. The principal–agent relationship theory suggests that organisational managers and top executives must be compensated through financial compensation (salary, bonuses, etc.), as well as non-financial compensation such as attractive working conditions, flexible hours, free holidays and car parking permits. The contingency theory literature assumes that an organisation's incentive plans depend on the particular circumstances within which it operates, such as business size, strategic focus, economic conditions and external environment. Contemporary incentive schemes should be based on both financial and non-financial performance. An effective incentive scheme provides strong motivation for the organisational managers and executives to achieve organisational goals.

Key terms to learn

Cash bonus
Compensation
Deferred bonus
Executives
Incentives
Monetary compensation

Participating units
Performance-related pay
Performance shares
Phantom stock plans
Profit-sharing
Stock appreciation rights

Discussion questions

14.1 Why organisations need to have an incentive plan.

14.2 What are the ideal conditions for an effective incentive system?

14.3 Compare the three methods used to determine the magnitude of the bonus pool.

14.4 When should an organisation use a pool based on the overall organisational performance?

14.5 What are the aims of incentive plans?

14.6 Compare and contrast the types of executive compensation schemes.

14.7 Explain the forms of monetary and non-monetary compensation plans.

14.8 What is a phantom stock plan? How does it differ from stock options?

14.9 What is the difference between a performance-related pay scheme for a long-run focus and a short-run focus?

14.10 Why is profit-sharing limited when it is applied to all organisational employees?

14.11 What is the relationship between strategy and profit sharing?

14.12 Based on the agency theory, which compensation plan gives more long-term benefit to the organisation? Explain.

14.13 Is there any relationship between the compensation plan and the balanced scorecard approach to performance measurement? Explain.

14.14 Explain why profit-sharing is considered as a short-run performance related pay scheme?

14.15 What is the role of MAS in incentive/compensation plans?

14.16 Explain this statement: 'There is a different incentive plan for different strategy typologies.'

Further reading

Banker, R., Potter, G. and Srinivasan, D. (2000) 'An empirical investigation of an incentive plan that includes non-financial performance measures', *Accounting Review*, vol. 75, no. 1, January, pp. 65–92.

Ittner, C.D., Larcker, D.F. and Rajan, M.V. (1997) 'The choice of performance measures in annual bonus contract', *Accounting Review*, vol. 2, no. 2, April, pp. 231–56.

Kohn, A. (1993), 'Why incentive plans cannot work?', *Harvard Business Review*, September–October, pp. 54–63.

Nelson, B. (1995) 'Motivating employees with informal rewards', *Management Accounting* (USA), November, pp. 30–4.

CHAPTER 15

Public sector management accounting and controls

Key learning objectives

After reading this chapter you should be able to:

- develop an understanding of the relationship between public sector reform and new public management;
- understand the implications of public sector reform for accounting;
- understand the concept of accrual reporting budgeting;
- describe the planning programming budgeting techniques;
- understand the concept 'zero-based budgeting'.

Introduction

Over the past few years many countries have embarked on a wide range of financial and administrative reforms which mainly place emphasis on improved monitoring and accountability. Management accounting plays a significant role herein. This chapter provides a brief introduction to this contemporary management accounting system in the public sector.

Public sector reform and new public management

In recent years, many countries have embarked on a wide range of financial and administrative reforms. These reforms have two broad themes: those which concentrate on the management control system by improving the information provided by the accounting systems, by clarifying roles and responsibilities, and by creating accountability; and those which account for stabilising the economy by exposing the public sector to competition. The two main objectives of the reform process are to promote a culture of performance, and to make the public sector more responsive to the needs of government by increasing the organisation's accountability, by promoting efficiency and effectiveness, by introducing participative decision-making and by adopting a customer focus. The financial reform agenda includes such things as financial reporting, accrual accounting, full cost pricing, purchaser/provider agreements and asset management. The administrative reform encompasses, but is not limited to, structural reforms, labour reforms, the review of information systems and accountability reforms. These reforms are centred on new public management (NPM) ideals (Hood, 1995).

The introduction of NPM in the public sector has seen a shift in focus from the adherence of formalised procedures to an emphasis on resource allocation and goal achievement. Briefly, NPM encompasses the following ideas:

- from management's perspective, the public and private sector are not dissimilar and therefore should be managed on the same basis;

- the refocus of process accountability to accountability for results;

- the separation of commercial and non-commercial business activities;

- an emphasis on improved financial reporting, monitoring and accountability;

- an increase in the contracting out of business activities using specific contracts for short-term work;

- the mimicking of private sector management practices such as the introduction of corporate plans, mission statements and strategic plans;

- a shift in preference from non-monetary incentives to monetary incentives;

- an emphasis on cost-cutting and efficiency.

A range of social, economic and technological pressures are forcing governments to become more effective, efficient and accountable in their use of publicly generated funds. In particular, Rivlin (1996), Sansom (1997) and Wensing (1997) claim that governments are under pressure from increased globalisation, the dissatisfaction of citizens with the current management and a curtailing of budget spending. Mellors (1995, p. 1) contends that there are six key forces driving the change in the public sector, including the following:

- changing attitudes to the role of government in the economy;

- the process of microeconomic reform;

- changing community and business expectations;

- resource constraints;

- the impact of technology;

- demands for greater accountability.

Implications of public sector reform for accounting

The government reforms have had substantial implications for accounting. Traditional accounting in the public sector focused on inputs and the control of expenditure. The reform of the public sector has changed the traditional role of accounting to one that is focused on accountability and the efficient allocation of resources. This implies that accounting should concentrate upon outputs, performance measurement, efficiency, cost saving, productivity and performance measurement (Broadbent and Guthrie, 1992; Guthrie, 1995). This in turn requires that new accounting technologies be employed such as planning programming budgeting, accrual accounting, performance indicators and annual reporting mechanisms (Guthrie, 1995). The following sections discuss some of these 'new' management accounting techniques.

Accrual accounting

The public sector has in recent years moved from cash-based accounting to accrual accounting in response to the adoption of commercial principles. Cash accounting requires the recording of inflows and outflows of cash. In contrast, accrual accounting requires revenue to be recognised in the period in which economic benefits can be measured reliably. Likewise, expenses are recognised when the consumption of goods is capable of reliable measurement. There are several reasons why the move to accrual accounting was inevitable. Firstly, accrual accounting offers the benefits of improved accountability and improved resource management (Funnell and Cooper, 1998). This claim has been supported by evidence that suggests a cash system provides inadequate information for the full costing of operations. Accrual accounting on the other hand is said to improve decision-making by providing information on the full cost of operations and the resources used to deliver services to the public. This is increasingly important for those business units that are commercialising to enable them to recover the costs of products and services. Finally, accrual accounting gives governments the opportunity to minimise their costs through cost identification (Guthrie, 1999).

Limitations identified from the adoption of accrual accounting include the fact that it can lead to the misallocation of resources and an inadequate disclosure of the size of assets and liabilities. This reduces the organisation's ability to account for the full cost of programmes due to fluctuations in costs. More importantly, perhaps, is the fact that accrual accounting enables organisations to defer liabilities such as long-service leave to future periods, therefore burdening future taxpayers with these costs. By contrast, the government can also charge the full costs of assets purchased during the year to the current taxpayers, instead of allocating these costs over the useful life of that asset (Ryan, 1998).

The introduction of accrual accounting in the public sector requires a change in the existing information techniques. This means that considerable amounts of money have to be invested in changing the management accounting system so that it can produce accrual reports and either training or recruiting individuals to support the new accrual management accounting system (Guthrie, 1999). Accrual budgeting refers to the preparation of budgets according to accrual concepts. Guthrie (1999, p. 145) suggests that the primary reason for this is the inconsistencies between measuring the full cost of a programme in inflated accrual terms when the cash allocated by governments is in smaller absolute dollar amounts. Organisations prepare operating budgets, a capital budget, a budget of cash flows and a budgeted statement of assets and liabilities using accrual principles.

In addition to the common use of revenue budgeting, some public sector entities also make use of the following management control techniques.

Planning programming budgeting system

The planning programming budgeting system (PPBS) attempts to link together plans, objectives, the environment in which the organisation is working, and the feedback from control information. The US President Johnson introduced the system in 1965 into the federal government.

Public sector accounting literature (Coombs and Jenkins, 1995; Jones and Pendlebury, 2000) discuss the following key objectives of PPBS:

- the careful identification and examination of goals and objectives in each area of government activity;

- analysis of the output of a given programme in terms of its objectives;

- measurement of the total costs of specific programmes, not just for one year but for several years into the future;

- the formulation of objectives and programmes extending beyond a single year to relate annual budgets to long-term objectives;

- analysis of alternatives to find the most efficient ways of reaching programme objectives for least cost;

- the establishment of analytical procedures to serve as a systematic part of the budget review process.

Zero-based budgeting

Zero-based budgeting (ZBB) is a technique whereby the total cost (base plus increment) of every item included in a proposed budget must be justified and approved. It suggests that no base or minimum expenditure level should be acceptable for any activity. Resources are not necessarily to be allocated in accordance with the previous year's pattern. The approach requires a re-evaluation of all expenditure and all activity; all activities start from a zero base.

Advantages of ZBB

- It allocates resources according to priorities, between the essential and the less essential.

- It improves decision-making because budgetary allocation is related to objectives.

- It makes managers plan ahead and defend their budgets; thereby it creates a greater feeling of ownership of those budgets (Coombs and Jenkins, 1995; Jones and Pendlebury, 2000).

Problems with ZBB

- It is a time-consuming exercise.

- It is impossible to appraise all activities each year.

- It is imposed for legislative and political reasons.

- It generates a mass of information that cannot be adequately assimilated by decision-makers (Coombs and Jenkins, 1995; Jones and Pendlebury, 2000).

Budgetary accounting

Budgetary accounting includes both budgeted and actual amounts within the double-entry system. Using budgetary accounting, budget reports for all departments are prepared prior to the commencement of the reporting period. The budgeted reports are then compared with actual reports for the period, and variances between the two established. Variance reports are an easy way to tell if budgets have been adhered to or if the individual departments have over- or under-spent compared to the budget.

Budgeted amounts are credited to the appropriate account and then, as the expense is incurred, debits are set against these credits. This results in a balance that represents the amount of the budget still unspent.

The reliance on budgets in the public sector stems from the nature of their funds. Governments collect taxes, levies, fees, etc. and allocate resources through the budget process to departments (e.g. health and education), which are subsequently limited by this allocation of funds to achieve their objectives. To enable efficient and effective operation in the department, the department has its own budget for spending. This process allows for effective spending of government funds, but does not allow for any efficiency measurements, as the only requirement is that all the money allocated is spent (for details, see Jones and Pendlebury, 2000).

The main disadvantage of budgetary accounting is the complexity involved in realising two sets of numbers. Common practice is to present the budget alongside operating accounts in the same format. This enables the presentation of comparative data that can be used for performance evaluation, controlling and planning resource allocation.

Chapter summary

In recent years, there have been pressures from government to produce a higher set of desired outcomes for the public sector. The pace of reform has had a coercive effect as government organisations have been forced to adopt methods such as managing for outcome, benchmarking, performance management and total quality management. In this 'new' world, public sector management has been transformed from being administrators and custodians of resources to being accountable managers empowered with greater delegated authority. The adoption of NPM has implications for management accounting. Traditional management accounting in the public sector focused on inputs and the control of expenditure. The NPM initiatives have changed this traditional role of accounting to one that focuses on accountability and the efficient allocation of resources. This implies that accounting should concentrate upon outputs/outcomes, performance measurement and efficiency and effectiveness. This in turn requires that new accounting technologies be employed such as planning programming budgeting, accrual budgeting and performance management.

Key terms to learn

Accrual accounting   Public sector
Accrual budgeting   Public sector accounting
New public management   Reform
Planning programming budgeting   Zero-based budgeting

Discussion questions

15.1 Should public sector entities be managed differently from private sector entities?

15.2 How the government can change the public sector to be more effective, efficient and accountable.

15.3 What are the two broad themes of public sector reforms worldwide?

15.4 Describe the concept 'new public management'. Why is this important for today's public sector organisations?

15.5 How has accounting been affected by public sector reforms?

15.6 Why has the public sector moved from cash- to accrual-based accounting?

15.7 What are the limitations of applying accrual accounting in the public sector?

15.8 What is zero-based budgeting (ZBB)? Discuss its strengths and weaknesses.

15.9 Do today's public sector organisations need to reform their management accounting systems? Explain.

15.10 What are planning programming budgeting systems (PPBS)? What are the benefits of PPBS to the organisation?

15.11 Discuss the role of budgets in today's public sector organisations.

Further reading

Hood, C. (1995) 'The "New Public Management" in the 1980s: variations on a theme', *Accounting, Organizations and Society*, vol. 20, no. 2/3, pp. 93–109.

Lapsley, I. (1999) 'Accounting and the new public management: instruments of substantive efficiency or a rationalising modernity?', *Financial Accountability and Management*, vol. 15, no. 3, pp. 201–7.

Lapsley, I. and Pettigrew, A. (1994) 'Meeting the challenge: accounting for change', *Financial Accountability and Management*, vol. 10, no. 2, pp. 79–92.

Parker, L. and Gould, G. (1999) 'Changing public sector accountability: critiquing new directions', *Accounting Forum*, vol. 23, no. 2, pp. 110–30.

Case studies

A   The Boeing Company (process and activity analysis at Propulsion Systems Division)

B   MosCo, Inc. (activity-based costing)

C   Cost centre management at Air Command (business planning and costing)

D   Target costing: when accounting and marketing collide

E   Using EVA at Outsource, Inc.

F   Dialysis Clinic, Inc. (treatment costing in managed care)

G   Tempest, Inc. (the balanced scorecard)

H   East River Manufacturing (implementing ABC and ABM)

I   Precision System, Inc. (quality costing)

Learning Resources
Centre

Learning Resources
Centre

CASE STUDY A

The Boeing Company

(Process and activity analysis at Propulsion Systems Division)

(Greg Anderson and Mikael Weigelt prepared this case under the direction of Professor Kavasseri V. Ramanathan. Copyright © 1998 by Institute of Management Accountants, Montvale, NJ. Reproduced with permission.)

Recently, Mike MacFarlane, a cost analyst, transferred from the Boeing Company's corporate headquarters to Propulsion Systems Division (PSD). His prior responsibilities at headquarters did not completely satisfy him because most of his work there was too far removed from actual airplane production for his liking. Given his background in engineering and accounting, he felt that PSD would provide exciting career opportunities.

Because of his spirited attitude, ability to work as a team player and knowledge of world-class accounting systems, he was assigned to a project team that examined the potential value of process and activity analysis. Mary Barclay, supervisor for programme cost targets and budgets, had been designated as the team leader of the process and activity analysis project team.

Joe Kelker, director of finance at PSD, explained to Mike the objective of the process and activity analysis project. 'As you know, a few years ago, Boeing launched several strategic initiatives to enhance our competitive standing. The central theme was to achieve continuous quality improvement in every aspect of the company's operation. Only by continuously improving the Boeing Company's competitive strengths will we prosper in an environment of rapid technological change, increasing competitive pressures and global markets.

'However, top management's commitment to continuous improvement can be realised only if we identify specific opportunities for improvement. Instead of just making statements about Boeing's competitiveness, we need to actually modify our manufacturing and service operations. I think that viewing cost data based on process and activity analysis is a key factor in enabling us to identify these opportunities.'

Joe further explained his ideas by quoting from one of Boeing's recent top management statements: 'Our objective is to realign the accounting system so that the cost information provided aligns with our understanding of the flow of resources in the processes at Boeing. Only then can we use with confidence our accounting data as an aid in targeting and measuring our CQI continuous quality improvement performance.'

After contemplating these notions for a while, Mike applied Joe's message to PSD: 'Currently we have a management accounting system that allows us to analyse cost variances interactively. However, the shortcoming of the cost visibility system is that it is structured largely along functional organisation lines (e.g. manufacturing, engineering, finance). If we want to identify opportunities for process improvement, we need to associate costs with processes and activities, not just functional organisations. Also, we need to be able to estimate the change in total cost, given a change in the manufacturing process. Taking a process view of the data will enhance our ability to identify improvement opportunities. We must then be able to compare their relative importance and to judge what leverage we have in making modifications. This will allow us to prioritise improvement opportunities.'

'Looking at the best manufacturing companies worldwide we discovered that many of them employed activity-based cost management to achieve this. Propulsion Systems Division has been selected for a pilot project examining the value of this concept for Boeing. We hope the lessons learned will lead to a refined methodology of analysis that can be used strategically throughout the Boeing Company.'

Joe continued by defining Mike's job: 'Your responsibility in this project will be to develop a database describing the activities in our division. Mary and I decided it would be best to get you started in this project by having you perform a process and activity analysis for the engine build-up (EBU) shop. This way you will learn our methodology from the ground up.'

The Propulsion Systems Division

Boeing's Propulsion Systems Division provided the link between the engine manufacturer and the airplane. The division defined its responsibility as 'everything under the wing'. Even though the engine itself was bought (according to airline customer specifications) from Pratt & Whitney, Rolls-Royce or General Electric, there were several variations to accommodate. PSD's functions included the design, procurement, build-up and installation of all the hardware associated with the engine. The hardware PSD provided included the cowls, thrust reverser, strut, strut fairings and exhaust sleeve depicted in Exhibit A.1, as well as the engine build-up components shown in Exhibit A.2.

PSD's assembly operations were fairly complex, since they included more than 20 possible different, basic engine–airplane combinations that were modified to customer specifications. This complexity was further increased by strict inspection requirements by Boeing's quality assurance organisation and the Federal Aviation Administration.

Mike's assignment involved the EBU shop at PSD. As can be seen from Exhibits A.1 and A.2, the EBU line took the engine core and added the wire bundles, hoses, ducts, engine mounts and components according to design specifications. Next the cowls, thrust reverser, plug and exhaust sleeve were added to meet functional and aerodynamic specifications. The engineering department listed the following considerations as the most important factors for the design of an engine: performance (i.e. thrust), reliability, maintainability and weight.

The process and activity analysis project

The division-wide process and activity analysis project grew out of a small pilot project considering only the EBU within PSD. In the fall of 1990, this initial project was completed. Since the results were extremely promising, management decided to extend the project to the whole division.

Carolyn Feller, the division general manager, summarised the outcome of the initial study: 'We gained a new appreciation of cost composition and activities in the EBU and of the gap between presently available cost data and the financial information that was needed for managing in an intensively competitive environment.'

One of the results of the pilot project included a definition of outputs for the division. The findings suggested there should be four process centres: engine build-up, strut, wire shop and new propulsion development.

Shop management contended that they had been doing activity analysis for years. They claimed that over time the company had placed a significant emphasis on improving detailed task efficiencies in the shop. While they recognised there were still opportunities for improvement in the shop, they believed there was additional benefit to be gained by analysing the support processes as well.

Propulsion Systems' senior management concurred, emphasising that once the entire business unit was analysed from a process perspective and value was assessed from the customer's point of view, PSD would have the information to identify high-leverage opportunities.

Since Carolyn believed that PSD could benefit significantly from this project, she wrote a memo to all supervisors at PSD, demonstrating commitment from top management and asking for consistent support throughout the division.

The methodology developed by the project team was referred to as *process and activity analysis*, rather than the popular industry term *activity-based costing*. While activity-based costing emphasised accounting, process and activity analysis emphasised Boeing's intention to apply the project's results to all business operations and not just to improve the cost management system. Process and activity analysis was like a comprehensive medical check-up, a labour-intensive diagnostic tool that pointed to the areas where high-leverage opportunities existed. Process and activity analysis did not provide the re-measurement capabilities of a costing system, which the term activity-based costing implied.

In its statement of work, the project team agreed to *five* objectives for the process and activity analysis project:

- increase cost visibility;

- identify major cost drivers;

- trace overhead cost to processes where possible;

- identify non-value-added activities;

- provide a process flow chart to help guide improvement measures.

First, Boeing's management felt that the current cost management system did not provide enough visibility. Specifically, when work crossed organisational boundaries, costs created by the underlying total production process remained largely hidden. Process and activity analysis would provide information that increased cost visibility.

Second, process and activity analysis would identify the major cost drivers so that Boeing could better identify items to be analysed and predict cost behaviour if a process were modified.

Third, the analysis would improve the traceability of overhead costs. A better understanding of the production process and its relation to total cost would improve management's ability to make each organisational unit responsible for the overhead resources it consumes.

Fourth, the project would support the continuous quality improvement initiative by identifying which activities add value to the end-product and which activities are non-value added. Reducing or eliminating non-value added activities would ensure the Boeing Company's ability to maintain its competitive advantage.

Process and activity analysis

In the first step of process and activity analysis each workgroup developed a list of activities and tasks. In Boeing's terminology, a task was defined as a generic operation, whereas an activity represented a group of tasks. For manufacturing, the operations and inspection records (O&IRs) provided a guideline for the development of the activity and task list because they contained the assembly instructions as defined by the Manufacturing Production Planning department (see Exhibit A.3). Bar-charts showed the sequence and time allowed for each activity that a shop employee must perform each day to meet schedule requirements (see Exhibit A.4).

Each task was characterised by its value, end-product (or process), activity type, task time, flow time and task dollars. The value was either primary external (PE), primary internal (PI), support external (SE) or support internal (SI). Primary tasks were value-added activities that changed the form, fit or function of the product, for which the customer was willing to pay. All other activities were support tasks (i.e. non-value added). External tasks were done for anyone outside the workgroup, such as customers or other workgroups, while internal tasks were performed to serve the same workgroup. Internal tasks were more easily modified than external tasks, since they were restricted to only one organisational unit. For tasks identified as internal, no party outside the organisation performing the task depended on its performance (see Exhibit A.5).

The instruction manual for the interviewer contained the following examples for the different task types: Manufacturing operations typically were classified as primary external tasks, because they usually modified the form, fit, or function of the product. Operations that prepared the product for the manufacturing process typically were primary internal tasks. So, for example, if hardware had to be removed to gain access to certain components, then its removal was considered primary internal.

Support tasks did not change the form, fit or function of the product. For instance, internal training or inspection procedures and quality control checks were typically support tasks in nature. If these tasks were performed for someone outside the workgroup, they were classified as external. Therefore, quality control was mostly support external. By default, all other tasks were support internal tasks. They included preparation of tools, preparation of internal flow control, training, group meetings and so on.

For each task, the workgroup estimated the task time, which was the number of hours spent on each task per product unit. The task time described the actual duration of the work performed. Task times were distinguished from flow times, which included task times as well as wait, transport and idle times. The hours spent per unit then were multiplied by the number of units produced to obtain estimated total hours. Since the estimates provided by the workgroups often did not add up to the total hours worked, the estimated hours were adjusted.

Data collection was performed mainly through interviews. Before conducting the interviews, all interviewers went through a two-day training programme set up by the process and activity analysis project team. This training ensured reliable and consistent interviews. Crucial to the success of the project was consistent classification of tasks into primary and support, as well as external and internal.

In addition, the project team collected all directly assignable costs for each workgroup. These costs included direct labour, indirect labour, overtime, fringe benefits and non-labour costs such as supplies, training, furniture and fixtures, shipping material, etc. (see Exhibit A.6). These costs were extracted from the current cost accounting system by the charge number, which uniquely identified each workgroup. That is, the only costs assignable to each workgroup were those that the group's supervisor could control.

Total labour hours were the base for measuring the cost of the activities (see Exhibit A.6). The rate for each workgroup was calculated as:

$$\text{Rate} = \text{Total \$} \div \text{Total hours}$$
$$= [\text{Direct labour \$} + \text{Indirect labour \$} + \text{Non-labour}]$$
$$\div [\text{Direct labour hours} + \text{Indirect labour hours}]$$

Multiplying the labour hours for each task by the rate gave a cost value for each activity (see Exhibit A.7). These rates were often different for each first-line supervisor's workgroup because the workers in each group had different labour rates and consumed different overhead cost elements.

Given the activities and their dollar values, Pareto charts were prepared that indicated the importance of each task in terms of its cost (see Exhibits A.8 and A.9). In general, a Pareto chart was a bar-chart that graphically represented the importance of a set of items. The length of the bar indicated the amount of resources expended on the associated item.

For the process and activity analysis project, Pareto charts provided an easily understood visual representation of the relative importance of activities. High-cost activities often provided the best opportunities for process improvements.

The 767 engine build-up group

Mike accompanied John Parker, a shop supervisor selected as one of the interviewers for the project, to meetings with the 767 EBU group. After several meetings, the operations group and the project team agreed on a list of activities performed by the operations group. The most difficult step was to find a good balance between specificity and generality of the activities identified. Too detailed activity lists were cumbersome to work with, whereas too general activity definitions did not describe the process accurately. The outcome of the meetings was a list (see below) that provided a framework within which to report the detailed task information collected through examining the operations and inspection records, and shop bar-charts. Exhibit A.5 shows the task breakdown and analysis for activity #6 from the list: 'Install exhaust plug and sleeve'.

767 Engine build-up list of activities

1. Assist shop personnel
2. Continuous quality improvement
3. Install core wire
4. Install electric wire
5. Install engine drain
6. Install exhaust plug and sleeve
7. Install fan case wire
8. Install fire detector
9. Hang engine
10. Install inlet
11. Install ECS controller
12. Install heat shields
13. Install left bracket
14. Meetings
15. Misc. supervision
16. Rejection tags
17. Rework
18. Install right bracket
19. Safety
20. Install starter systems
21. Vendor rework
22. Install wire

After combining data received from interviews, the shop bar-charts and operations and inspection records (see Exhibits A.3 and A.4) with the cost analysis data included in Exhibit A.6, the process and activity analysis project group prepared a Pareto chart for all the activities of the operations workgroup (see Exhibit A.10). The Pareto chart showed that the activities 'Install fire detector' and 'Install wire' were the most significant in terms of resource consumption.

The 737 engine build-up group

After going through the process and activity analysis for the 767 EBU group, Mike understood the process well enough to lead the analysis effort in another operations group. Mike scheduled a meeting with Erik Olson and the 737 EBU group. Erik had been a supervisor on the EBU line for five years. He was recruited as an interviewer for the process and activity analysis project. His experience with the EBU process helped him to communicate with the workers and their supervisor. The meeting concentrated on the activity 'Install wire bundle'. As shown in Exhibit A.11, this activity consumed the most resources within the 737 EBU workgroup.

Mike contacted Joanne Nguyen, a methods analyst in industrial engineering and a fellow team member on the process and activity analysis project, who supplied him with the relevant shop bar-charts, and operations and inspection records (see Exhibits A.12 and A.13).

Mike and Erik interviewed Tyrone Washington, the supervisor for the 737 EBU group, who described the work routine as follows: 'First, we check to see if we have the right wire bundles. To do this, we compare the wire cards with our call sheets. Removing the wire cards and checking the call sheets requires 0.2 hour in total. Second, wire bundles W1504 and W1506 are routed over the oil return line and through the 6 o'clock position' (see Exhibit A.14). The total task time here is 1.0 hour. Completing the wire bundle and hardware installation requires 8.0 hours. To perform this activity, the employee must go to the rotobin to pick up p'. This requires an additional 0.3 hour.

'Next, wire bundles W1502 and W0200 are installed with the required brackets and fillers. The total time to complete this installation is 2.0 hours, with an additional 0.3 hour necessary to go to the rotobin to pick up parts. Then the mechanic installs the deflector assembly and installs wire bundle W1508, requiring 1.5 hours, with an additional 0.1 hour required to go to the rotobin, 0.2 hour to go to the tool-room for parts and 0.1 hour to go to the call sheet. Finally, the quality control inspector must verify that wire bundle installation is complete. This activity takes 0.3 hour.'

Tyrone went to the delivery schedule and determined that YSO ship sets (of two engines per ship set) were built up in one year's time. By multiplying the number of ship sets by the number of engines in each ship set, Mike determined that the tasks in this workgroup were performed 300 times per year.

After the meeting with the EBU workgroup, Mary provided Mike with cost information about the workgroup. Total direct labour hours in the 737 EBU shop last year were 22,808, which translated into $273,696. The breakdown of the labour components and corresponding costs were:

	Hours	Costs ($)		Hours	Costs ($)
Fabrication	6	82	Minor assembly	21	283
Major assembly	21,269	254,502	Rework	443	5,531
Developmental work	189	2,238	Tooling	13	186
Vendor rework	867	10,874			

The indirect labour consumed was 4,192 hours, for a total of $73,616. Overtime, fringe benefits and bonus payment for the workers in the shop totalled $205,996. In addition, the following overhead costs were identified:

Perishable tools	$11,412
Tool and shop equipment	$6,734
Electrical, mechanical and miscellaneous shop supplies	$5,485

Resource support from support services	$1,291
Group-administered training	$1,176
Telephones	$410
General travel	$282
Business meeting expense	$208
Undergraduate and graduate study	$64
Promotional items	$53
Entertainment	$24
Data processing supplies	$22
Office supplies	$21
Conferences and seminars	$10

After several meetings, the group agreed to the list of activities shown below which the 737 EBU group performed. With this information about the workgroup, Mike went to his office to complete the process and activity analysis.

737 engine build-up list of activities

1.	Assist shop personnel	12.	Install hydraulic plumbing
2.	Install left bracket	13.	Install hydraulic pump
3.	Install right bracket	14.	Install IDG & plumbing
4.	Continuous quality improvement	15.	Misc. administrative
5.	Install control and tubing	16.	Misc. supervision
6.	Install duct	17.	Pre-assembly
7.	Install exhaust plug and sleeve	18.	Rejection tags
8.	Install extension ring	19.	Safety
9.	Install aft mount 1 fan case support	20.	Install starter systems
10.	Install fire detector	21.	Vendor rework
11.	Hang engine	22.	Install wire bundle

Required questions

1. For the workgroup 737 engine build-up analyse the activity 'install wire bundle'. Analyse the tasks of the activity in terms of value, time, frequency and cost. Use the worksheets in Exhibit A.12, A.13, A15, A16 and A.17 for this problem.

2. Create two Pareto charts for the tasks of the workgroup: one showing the total dollar values of all the tasks and one showing the dollar values of

only the support tasks. For the support tasks Pareto chart, list the support internal tasks by support internal category as defined on the worksheet, for example 'Get drawings', 'Go to rotobin', 'Go to toolroom', etc. (see Exhibit A.15). Use the data you developed in the Exhibit A.17 worksheet to assist you. Discuss the usefulness of your Pareto charts.

3. Discuss the choice of direct and indirect labour hours as a measurement base for the resources consumed by each task.

4. Discuss the difference between process and activity analysis, and functional organisation costing. Is the insight gained from process and activity analysis valuable? Why?

5. What are the potential pitfalls of looking at the activity data from a functional organisation perspective rather than focusing on the activity data as they relate to the entire EBU assembly process? What additional insight can we gain by taking the process perspective?

6. Once the process and activity analysis information is collected for the entire division, how can it best be used as a tool for decision-making?

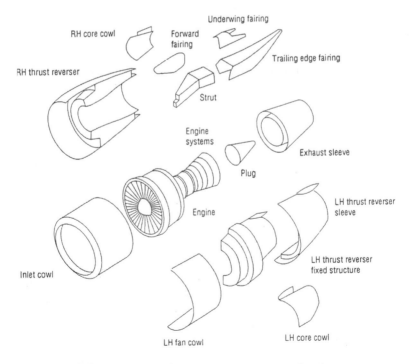

Exhibit A.1 Propulsion Systems Division hardware.

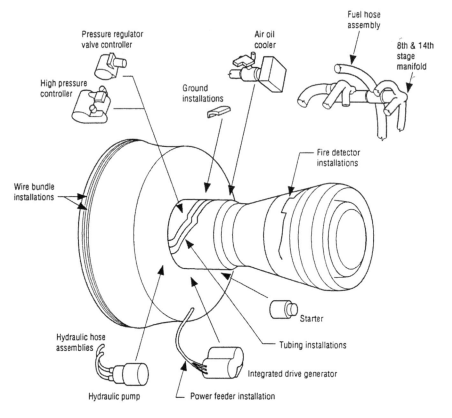

Exhibit A.2 Engine build-up components.

Part #	Name	Quantity
314T3310-5	Sleeve	1
314T320-13	Plug	1
333T4000-2	Bracket	2
69B97200	Pin	1
BACB30PN4-5	Bolt	66
BACB30PN4-7	Bolt	18
BACN10HR4C	Nut	67
NAS1587-4C	Washer	84

Reference drawings

301T4700 Sheet 1, 2, 4

333T4000 Plan Sheet 1

Tool requirements

Ohme 314T33120-Sleeve Sting

Work to be performed

Operation	Description
010.00	Receive sleeve and plug and route packaging sheets to QC
020.00	Record exhaust part number and serial number
030.00	Inspect – OK to install exhaust plug and sleeve
040.00	Install fasteners (16) places and torque per reference drawing
050.00	Inspect – witness/record torque on 10% of fasteners
060.00	Install index pin on outer flange
070.00	Install fasteners (66) places per drawing. Inspect – witness/record torque on 10% of fasteners
080.00	Remove Ohme sling
090.00	Note any fit or fair problem

Exhibit A.3 Exhibit A.2 engine build-up.

Operation plan	Crew	6:00am	2:30pm	6:00am	2:30pm	6.00am	2.30pm
Shop: P4111	A	High engine 14006 / F1 O4 D007	Purchase equipment 14116	Install left bracket 14826	Install drain 14845	Install exhaust plug and sleeve 14662	
					Install fire detectors 14823		
See: EBU	B			Install right bracket 1482	Install fan case wire 14925	Install ECS control 14658	Install core wire 14926
Area: 767 CC: 925/581 Model/ customer: PW 4000							

Exhibit A.4 767 Engine build-up shop bar-chart.

Shop: P-4111 **Model:** 767 **Engine Type:** P&W 4000
O&IR# 14662
O&IR (Activity) Title: Install exhaust plug & sleeve
Major Activity: Inlet & exhaust

Operation	Task description	PE	PI	SE	SI Get drawings	SI Go to rotobin	SI Go to tool-room	SI Go to call sheet	SI Get test equip	SI Uncrate	Task total	Freq/yr
010.00	Receive plug/sleeve	.5			.2	.2	.2			.5	1.6	200
020.00	Record pin # & serial #			.2			.2				0.4	200
030.00	Inspect – OK to install plug and sleeve						.2				0.2	200
040.00	Install bolts & torque	.7									0.7	200
050.00	Inspect/witness/record torque on 10% of fasteners	.7									0.7	200
060.00	Install index pin	.2									0.2	200
070.00	Install fasteners (66) places/inspect/witness torque on 10% of fasteners	3.1					.2	.2			3.5	200
080.00	Remove sling				.5						0.5	200
090.00	Note any fit or fair problems								.2		0.2	200
	Analysis totals:	5.2		0.2	0.7	0.2	0.8	0.2	0.2	0.5	8.0	
		PE	PI	SE	SI						**Total**	
					2.6 SI							

Exhibit A.5 767 engine build-up – task analysis worksheet.

Description	$%	Dollars	Hours	Rate
Direct labour				
Quality assurance	0	36	3	
Fabrication	0	21	2	
Minor assembly	0	180	16	
Major assembly	37	185,652	15,650	
Rework	1	7,361	568	
Development	0	836	61	
Vendor rework	5	27,578	2,174	
Total direct labour	44	221,664	18,473	
Indirect labour	15	74,791	4,892	
Overtime fringe benefit bonus	34	173,736		
Total labour	93	$469,891	23,302	
Non labour				
Tools shop equipment	3	13,496		
Perishable tools and equipment	2	9,549		
Shop supplies	1	6,275		
Travel general	0	1,925		
Group administrated training	0	1,775		
Undergraduate and graduate study	0	1,125		
Telephone	0	925		
Support from support service	0	765		
Office machine and equipment	0	520		
Office furniture and fixtures	0	450		
Misc expense	0	200		
Office supplies	0	75		
Data processing supplies	0	20		
Conference and seminars	0	12		
Business meeting expense	0	9		
Total non-labour ($)	7	37,030		
Total	100	$506,921	23,302 =	21.75

Exhibit A.6 767 engine build-up cost analysis.

Operation	Task description	Value	Task time	×	Frequency /yr	×	Rate	=	Dollars
010.00	Receive plug & sleeve	PE	0.5		2000		$21.75		$2,175
010.00	Get drawing	SI	0.2		2000		$21.75		$870
010.00	Go to rotobin	SI	0.2		2000		$21.75		$870
010.00	Go to call sheet	SI	0.2		2000		$21.75		$870
010.00	Uncrate	SI	0.5		2000		$21.75		$2,175
020.00	Record pin # & serial #	SE	0.2		2000		$21.75		$870
020.00	Go to call sheet	SI	0.2		2000		$21.75		$870
030.00	Inspect to install plug & sleeve								
030.00	Go to call sheet	SI	0.2		2000		$21.75		$870
040.00	Install bolt & torque	PE	0.7		2000		$21.75		$3,045
050.00	Inspect/witness torque – 10% fasteners	PE	0.7		2000		$21.75		$3,045
060.00	Install index pin	PE	0.2		2000		$21.75		$870
070.00	Install fasteners/ witness torque	PE	3.1		2000		$21.75		$13,485
070.00	Go to call sheet	SI	0.2		2000		$21.75		$870
070.00	Get test equipment	SI	0.2		2000		$21.75		$870
080.00	Remove sling	SI	0.5		2000		$21.75		$2,175
090.00	Note problems	SI	0.2		2000		$21.75		$870
Total	Install exhaust plug and sleeve		8.0		2000		$21.75		$34,800

Exhibit A.7 767 engine build-up activity: install exhaust plug and sleeve – value analysis worksheet.

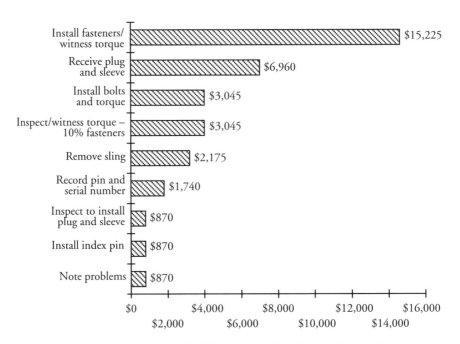

Exhibit A.8 767 engine build-up – install exhaust plug and sleeve total activity = $34,800.

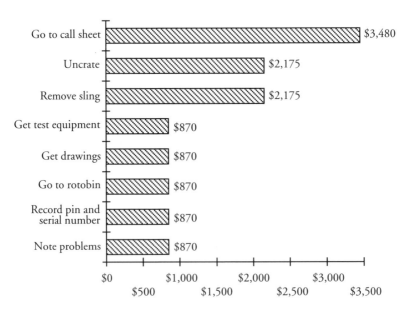

Exhibit A.9 767 engine build-up – install exhaust plug and sleeve total support tasks = $12,180.

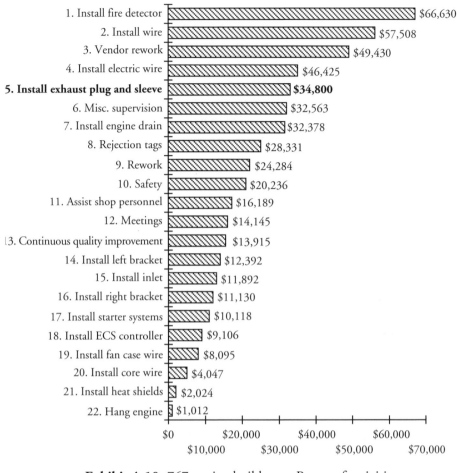

Exhibit A.10 767 engine build-up – Pareto of activities total = $506,920.

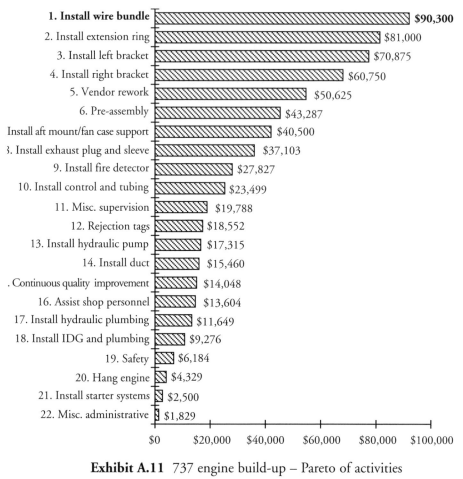

Exhibit A.11 737 engine build-up – Pareto of activities total = $580,500.

Operation plan	Crew	Skill	6:00am		2:30pm	6:00am	2:30pm	6:00am		2:30pm
Shop: P4112	A	Mechanic	High engine 14006	F1 O4 D007	Purchase equipment 14116	Install left bracket 14826	Install hydraulic pump 24971	Install control & tube 24663	Install duct 24659	Install hydraulic plumbing 24838	Install IDG & plumbing 24824
Sec: EBU	B	Mechanic				Install right bracket 24827	Install wire bundle 24925			Install ECS control 14658	Install core wire 14926
Area: 767 CC: 925/581 Model/ customer: ECM										

Exhibit A.12 737 Engine build-up – shop bar-chart.

Part #	Name	Quantity
W1504	Wire Bundle	1
W1506	Wire Bundle	1
W1508	Wire Bundle	1
W1502	Wire Bundle	1
W0200	Wire Bundle	1
BACC10GU104	Clamp	19
BACC10GU106	Clamp	17
NAS1802-3-9	Screw	52
NAS1805-3	Nut	11
NAS43HT3-16	Spacer	2
MAS6703U2	Bolt	10

Reference drawings

330A8893

330A8894

330A8895

330A8896

Work to be performed

Operation	Description
020.00	Verify wire bundle cards with wire bundle number list
030.00	Route wire bundle W1504 & W1506 over oil line and through 6 o'clock position & install bracket
040.00	Complete wire bundle & hardwire installation
050.00	Install wire bundle W1502 & W0200 with brackets and fillers Complete wire bundle installation
060.00	Install deflector assembly component & torque Install wire bundle W1508
070.00	Shop verify wire bundle installation

Exhibit A.13 767 engine build-up operation and inspection record: wire bundle installation.

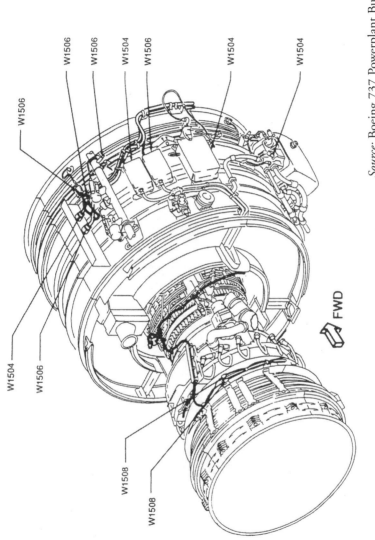

W1506

W1506

W1506

W1504

W1504

W1506

W1504

W1504

W1506

W1504

W1506

FWD

W1508

W1508

Source: Boeing 737 Powerplant Buildup Manual

Exhibit A.14 Wire bundle installation.

Shop: P-4112   **Model:** 737   **Engine Type:** CFM
O&IR# 24925
O&IR (Activity) Title: Install wire bundle
Major Activity: Install wire bundle

Operation	Task description	PE	PI	SE	SI	SI	SI	SI	SI	SI	SI	SI	Task total	Freq/yr
					Get drawings	Go to rotobin	Go to tool-room	Go to call sheet	Get test equip	Uncrate				

Analysis totals:

		PE	PI	SE	SI	Total

Exhibit A.15 737 engine build-up – task analysis worksheet.

Description	Dollars	Hours	Rate

Exhibit A.16 737 engine build-up – cost analysis worksheet.

Operation	Description	Value	Task time	×	Frequency /yr	×	Rate	=	Dollars

Exhibit A.17 737 engine build-up activity: wire bundle – value analysis worksheet.

CASE STUDY B

MosCo, Inc.

(Activity-based costing)

(Richard J. Block (Digital Equipment Corporation) and Lawrence P. Carr (Babson College) prepared this case. Copyright © 1998 by Institute of Management Accountants, Montvale, NJ. Reproduced with permission.)

The evening before the annual two-year budget review, Cosmos 'Chip' Offtiol, MosCo's director of operations, was confident. While he waited for the latest financial estimates, he thought of the plan he and his staff had methodically prepared, which successfully addressed all the crises this new business unit was facing: developing competitive transfer pricing on an ageing product, developing and marketing new products to external customers against an established market leader, reducing manufacturing costs, improving manufacturing utilisation and improving its slim levels of profitability.

When Jonathan Janus, MosCo's controller, solemnly delivered the requested pro forma income statements, Offtiol' s mood changed dramatically. Instead of sustained profit, Offtiol was shocked to see significant projected operating losses. He wondered why his extensive planning had not improved MosCo's 1995 and 1996 financial results. With less than 24 hours before he was to offer senior management a viable business plan, he felt abandoned and hopeless.

Background

MosCo, a semiconductor design and manufacturing company, is a wholly owned subsidiary of Computer Systems, Inc. (CSI), a leading manufacturer of client/server systems, workstations and personal computers. During 1993 and 1994, MosCo manufactured and sold to CSI a single product – the x100 a 100 MHz, 10 nanosecond microprocessor. The x100 is a .75 micron device packaged in a 339 pin grid array (PGA) and is used in CSI's servers and workstations. MosCo has sold CSI 150,000 units of the x100 in each of the past two years.

Although MosCo sells entirely to its corporate parent, the company was required to establish competitive prices for its devices by Q3 94. Previously, the x100 had been sold to CSI at full cost. Establishing competitive prices was but one of many changes CSI required MosCo to make. In 1995, CSI planned to change all its major business units into profit centres. CSI management felt each business unit needed flexibility and independence to react to rapidly changing market conditions. CSI believed that if its business units were profit centres, they would be more accountable for their own financial success. Their strategies and annual performance would be more visible and measurable as well. This change meant they could sell their devices to external customers using available manufacturing capacity. MosCo could also recover the large development costs for future products and control their destiny.

MosCo established the competitive market selling price of the x100 at $850, based on industry price/performance comparisons. CSI approved of this market-based method of establishing transfer prices, which ensured that CSI could purchase internally at a competitive price while placing the burden of cost management appropriately on MosCo. Jonathan Janus, MosCo's controller, prepared revised financial statements applying the $850 transfer price to MosCo's 1993 and 1994 shipments (see Exhibit B.1). Gordon Scott, MosCo's vice-president and general manager, was pleased to see MosCo had generated profits of $4.9m and $1.9m for 1993 and 1994, respectively, on annual revenues of $127.5m, after applying the newly established transfer price. The profit decline in 1994 reflected the establishment and staffing of MosCo's new marketing department. This department was created to identify and open external market opportunities for new products currently under development.

As FY95 approaches, MosCo management is faced with a number of pressures and unknowns. CSI is under severe competitive pressures in their server and workstation product lines and is already demanding a price reduction on the x100. They also insist MosCo remain profitable. Carlotta Price, head of MosCo's new marketing department, determined from industry studies that the price/performance for microprocessors halves every 18 months (Moore's law). To remain competitive, merchant semiconductor companies consistently were offering some combination of price reductions and/or performance improvements, so that their products' price/performance (price per unit of speed) halved every 1.5 years. Thus, for the x100 and for every CPU MosCo developed and manufactured, Price believed the market would require similarly timed price/performance offerings. Price knew any price reductions would require offsetting cost reductions if MosCo was to remain profitable and wondered what the manufacturing organisation was thinking.

As product development was no longer working on any x100 performance improvements, Price computed required price reductions on the x100 following the industry model. The x100 would continue at the $850 price through Q1 95, then drop to $637.50 at the start of Q2 95, drop to $425.00 at the start of Q1 96 and to $318.75 at the start of Q4 96. Price was troubled by these prices as she knew CSI was requesting 150,000 units in FY95, but only 75,000 in FY96. CSI indicated it expected a customer shift away from workstations and into CSI's new personal computer line. (Appendix B1 presents an overview of the semiconductor manufacturing process typically found in a microprocessor supplier such as MosCo. Appendix B2 presents an overview of the product costing process used by MosCo.) Product cost for the x100 had remained constant during FY93 and FY94 at approximately $665 (see Exhibit B.2). Price computed cost reductions of approximately $166.25 per year (to $498.75 in FY95 and $332.50 in 1996) would be necessary to maintain the x100's current gross margin of –22%. She wondered if manufacturing could achieve a cost reduction that steep.

Concurrent with the x100 pricing activities, P.J. Watt, head of product development, sent an urgent request to Scott, Price, Janus and Offtiol for $3m in funding. This funding would accelerate the completion of an integer-only microprocessor, the x50 and the follow-on CPU, the x75. The x50, a new product already under development, could be completed with $1m of the additional funding and made available for volume shipment by the beginning of FY95. The remaining $2m would be spent during FY95 and FY96 to complete development and ready the x75 for volume shipment by the beginning of FY97.

The x50 is a 50 MHz, 20 nanosecond CPU, manufactured like the x100, using the present .75 micron technology, but unlike the x100, the x50 does not have a floating-point processor. The elimination of the floating-point processor reduces the size and power requirements of the CPU. The x50 and x75 can be packaged in a 168 pin grid array (PGA) that costs $15, that is $35 less than the 339 PGA used by the x100. However, the testing parameters of the x50 and x75 are significantly different than for the x100 and require a Bonn tester, which MosCo does not currently own. This $2m tester, if purchased, will add $1.2m in annual depreciation and other direct operating costs, and $800,000 in incremental annual support costs to the present level of manufacturing spending.

The x50 and x75 are targeted as entry devices for CSI's personal computer business. NoTel is the market leader in .75 micron integer-only microprocessors. Their N50 CPU (also 50 MHz, 20 nanoseconds) sells for $500. The N50 has just been announced with volume shipments to coincide with the beginning of MosCo's FY95. MosCo's new marketing department estimates the demand for the x50 from CSI and potential new external customers could easily exceed 1,000 units per year. To break into this market, Price recommended heavy market promotion and a price/performance two times the competition's. Estimates for unit sales potential from advertising are 100,000 for the first $1,000, up to 500,000 for the second $1,000 and over 1m for a third million-dollar advertising expenditure.

With the increased pricing pressures from both CSI and the external marketplace, product cost reduction became critical. This fact, coupled with the request from product development for additional funding, had Gordon Scott very concerned. He knew it was important to bring out the x50 and x75 quickly, but the pricing pressures for their market entrance and the pricing pressures from CSI on the x100 seemed almost impossible to meet and still achieve a profit in FY95 and 96. He knew, however, if he didn't maintain a profitable operation, his tenure would be short.

Reduced product costs leading to competitive manufacturing appeared to be the critical factor necessary to sustain MosCo's slim profit levels. Scott asked Offtiol, the director of operations, to formulate a series of recommendations for developing and manufacturing an expanded CPU product line in FY95 and FY96. He asked that the recommendations be completed by the annual two-year budget review, scheduled to commence in a month. Scott knew that soon after MosCo's budget review he would have to present a credible business plan to CSI management. He worried how he could develop a viable plan in light of the obstacles.

The Offtiol plan

Offtiol started his preparation by reviewing the detailed x100 product cost (see Exhibits B.2, B.3 and B.4). He immediately assembled a team comprising Janus from finance, T.Q. Marcel from quality and Beeb Ruby from training. The team, led by Marcellus DeStepper, manager of wafer fabrication, conducted a cost review by activity. Offtiol, like Scott, believed significant cost reductions would be necessary to maintain profitability. He had recently taken an executive development course in activity-based costing and knew it was a proven method for better understanding cost structures and cost drivers, and highlighting non-value-added work. Offtiol was excited, given the size of the assignment and his belief there were both cost reduction opportunities in manufacturing and necessary improvements in the current standard cost system. He felt the current standard cost system did not properly capture the complexity of MosCo's production process. He felt an ABC analysis could provide the insight necessary to reduce the x100 product cost by the $166 marketing had requested.

The team mapped the processes of the entire operation and then reassigned costs to the newly defined activities (see Exhibits B.5a–c). The direct manufacturing operation was now better delineated by equipment use (see Exhibit B.5b). The manufacturing support organisations were also better understood. Their key activities were costed, then each was aligned to the manufacturing operation it supported (see Exhibit B.5c). MosCo's ABC team reset the x100 product cost in line with the true practical capacity of the manufacturing process. The team saw capacity utilisation as a major driver of product cost. The old product costing methodology was based on the planned utilisation of each manufacturing process with underutilised manufacturing costs absorbed into product costs.

The revised x100 product cost (see Exhibits B.6 and B.7) was pleasing, but not totally surprising to Offtiol. It confirmed his belief in the inaccuracies of the old costing method. The new x100 product cost of $437.50 was $227.61 lower than the $665.11 original cost shown by the old system. It did not make sense to charge the x100 for the costs of resources it did not consume. Offtiol felt he could commit immediately to Price's 1995 product cost reduction request of $166.

To achieve the 1996 product cost goal of $332.50, Offtiol and his team looked further into the activity-based costing results. The study clearly showed that wafer fabrication was the largest area of manufacturing cost. Offtiol, with the help of Janus, computed that if the x100 wafer cost was reduced from the 1995 level of $3,000/wafer to $1,866/wafer, the x100 total product cost would be lowered by $105, achieving the desired $332.50. To obtain a wafer cost of $1,866, spending reductions of –$25.5m or 38 per cent in wafer fabrication would have to be achieved (see Table B.1). Offtiol again asked DeStepper to review the fabrication area for further cost reduction opportunities. He asked deStepper to formulate a plan that could reduce direct wafer fabrication spending by –$25.5m (from $67.4m to $41.9m).

Table B.1 x100 1996 target product cost analysis (x100 gross die/wafer = 50)

Manufacturing area	Cum. wafer	Cost/die	Cum. cost die
Desired wafer cost	$1,866.00	$37.32	$37.32
Yielded raw wafer cost	$50.00	$1.00	$38.32
Probe cost/wafer	$500.00	$10.00	$48.32
Probe yield		25.0%	$193.28
339 PGA package cost		$50.00	$243.28
Assembly cost		$8.00	$251.28
Assembly yield		90.0%	$279.20
Test cost		$40.00	$319.20
Test yield		96.0%	$332.50
Current fabrication spending:		$67,392,000	
Desired level of spending:			
(22,464 annual wafer			
production @ $1,866)		$41,917,824	
Required spending reduction:		$25,474,176	
		38%	

DeStepper returned in two weeks with an alternative plan (see Table B.2). His team found nominal spending opportunities by: (1) reducing monitor wafer usage, (2) redesigning wafer lot handling procedures and (3) better placement of inspection stations. DeStepper's most significant discovery was the 64 per cent increase in capacity attained by increasing equipment uptime (the time equipment is not undergoing repair or preventive maintenance). Higher uptime, however, required an annual investment of –$1.8m in additional equipment engineers. While this investment would increase wafer fabrication spending to –$69.2m, wafer fabrication capacity would increase from 26,000 to –42,700 in annual wafer starts. The increased capacity actually decreased the cost/wafer to $1,845, which was $21 lower than Offtiol had requested.

Table B.2 DeStepper alternative capacity and spending plan

	Current level	Proposed level
Total wafer start capacity	26,000	42,707
Engineering wafer starts	1,040	1,040
Production wafer starts	24,960	41,667
Fabrication line yield	90%	90%
Annual wafer completions	22,464	37,500
Annual spending level	$67,392,000	$67,392,000
DeStepper's added spending		$1,797,120
Proposed spending level		$69,189,120
Cost/wafer	$3,000	$1,845

Offtiol dismissed DeStepper's alternative plan outright. 'Spending needed to decrease, not *increase*!' Offtiol exclaimed, and reiterated his request to reduce fabrication spending by 38 per cent. Offtiol then focused his team's cost reduction efforts on packaging costs, another major cost component of the x100. (MosCo had spent close to $8.8m annually on chip packages.) He asked MosCo's purchasing manager, Nomial, to pressure MosCo's 339 PGA supplier to lower their $50 price. Nomial told Offtiol she had already made this request and was reminded by the vendor that the 339 PGA was a unique design, used only by MosCo for the x100. With order volumes declining by 50 per cent in a year, Nomial said it would be difficult to keep the $50 package price from increasing.

The final area of review was the x50 proposal. Offtiol and the team reviewed its product cost, necessary manufacturing process and spending requirements (see Exhibits B.8 and B.9). Offtiol compared the x50 product cost (computed assuming all production capacity was used to manufacture the x50) with the product cost of the x100 and noted a few significant cost differences. The reduced size of the x50 (no floating point processor) increased the number of dies able to be placed on each wafer, thus reducing the fabrication cost/die 67 per cent from the x100 ($61.00 for the x100; $20.33 for the x50). The increase in the number of dies on each wafer increased the probe time, however, and increased the probe cost per wafer by 25 per cent ($500 for the x100; $625 for the x50). He was pleased with the doubling of assembly capacity resulting from the smaller package required by the x50 (202,500 annual assembly starts for the x100; 405,000 for the x50). The increase in assembly throughput reduced the x50 assembly costs by 50 per cent. Offtiol was pleasantly surprised at the x50's lower test costs. Even though the x50 required a new tester, the lower annual operating costs versus the x100, along with the reduced testing time from the elimination of the floating point unit, resulted in a per unit test cost of only $5 versus $40 for the x100.

With the x50's cost structure now soundly understood, Offtiol could better appreciate the high but achievable profit margins of the x50. The margins ranged from 75 per cent during Q1–Q3 95 to –67 per cent in Q4 95 when the marketing-required price reduction took effect (see Table B.3). If DeStepper could achieve the $1,866 wafer cost by the start of 1996 (see Exhibits B.10 and B.11), the x50 could obtain a very respectable margin of –59 per cent in the second half of 1996 at the required price of $125. Using the capacity available in 1995 and 1996 to produce 50,000 and 215,000 units, respectively, easily convinced Offtiol to fund the x50 development effort and purchase the new tester. While the product specifications for the x75 were not yet available, he also agreed to fund its development effort. He felt the x75 would achieve the same product margins the x50 demonstrated.

Table B.3

	Q1 95 Q3 95	Q4 95 Q2 96	Q3 96 Q4 96
Price	$250.00	$187.50	$125.00
Cost	$62.50	$62.50	$51.02
Margin $	$187.50	$125.00	$73.98
Margin %	75.0%	66.7%	59.2%

Just as Offtiol was completing his x50 product development meeting, Nomial called and suggested outsourcing and then disinvesting MosCo's assembly operations. She had found an assembly house that could assemble the x50 in its required 168 PGA for $5 per device (in volume levels of 500,000) with equivalent yields to those MosCo projected; Offtiol thought this idea had merit until he compared the $5 external assembly cost/device to the internal cost estimate of $4. He quickly concluded outsourcing would only increase the overall product cost and therefore was not a viable option.

A week before the budget review, Offtiol asked Janus to prepare new pro forma income statements for FY94, FY95 and FY96. He wanted to reflect all his cost reduction targets and product-funding levels. He was curious to see the levels of profit he would generate in 1995 and 1996 from: (1) the revised x100 product cost, (2) the 1996 cost reduction targets in wafer fabrication and their effect on the x100 and x50, (3) the funding of the x50 and x75, (4) the purchase of the Bonn tester the x50 required, (5) the utilisation of 1995 and 1996 capacity for manufacturing the x50, (6) the additional advertising expense necessary to promote the x50 fully in the marketplace and (7) the selling of the x100 and x50 using the marketing department pricing model. Offtiol was confident his decisions would prove sound and keep MosCo profitable in 1995 and 1996.

Now, after a second review of Janus's pro forma income statements (see Figures B.12a–c), Offtiol had become very anxious. He had to present a viable set of recommendations to MosCo's senior management the following day. He thought he and his team had explored and included all viable options in Janus's statements. Finally, Offtiol concluded the cause of the projected FY95 and FY96 losses was the overly aggressive pricing model. He decided he would present Janus's projections, highlight the losses in spite of the cost reductions reflected and suggest keeping the x100 price at $850 for all of 1995 and at $637.50 for all of 1996. The $23.9m increase in FY95 revenue would turn the –$(15.2m) loss into an $8.7m profit. But the $17.9m increase in FY96 revenue would only improve the loss of –$(40.5m) to –$(22.6m). Offtiol was convinced Scott would also agree Price's pricing model was too aggressive. He was certain Scott would approve a revised x100 price and be receptive to a higher price for the x50, which could offset the remaining projected 1996 loss. Offtiol felt it would take a combination of his cost reduction efforts and higher prices to maintain MosCo's profitability and thus demonstrate to CSI MosCo's ability to transform itself into a competitive business unit.

Discussion questions

In reviewing Offtiol's assessments and conclusions, has he proposed the optimal recommendations? Specifically:

1. What caused the 1995 x100 product cost to drop by $227 after reflecting the ABC review and the new costing approach? Did spending decrease or just shift?

2. What is the impact of using the full utilisation approach to product costing versus applying manufacturing cost to the amount produced?

3. What are the drivers of manufacturing cost? Of product cost?

4. Was it practical or plausible to reduce direct wafer fabrication by 34 per cent or $23m?

5. Should Offtiol have looked at areas other than wafer fabrication to identify further cost reductions?

6. Why is there still underutilised manufacturing capacity when the x50 is being manufactured? Is the pricing model in fact too aggressive? Should Offtiol propose increasing the prices of the x100 and x50?

7. What pricing advantages does Mosco's competitor, NoTel, have, knowing their N50 (see Exhibit B.10) has 33 per cent more die/wafer than the x50? (Assume the same wafer, probe, assembly and test costs and yields as the x50.)

Appendix B.1

Overview of the semiconductor manufacturing process

Semiconductor devices are made from silicon, which is material refined from quartz. Silicon is used because it can be altered easily to promote or deter electrical signals. Electronic switches or transistors which control electrical signals can be formed on the surface of a silicon crystal by the precisely controlled addition of certain elements designed in microscopically small patterns.

Silicon is first melted to remove impurities and grown into long crystals (ingots), which vary in size from 9.5 inches to 16 inches in diameter (typical sizes in use today are 6- and 8-inch). The purified silicon is sliced into wafers on which integrated circuits will be patterned. As the size of an integrated circuit is extremely small, hundreds, even thousands, of circuits can be formed on a wafer at the same time.

Integrated circuits (typically referred to as 'chips' or 'dies') are an array of transistors made up of various connected layers, designed to perform specific operations. Each layer is a specific circuit pattern (approximately 20 are used in present processes). A glass plate (called a reticle) is used to pattern each layer on the wafer during the fabrication process.

Fabrication

In the fabrication process, blank wafers are first insulated with a film of oxide, then coated with a soft, light-sensitive plastic called photoresist. The wafers are masked by a reticle and flooded with ultraviolet light, exposing the reticle's specific circuit pattern on the unmasked portion of the wafer. Exposed photoresist hardens into the proper circuit layer outline. Acids and solvents are used to strip away unexposed photoresist and oxide, baring the circuit pattern to be etched by either chemicals or superhot gases. More photoresist is placed on the wafer, masked and stripped, then implanted with chemical impurities, or dopants, that form negative and positive conducting zones. Repeating these steps builds the necessary layers required for the integrated circuit design to be completed on the wafer.

Probe

In the probe process, an electrical performance test of the functions of each of the completed integrated circuits is performed while each die is still on the wafer. The non-functioning dies are marked with ink; the functioning dies are left unmarked and moved to assembly.

Assembly

In the assembly process, each die is cut from the wafer with a diamond saw. The good dies are placed in the cavity of a ceramic package. The bonding pads from the dies are connected by very thin aluminum wires into the leads of the package, creating the necessary electrical connection from the chip to the package. The package is then sealed, with a metal lid placed over the exposed dies in the package.

Test

Once the device is completely packaged, it is tested to ensure all electrical specifications of the integrated circuit are met. The completed, packaged semiconductor device is now ready to be soldered to a printed circuit board (PCB), which in turn will be installed into a computer system.

Appendix B.2

Overview of the product costing process

Semiconductor product costing is a multiple-step process in which manufacturing costs measure value added to raw material as it is processed. Value-added typically is defined as production or capacity throughput divided by spending. The cost system collects, accumulates and yields material and manufacturing costs through each stage of production.

- First, the costs of raw materials used and the unit costs of each stage of manufacturing are established.

- Next, raw wafer and wafer production costs are converted to die costs. In wafer fabrication and probe, manufactured material is in wafer form.

- Costs of the raw wafer and manufacturing in these stages are captured initially as cost/wafer. In assembly, where the wafer is cut into dies, the unit of measure also changes to dies. Thus, to complete the costing of the final product, which is in die form, cost/wafer must be converted to cost/die.

- Finally, the unit die costs are accumulated in the sequence of the manufacturing process and yielded at each stage. Yield refers to the production units successfully manufactured in each stage. The semiconductor manufacturing process typically loses much of its production due to misprocessing or non-functioning dies. Yielding the accumulated unit cost at each manufacturing stage applies the cost of lost production units to the cost of good production units.

At MosCo, the unit production cost of each major manufacturing stage (wafer, fabrication, probe, assembly, test) has been determined by applying that stage's annual spending to the annual volume of production (see Exhibits B.2 and B.3) or capacity (see Exhibits B.6 and B.7).

Exhibits B.3 and B.7 highlight the computation of unit cost at each stage of manufacturing. In wafer fabrication and probe, the production unit is a wafer. Unit cost through these two stages is computed as wafer cost. In assembly and test, the wafer has been diced to remove the dies. The good dies continue through assembly; the non-functioning dies are discarded. Unit cost through these two manufacturing stages is computed as die cost.

At each stage of production, production loss (or yield) is experienced. Yield loss is typically greatest during probe, when each die on the wafer is first tested to determine if it is functioning as designed. At probe, the effectiveness and quality of the wafer fabrication process, through which the multiple circuit layers have been placed on the wafer, is revealed. In wafer fabrication, the wafers used solely for engineering testing (to ensure equipment is properly calibrated and not used for production) are also eliminated (treated similar to production yield loss) in the calculation of wafer cost.

Exhibits B.2 and B.6 highlight the computation of product cost. The unit cost of each manufacturing stage is listed. For the raw wafer, wafer fabrication and probe, the unit cost (wafer) is converted to die cost. The material cost is reflected at the manufacturing stage at which it is introduced. To determine a final or complete product cost, the cost per die is accumulated through each manufacturing stage and yielded for the production loss experienced in that stage. Yielding the accumulated die cost has the effect of placing the total cost of manufacturing on the good production units (or expected good production units if the total production capacity costing method is used).

Exhibit B.2 highlights the accumulation of costs the x100 incurs during manufacturing. The cost and application of raw material can be seen at the start of wafer fabrication and assembly. Wafer to die conversion, based on the x100's specification of 50 die on each wafer, is used to compute the equivalent die cost from the raw wafer and at wafer fabrication and probe. Finally, the treatment of production loss (yield) can be seen throughout the costing process, as the accumulated cost at each stage of production is increased by the planned or expected yield at that stage, resulting in an accumulated cost that reflects the total cost of production applied to the good dies produced or expected after each stage.

Revenue	1993	1994
x100: 150,000 @ $850	$127,500,000	$127,500,000
Cost of sales:		
Wafers: (16,595 @ $45)	$746,775	$746,775
Packages: (175,000 @ $50)	$8,750,000	$8,750,000
Mfg. spending	$91,112,000	$91,112,000
Total cost of sales	$100,608,775	$100,608,775
Gross margin ($)	$26,891,225	$26,891,225
Gross margin (%)	21%	21%
Process development	$14,000,000	$14,000,000
Product development	$5,000,000	$5,000,000
Marketing & administration	$3,000,000	$6,000,000
Operating profit	$4,891,225	$1,891,225

Exhibit B.1 MosCo, Inc. income statement.

Description	Cost/wafer	Cost/die	Cum. cost/die
Yielded raw wafer	$50.00	$1.00	$1.00
Wafer production cost	$5,245.15	$104.90	$105.90
Probe production cost	$785.71	$15.71	$121.62
Probe yield		25%	$486.47
339 PGA package cost		$50.00	$536.47
Assembly production cost		$9.26	$545.73
Assembly yield		90%	$606.36
Test production cost		$32.14	$638.51
Test yield		96%	$665.11
Total x100 product cost			$665.11

Exhibit B.2 MosCo, Inc. – FY94 product cost worksheet x100 – gross die/wafer: 50.

Operation	Per year	Mfg. spending	Cost/unit
Planned wafer capacity	16,595		
Engineering test wafers	1,040		
Planned wafer starts	15,555		
Wafer fabrication yield	90%		
Planned wafer production	13,999.50	$73,429,500	$5,245.16
Planned probed wafer starts	14,000	$11,000,000	$785.71
Gross die/wafer (x100 = 50)	50		
Total gross die thru probe	700,000		
Probe yield for x100	25%		
x100 probed die output	175,000		
Planned assembly starts	175,000	$1,620,000	$9.26
x100 assembly yield	90%		
Planned assembly completions	157,500		
Planned test start	157,500	$5,062,500	$32.14
x100 test yield	96%		
Planned test output	151,200		
Total manufacturing spending		$91,112,000	

Exhibit B.3 MosCo, Inc. – FY94 used capacity and process costs worksheet x100.

Organisation	Manufacturing				R&D		SG & A	Total
	Fabrication	Probe	Assembly	Test	Prod Devp	Proc Devp	Mkt & Adm	
Direct Mfg.	$57,000,000	$11,000,000	$1,620,000	$5,062,500				$74,682,500
Res. & Devp.					$2,000,000	$9,000,000		$11,000,000
Mkt & Admin							$5,000,000	$5,000,000
Support Org's								
Facilities	$5,500,000				$1,000,000	$3,000,000	$500,000	$10,000,000
Yield Eng.	$2,000,000							$2,000,000
Cimt	$4,000,000				$2,000,000	$2,000,000	$500,000	$8,500,000
Qual. & Rel.	$3,537,500							$3,537,500
Purchasing	$1,392,000							$1,392,000
Tot. Support	$16,429,500				$3,000,000	$5,000,000	$1,000,000	$25,429,500
Tot. Spending	$73,429,500	$11,000,000	$1,620,000	$5,062,500	$5,000,000	$14,000,000	$6,000,000	$116,112,000

Fabrication	$73,429,500
Probe	$11,000,000
Assembly	$1,620,000
Test	$5,062,500
Tot. mfg. spending	$91,112,000

Exhibit B.4 MosCo, Inc. – FY94 spending summary by organisation.

Activity	Manufacturing				R&D		SG & A	Total
	Fabrication	Probe	Assembly	Test	Prod Devp	Proc Devp	Mkt & Adm	
Direct Mfg. (See Exhibit B.5b)	$57,000,000	$11,000,000	$1,620,000	$5,062,500				$74,682,500
Res. & Devp.					$2,000,000	$9,000,000		$11,000,000
Mkt & Admin								$5,000,000
Marketing							$3,000,000	$3,000,000
Administration							$1,000,000	$1,000,000
Finance/HR							$1,000,000	$1,000,000
Total							$5,000,000	$5,000,000
Total Support	$10,392,000	$2,000,000		$3,037,500	$3,000,000	$6,000,000	$1,000,000	$25,429,500
See Exhibit B.5c								
Total Spending	$67,392,000	$13,000,000	$1,620,000	$8,100,000	$5,000,000	$15,000,000	$6,000,000	$116,112,000

Fabrication	$67,392,000
Probe	$13,000,000
Assembly	$1,620,000
Test	$8,100,000
Tot. mfg. spending	$90,112,000

Exhibit B.5a MosCo, Inc. – FY94 activity-based spending summary by organisation.

Activity	Manufacturing				R&D		SG & A	Total
	Fabrication	Probe	Assembly	Test	Prod Devp	Proc Devp	Mkt & Adm	
Equipment capacity:	: Driven by Equipment Installation							
Depreciation	$30,000,000	$3,500,000	$520,000	$1,400,000				$35,420,000
Utility costs	$5,000,000	$1,000,000	$50,000	$500,000				$6,550,000
Property/site	$5,000,000	$5,000,000	$50,000	$100,000				$5,650,000
Total	$40,000,000	$5,000,000	$620,000	$2,000,000				$47,620,000
Equipment capacity:	: Driven by Equipment Uptime							
Equip engn'rs	$8,000,000	$2,000,000		$1,762,500				$11,762,500
Monitor wafer	$1,000,000							$1,000,000
Op'n supplies	$1,000,000	$1,000,000	$100,000	$300,000				$2,400,000
Total	$10,000,000	$3,000,000	$100,000	$2,062,500				$15,162,500
Equipment capacity:	: Driven by production							
Direct labour	$5,000,000	$2,000,000	$800,000	$700,000				$8,500,000
Monitor wafer	$1,000,000							$1,000,000
Op'n supplies	$1,000,000	$1,000,000	$100,000	$300,000				$2,400,000
Total Support	$7,000,000	$3,000,000	$900,000	$1,000,000				$11,900,000
Tot. dir. mfg.	$57,000,000	$11,000,000	$1,620,000	$5,062,500				$74,682,500

Tot. dir. mfg.: (new Bonn tester) $1,215,000

Exhibit B.5b MosCo, Inc. – FY94 direct manufacturing activity-based spending summary.

Activity	Manufacturing				R&D		SG & A	Total
	Fabrication	Probe	Assembly	Test	Prod Devp	Proc Devp	Mkt & Adm	
Facilities							$5,000,000	
D/I water	$1,000,000					$500,000		$1,500,000
Site support	$500,000			$100,000	$5,000,000	$5,000,000		$2,100,000
Utilities	$3,000,000			$400,000	$5,000,000	$2,000,000		$5,900,000
Chemicals	$500,000							$500,000
Total	$5,000,000			$500,000	$10,000,000	$3,000,000	$5,000,000	$10,000,000
Yield eng.: yield improvement		$2,000,000						$2,000,000
Cimt:								
Shop-floor system	$1,000,000			$1,000,000	$1,000,000			$2,000,000
Networks	$500,000			$500,000	$500,000	$500,000	$250,000	$2,750,000
Field svc	$500,000			$500,000	$500,000		$250,000	$1,750,000
System devp						$500,000		$1,000,000
Equip. connection						$1,000,000		$1,000,000
Total	$2,000,000			$2,000,000	$2,000,000	$2,000,000	$500,000	$8,500,000
Quality:								$1,000,000
Doc. control	$1,000,000				$1,000,000			
Fail analysis	$500,000			$100,000		$250,000		$850,000
Equip. calibrate	$500,000			$437,500		$750,000		$1,687,500
Total	$2,000,000			$537,500	$1,000,000	$1,000,000		$3,537,500
Purchasing	$1,392,000							$1,392,000
Total Sup. spend	$10,392,000	$2,000,000		$3,037,500	$3,000,000	$6,000,000	$1,000,000	$25,429,500
Total Sup. spend: (new Bonn tester)				$810,000				

Exhibit B.5c MosCo, Inc. – FY94 support group activity-based spending summary.

Description	Cost/wafer	Cost/die	Cum. cost/die
Yielded raw wafer	$50.00	$1.00	$1.00
Wafer production cost	$3,000.00	$60.00	$61.00
Probe production cost	$500.00	$10.00	$71.00
Probe yield		25%	$284.00
339 PGA package cost		$50.00	$334.00
Assembly production cost		$8.00	$342.00
Assembly yield		90%	$380.00
Test production cost		$40.00	$420.00
Test yield		96%	$437.50
Total x100 product cost			**$437.50**

Exhibit B.6 Mosco, Inc. – FY94 revised product cost worksheet x100
– gross die/wafer: 50.

Operation	Per year	Mfg. spending	Cost/unit
Planned wafer capacity	26,000		
Engineering test wafers	1,040		
Planned wafer starts	24,960		
Wafer fabrication yield	90%		
Planned wafer production	22,464	$67,392,000	$3,000.00
Planned probed wafer starts	26,000	$13,000,000	$500.00
Gross die/wafer (x100 = 50)	50		
Total gross die through probe	1,300,000		
Probe yield for x100	25%		
x100 probed die output	325,000		
Planned assembly starts	202,500	$1,620,000	$8.00
x100 assembly yield	90%		
Planned assembly completions	182,250		
Planned test starts	202,500	$8,100,000	$40.00
x100 test yield	96%		
Planned test output	194,400		
Total manufacturing spending		$90,112,000	

Exhibit B.7 Mosco, Inc. – FY94 used capacity and process costs worksheet
x100.

Description	Cost/wafer	Cost/die	Cum. cost/die
Yielded raw wafer	$50.00	$0.33	$0.33
Wafer production cost	$3,000.00	$20.00	$20.33
Probe production cost	$625.00	$4.17	$24.50
Probe yield		70%	$35.00
168 PGA package cost		$15.00	$50.00
Assembly production cost		$4.00	$54.00
Assembly yield		96%	$56.25
Test production cost		$5.00	$61.25
Test yield		98%	$62.50
Total x50 product cost			**$62.50**

Exhibit B.8 Mosco, Inc. – FY94 product cost worksheet x50 – gross die/wafer: 150.

Operation	Per year	Mfg. spending	Cost/unit
Planned wafer capacity	26,000		
Engineering test wafers	1,040		
Planned wafer starts	24,960		
Wafer fabrication yield	90%		
Planned wafer production	22,464	$67,392,000	$3,000.00
Planned probed wafer starts	20,800	$13,000,000	$625.00
Gross die/wafer (x50 = 150)	150		
Total gross die through probe	3,120,000		
Probe yield for x50	70%		
x50 probed die output	2,184,000		
Planned assembly starts	405,000	$1,620,000	$4.00
x50 assembly yield	90%		
Planned assembly completions	364,500		
Planned test starts	405,000	$2,025,000	$5.00
x50 test yield	96%		
Planned test output	388,800		
Total manufacturing spending		$84,037,000	

Exhibit B.9 Mosco, Inc. – FY94 projected capacity and process costs worksheet x50.

Description	Cost/wafer	Cost/die	Cum, cost/die
Yielded raw wafer	$50.00	$0.33	$0.33
Wafer production cost	$1,866.00	$12.44	$12.77
Probe production cost	$625.00	$4.17	$16.94
Probe yield		70%	$24.20
168 PGA package cost		$15.00	$39.20
Assembly production cost		$4.00	$43.20
Assembly yield		96%	$45.00
Test production cost		$5.00	$50.00
Test yield		98%	$51.02
Total x50 product cost			**$51.02**

Exhibit B.10 Mosco, Inc. – FY94 revised product cost worksheet (reflecting requested wafer fabrication spending reduction) x50.

Operation	Per year	Mfg. spending	Cost/unit
Planned wafer capacity	26,000		
Engineering test wafers	1,040		
Planned wafer starts	24,960		
Wafer fabrication yield	90%		
Planned wafer production	22,464	$41,917,824	
Planned probed wafer starts	20,800	$13,000,000	$625.00
Gross die/wafer (x50 = 50)	150		
Total gross die through probe	3,120,000		
Probe yield for x50	70%		
x50 probed die output	2,184,000		
Planned assembly starts	405,500	$1,620,000	$4.00
x50 assembly yield	90%		
Planned assembly completions	364,500		
Planned test starts	405,000	$2,025,000	$5.00
x50 test yield	96%		
Planned test output	388,800		
Total manufacturing spending		$58,562,824	

Exhibit B.11 Mosco, Inc. – FY94 projected capacity and process costs worksheet (reflecting requested wafer fabrication spending reduction) x50.

	1994 revised	1995 recom'd	1996 recom'd
	$127,500,000	$115,312,500	$63,476,562
Revenue:			
Cost of sales:			
Raw material costs	$9,496,775	$10,348,010	$8,282,255
Production costs	$90,112,000	$59,063,500	$27,788,853
Total product cost	$99,608,775	$69,411,510	$36,071,108
Product gross margin	$27,891,225	$45,900,990	$27,405,454
%	21.9%	39.8%	43.2%
Underutilised costs	$0	$33,073,500	$38,873,971
Total cost of sales	$99,608,775	$102,485,010	$74,945,079
Gross margin:	$27,891,225	$12,827,490	($11,468,516)
%	21.9%	11.1%	−18.1%
Process developement:	$15,000,000	$15,000,000	$15,000,000
Product developement:	$6,000,000	$6,000,000	$6,000,000
Marketing & administration:	$6,000,000	$7,000,000	$8,000,000
Operating profit/(loss):	$891,225	($15,172,510)	($40,468,516)

Exhibit B.12a Mosco, Inc. – 'OFmOL' pro forma income statement.

	x100	x50	FY95
Revenue:			
Q1: (37,500 @ $850)	$31,875,000		
Q2–Q4: (112,500 @ $637.50)	$71,718,750		
Ql–Q3: (37,500 @ $250)		$9,375,000	
Q4: (12,500 @ $187.50)		$2,343,750	
	$103,593,750	$11,718,750	$115,312,500
Raw material costs:			
Wafers: (16,595 @ $45)	$746,775		
(583 @ $45)		$26,235	
Packages: (175,000 @ $50)	$8,750,000		
(55,000 @ $15)		$825,000	
	$9,496,775	$851,235	$10,348,010
Production costs:			
Fabrication: (14,000 @ $3,000)	$42,000,000		
(524 @ $3,000)		$1,572,000	
Probe: (14,000 @ $500)	$7,000,000		
(524 @ $625)		$327,500	
Assembly: (175,000 @ $8)	$1,400,000		
(55,000 @ $4)		$220,000	
Test: (157,000 @ $40)	$6,280,000		
(52,800 @ $5)		$264,000	
	$56,680,000	$2,383,500	$59,063,500
Underutilisation costs:			
Fabrication: ($67,392,000 – ($42,000,000 + $1,572,000)			$23,820,000
Probe: ($13,000,000 – ($7,000,000 + $327,500)			$5,672,500
Assembly: ($1,620,000 – ($1,400,000 + $220,000)			$0
Test: ($8,100,000 – $6,280,000) + ($2,025,000 – $264,000)			$3,581,000
			$33,073,500

Exhibit B.12b Mosco, Inc. – FY95 'OFTIOL' pro forma income statement worksheet.

	x100	x50	FY95
Revenue:			
Q1–Q3: (56,250 @ $425)	$23,906,250		
Q4: (18,750 @ $318.75)	$5,976,562		
Ql–Q2: (107,500 @ $187.50)		$20,156,250	
Q3–Q4: (107,500 @ $125)		$13,437,500	
	$29,882,812	$33,593,750	$63,476,562
Raw material costs:			
Wafers: (7,991 @ $45)	$359,595		
(2,448 @ $45)		$110,160	
Packages: (86,875 @ $50)	$4,343,750		
(231,250 @ $15)		$3,468,750	
	$4,703,345	$3,578,910	$8,282,255
Production costs:			
Fabrication: (6,950 @ $1,866)	$12,968,700		
(2,203 @ $1,866)		$4,110,798	
Probe: (6,950 @ $500)	$3,475,000		
(2,203 @ $625)		$1,376,875	
Assembly: (86,875 @ $8)	$695,000		
(231,250 @ $4)		$925,000	
Test: (78,187 @ $40)	$3,127,480		
(222,000 @ $5)		$1,110,000	
	$20,266,180	$7,522,673	$27,788,853
Underutilisation costs:			
Fabrication: ($41,917,824 – ($12,968,700 + $4,110,798)			$24,838,326
Probe: ($13,000,000 – ($3,475,000 + $1,376,875)			$8,148,125
Assembly: ($1,620,000 – ($695,000 + $925,000)			$0
Test: ($8,100,000 – $3,127,480) + ($2,025,000 – $1,110,000)			$5,887,520
			$38,873,971

Exhibit B.12c Mosco, Inc. – FY96 'OFFrIOL' pro forma income statement worksheet.

	x100	x50	N50
Function:	CPU/CISC	CPU/CISC	
Technology:	CMOS .75U	CMOS .75U	CMOS .75U
Frequency:	100mhj	50mhj	50mhj
Selling price			
Actual: 1994 Q1:			
1994 Q2:			
1994 Q3:			
1994 Q4:	$850.00		
Proposed: 1995 Q1:		$250.00	$500.00
1995 Q2:	$637.50		
1995 Q3:		£187.50	$375.00
1995 Q4:			
1996 Q1:	$425.00	$125.00	$250.00
1996 Q2:			
1996 Q3:	$318.75		
1996 Q4:			

	x100	x50	N50
Raw wafer costs:	$45	$45	$45
Wafer production cost:	$3,000	$3,000	
Probe cost/wafer:	$500	$625	
Gross die/wafer:	50	150	200
Good die thru test (EQS):	10.8	98.8	141.0
Probe yield	25%	70%	75%
Package type:	339PGA	168PGA	168PGA
Package cost:	$50	$15	$15
Assembly cost:	$8	$4	
Assembly yield:	90%	96%	
Test cost:	$40	$5	
Test yield:	96%	98%	

Exhibit B13 MosCo, Inc. – product specification.

(w) wafer (d) die	Total capacity available	x100 capacity used FY95 (150,000)	x100 capacity used FY96 (75,000)	Available capacity for x50 FY95	Available capacity for x50 FY96	Maximum used by x50 FY95	Maximum used by x50 FY96	Available capacity FY95	Available capacity FY96
FAB starts	26,000(w)	16,595	7,991						
Engineering **Starts**	1,040(w)	1,040	1,040						
Production starts	24,960(w)	15,555	7,723	9,405	17,237	582	2,447	8,823	14,790
Production **Completes**	22,464(w)	14,000	6,950	8,464	15,514	524	2,202	7,940	13,312
x100 probe starts	26,000(w)	14,000	6,950	12,000	19,050				
x50 probe starts	20,800(w)			9,600	15,240	524	2,202	9,076	13,038
339 PGA assembly **Starts**	202,500(d)	175,000	68,875	27,500	115,625				
339 PGA assembly **Completes**	188,250(d)	157,500	78,187						
168 PGA assembly **Starts**	405,000(d)			55,000	231,250	55,000	231,250	0	0
168 PGA assembly **Completes**	388,800(d)			52,800	222,000	52,800	222,000	0	0
x100 test starts	202,500(d)	157,500	78,187					45,000	124,313
x100 test completes	194,400(d)	151,200	75,060					43,200	119,430
x50 test starts	405,000(d)			405,000	405,000	52,800	222,000	352,200	183,000

Exhibit B.14 MosCo, Inc. – FY95 and FY96 capacity available.

CASE STUDY C

Cost centre management at
Air Command

(Business planning and costing)

(Howard Armitage and Wendy Osborne prepared this case. Copyright © 1998 by Institute of Management Accountants, Montvale, NJ. Reproduced with permission.)

In December 1993, Colonel R.J. Smith, command comptroller, Air Command, received a pilot business model that had been prepared for 7 Wing Construction Engineering in Ottawa. On 22 February 1994, the government of Canada introduced a budget recommending several military bases, including 7 Wing, be closed.

Colonel Smith commented:

> We started this project in 1992. The Canadian military, like all government departments, had experienced a long series of budget reductions. Fiscal restraint demanded effective resource management, but the disconnect between spending and consuming in the military made this difficult. We started the cost centre management project to determine if we could give consumers budgetary responsibility for resources consumed. This pilot business model was our first effort in implementing 'user pay'. The pilot project at 7 Wing took months. We

had planned to expand the model from just Construction Engineering to all of 7 Wing. Now we have to do the next phase at an entirely new site! This will be the proof of the concept of business model migration.

Public Service 2000

Throughout the 1980s, deficit reduction was a major goal of the Canadian federal government. In 1990, the public service had more than 500,000 people working in about 400 different organisations. That year, Prime Minister Brian Mulroney announced a government initiative, Public Service 2000 (PS2000), to enable the public service to function effectively in the context of continuing restraint.

PS2000, which became law in early 1992, directed government departments to delegate authority to those delivering services to clients and to assist managers in developing the necessary knowledge and skills to use that increased authority. With increased authority came increased accountability for funds spent. The departments, in turn, developed policies to act on PS2000. The initiative developed by the Department of National Defence was Defence 2000.

The Department of National Defence

In 1992, the Department of National Defence (DND) was one of 26 government departments directly presided over by a minister. It had a budget of $12.2 billion[1] (8 per cent of major government expenditure,[2] 40 per cent of the government's operating budget, 1.8 per cent of GDP[3]) and 85,000 military and 36,000 civilian employees.[4] The minister was responsible for the management and control of the Canadian Forces and for all matters relating to national defence. DND's objective was to deter the use of force or coercion against Canada and Canadian interests, and to be able to respond adequately should deterrence fail.

A deputy minister (DM), responsible for the financial and personnel administration of civilian employees, and the Chief of the Defence Staff (CDS) reported to the minister. The CDS was the senior military advisor to the minister and was responsible for the control and administration of the Canadian Forces. Six senior managers reported directly to the DM and CDS at National Defence Headquarters (NDHQ) in Ottawa (see Exhibit C.1). In addition, four commanders reported directly to the CDS. NDHQ senior management and the commanders of each command shared managerial responsibility for spending through a committee structure. Personnel were stationed at 29 Canadian Forces bases (CFBS) across Canada as well as abroad on NATO and UN missions. DND's budget was $12 billion (shown in thousands of dollars):

Air Command	3,030,864
Maritime Command	2,312,799
Land Force Command	1,936,139
Canadian Forces Europe	1,262,994
Personnel Support	446,107
Materiel[5] Support	4,615,115
Communication Services	834,564
Policy Direction Management Services	711,217
TOTAL	$12,185,819[6]

Defence 2000

At DND the public expectation for a better return on its tax dollar meant no budget increases and reducing the size of the permanent force while modernising ageing equipment and meeting increasing international commitments. Defence 2000, a department-wide strategic framework, was issued in November 1992 to provide the foundation for continuous improvement in providing good quality, cost-effective defence services to Canada. Its strategic goals were to:

• delegate authority, with attendant accountability;

• make service and cost-effectiveness driving forces;

• create an environment where all personnel felt empowered and committed to improving defence capability, managing costs, and making their organisation a better place to work for.

Various studies had identified support service areas (such as supply, maintenance, transportation, construction engineering and administration) where commands could achieve significant savings. The studies showed that commanders were resource custodians rather than resource managers, as they effectively controlled, on average, only 20 per cent of the value of resources they used. Colonel Smith recounted an example:

> Most bases run a 'taxi' service, where a military driver picks up and drops off people in a military vehicle. The only cost to the base is the cost of fuel. The Materiel Group at NDHQ supplies and pays for the cars, the Personnel Group at NDHQ pays for the drivers and the NDHQ legal staff control the funds to settle claims against the Crown resulting from accidents. A few dollars for gas appears to be cheaper than an $8 to $10 taxi fare. If you took the time to sit down and figure it out, it costs the military as a whole $36 in consumed resources for an equivalent trip.

A committee composed of top management was struck to develop and execute plans to achieve Defence 2000 goals. The committee examined current literature to find new information that could be of use to them. Two models of interest were the business planning process and activity-based costing/activity-based management (ABC/ABM).

Business planning process

Defence 2000 mandated that commands should implement a business planning process. A business plan was a contract between a superior and a subordinate specifying what activities the subordinate would carry out and what resources the superior would provide to allow him or her to do so. Attaching costs to each activity would allow subordinates to use resources effectively. The business planning concept would facilitate the implementation of ABC (attaching costs to the activities that created the demand for those costs).

Air Command

Air Command's objective was to maintain combat-ready general-purpose air forces to meet Canada's defence commitments. Air Command (AIRCOM) accounted for 25 per cent of DND's budget and 23 per cent of total person years. Five functional air groups and three wings reported to AIRCOM Headquarters (ACHQ) in Winnipeg (see Exhibit C.2). The commander of Air Command was responsible for accomplishing Air Command's objective and exercised command over all groups and wings reporting to him. The breakdown of Air Command spending in 1991–92 (in thousands of dollars) was:

Operating expenditures:

Personnel	1,230,125
Operations and maintenance	1,263,299
Operating requirement	$2,493,424
Capital	646,807
Total requirement	3,140,231
Less: Revenue[7]	109,357
Total funding	$3,030864

Colonel Smith highlighted Air Command's lack of responsibility for resource spending:

> In 1991/92, the Air Force spent about $2.5 billion on people, operations and maintenance (this doesn't include capital spending) to deliver our product – maintaining a combat-ready air force. A little more than half of this $2.5 billion (about $1.3 billion) is directly attributable to flying aircraft. (The rest is for support activities such as operating bases, headquarters, etc.) The only expenses in this entire $1.3 billion that Air Command manages are the cost of aviation fuel, which accounts for about $1.15 million and a few million for crew travel costs. Various staffs at NDHQ manage the rest.

The sole person responsible for the delivery of flying operations is the commander of Air Command. Yet he has spending responsibility for less than 10 per cent of the necessary resources. This relationship is fundamentally wrong.

Cost centre management project

In 1991, Lieutenant-General Huddleston, deputy chief of defence staff in Ottawa, was named commander of AIRCOM in Winnipeg. Almost immediately, he became dissatisfied with the effects of centralised defence reductions. Not only was NDHQ staff deciding how much had to be cut from budgets, but financial reduction targets were accompanied by specific directions on how AIRCOM would achieve the savings. The easiest targets for reductions were the operational capabilities of the air force (i.e. flying the various fleets). As a result AIRCOM was meeting its financial reduction targets by reducing flying rates, retiring some fleets and cancelling capital acquisitions.

General Huddleston was responsible for maintaining the combat capability of the air force to the maximum extent possible. He was convinced that substantial savings were possible by working smarter and empowering appropriate personnel to reduce costs in support operations. He believed AIRCOM could meet most, if not all, financial reduction targets in support operations and still maintain a credible combat capability. However, he had no way of analysing total support costs in a systematic and accurate way. Although DND had an extensive financial management information system, there was no way he could provide managers with the information to make informed financial decisions about their activities. Obviously, if he was going to ask his subordinates to manage their costs better, he would have to provide them with the tools to do so.

In July 1992, the Canadian Forces supply organisation at NDHQ announced that from 1 April 1993 it would be introducing an automated cost capturing system – customer consumption awareness (CCA). This system would allow each unit to track the cost of the materiel it used. The supply organisation hoped that when people became aware of how much they were spending and how much it was costing the armed forces and the Canadian government for some of their activities, they would try to find a less expensive way to do them. General Huddleston saw CCA as a first step to providing the information he was looking for. Its major shortcoming was that it provided cost information about the supply operation only.

In the military, operational units (such as a wing) carried out organisational objectives, such as flying fighter aircraft. Support organisations (such as supply) existed to support the operational units. Operational commanders (e.g. the commanding officer of a transport squadron) who actually used the resources had no awareness of or responsibility for their cost. The disconnect between consumption and management resulted in a 'horn of plenty' mindset, where commanders who wanted something simply ordered it without regard for cost. This led to overordering. Colonel Smith described how overconsumption had become a way of life:

> Because of our highly centralised approach to resource management, which is input- rather that output-oriented, we have ended up with a system that uses bureaucracy to control costs. The only way you can control costs when

managing inputs is to put barriers in the way of getting at the inputs. We have highly developed entitlement and approval processes that make it difficult for consumers to get anything new/changed/different without going through layers of process. For example, if you need a person with different qualifications, you have to go through an 'establishment change' process; if you need a new type of equipment, you need to go through a 'materiel authorisation change request' process, etc. Once established, however, you continue to have access to that resource – free and forever. There is no incentive to save. And once you get to the 'front of the line', you take as much as you can, because it may be a while before you get back to the front of the line. For example, if you think you need a piece of equipment to perform some task, but are unsure whether you will need one or two of the item, you are likely to order three. The bureaucracy is the same and you only want to go through it once.

General Huddleston wanted to shift the management of and budgetary responsibility for resources to the people who were consuming them. He directed his chief of staff support, Brigadier-General Popowich, to set up a committee with the command comptroller, the deputy chief of staff logistics and the deputy chief of staff support operations, to develop a system that would push resource management down to the level of the people using the resources and give people the tools required to operate such a system. The aim, objectives and scope of the cost centre management project (CCMP) are shown in Exhibit C.3. CCMP was seen as developing an information system that could be used to support business planning.

AIRCOM did not have the manpower to develop and implement CCMP. It needed an external consultant with a good knowledge of costing and organisation systems, and who was well-versed in DND funding and procurement policies, procedures and information systems at NDHQ, ACHQ and CFB levels. In November 1992, AIRCOM hired Consulting and Audit Canada.

Consulting and Audit Canada

Consulting and Audit Canada (CAC) is a special operating agency[8] of Government Services Canada, that offers professional audit and management consulting services focused solely on the needs of the public sector. It became an operating agency in 1989, but its professional services date back more than 50 years.

William Reid, principal consultant at CAC, assembled a team of CAC and AIRCOM people to study AIRCOM's structure and information systems. The team's initial report confirmed that there was a lack of accountability and information at all managerial levels. It was impossible for commanders (either operational or support) to determine the total costs of resources consumed by their organisation. The team believed that preparing a business model for each military unit[9] would aid the business planning process. A business model described the functions a unit performed and the cost elements it used to achieve its purpose or mandate. Functions were operating activities performed by a unit. Cost elements were inputs necessary to carry out each function, such as human resources, materiel and equipment. The business model concept would provide the basis for a 'user pay' policy. Reid summarised the work:

> This is an important project for Air Command. It makes sense to match budgetary responsibility with the responsibility for carrying out the related functions. This is the logical first step to take in an environment of fiscal restraint. The project represents a major cultural change for the Command.

In March 1993, Reid submitted a preliminary report suggesting they proceed with the CCMP on an incremental basis. He suggested the team prepare a business model for one support organisation. The model would define the functions the organisation performed and would determine the costs associated with each function. A key element of CCMP would be to develop a prototype information system to determine these costs.

7 Wing Construction Engineering

The Commander of 7 Wing Ottawa, Colonel Rick Findley, was very interested in innovative approaches to management. He volunteered his wing for the prototype business model. The organisation selected was Construction Engineering (CE), headed by the Wing Construction Engineering officer, Lieutenant Colonel Gord Brown (see Exhibit C.4). Some of the reasons for selecting Construction Engineering were that it had its own (military-wide) information system, it provided a specific service (the construction and maintenance of 7 Wing infrastructure) to a well-defined customer base and it was close to CAC (and DND) headquarters. Phase 1 began in May 1993.

7 Wing Construction Engineering (7 Wg CE) had approximately 410 full-time personnel – 160 military and 250 civilian – plus up to 100 term or casual employees at any given time. Lieutenant Colonel Brown commented: 'Construction Engineering is probably one of the most conscientious groups within the armed forces for keeping track of costs. When the project started, Colonel Findley asked me what I thought CE's annual costs were. I could track approximately $24 million from our information system and I estimated there was probably another $25–26 m spent by outside agencies on our behalf.'

Construction Engineering was the property manager for 7 Wing. It was responsible for constructing, maintaining and purchasing utilities for all Wing infrastructure, which had a replacement value of more than $800 million. It also provided fire, environmental and safety services to the Wing. 7 Wg CE had seven sections: Requirements; Engineering; Production; Utilities; Fire Services; Environment and Safety; and Administration. Requirements, Engineering and Production focused on construction and maintenance projects from initial planning and funding through to design and construction. These three sections provided a wide range of construction and maintenance services for the Wing infrastructure, which included buildings, married quarters, plants and distribution systems.

Utilities provided all utility services to the Wing, through direct operation of plants and systems, and purchases of utilities. Fire Services provided fire and crash response when needed and fire prevention services, such as inspection and training, to the Wing and selected other sites. Environment and Safety provided preventive and responsive environmental protection services for the Wing. Administration performed internal support functions to 7 Wg CE. It managed finances, personnel, supplies and equipment, and provided general administrative and property management support.

7 Wg CE also provided military personnel for deployed operations at missions abroad and for specific tasks within Canada. Lieutenant Colonel Brown determined that 2,700 person days (approximately $600,000) had been reassigned from CE in 1991/92.

Prototype business model

Preparing the business model involved defining the functions 7 Wg CE performed and determining the costs associated with each function. CAC determined that 7 Wg CE performed six functions as follows:

1. *Construct and maintain infrastructure.* CE Squadron provided a wide range of construction and maintenance services for the infrastructure on the Wing, including buildings, married quarters and works such as plants and distribution systems.

2. *Protect the environment.* CE Squadron provided preventive and responsive environmental protection services to the Wing. CE Squadron also served as a focal point and coordinator of broader Wing environmental services.

3. *Deliver utilities.* CE Squadron provided all utility services to the Wing, through direct operation of utility plants and systems, and through purchases of utilities by contracts.

4. *Provide fire service.* CE Squadron provided fire and crash response when needed and fire prevention services, such as inspection and training, to the Wing and selected other sites.

5. *Provide support.* CE Squadron had an internal group that provided it with support services, such as finance, personnel, supplies and equipment. In addition the Squadron provided general administrative and property management support to the Wing.

6. *Support deployed operations.* CE Squadron provided military personnel for missions abroad and specific tasks in Canada.

Using information available from DND's corporate and functional systems as well as estimates, CAC determined that 7 Wg CE annual costs were about $74,000,000, which could be categorised into eight cost elements (a breakdown of these costs is provided in Exhibit C.5 and a brief explanation of the sources for the costs is provided in Exhibit C.6):

1. *People – salary plus allowances, benefits and training.* Could be divided into military and civilian and regular hours. A more complex breakdown would separate direct and indirect costs.

2. *Material – the costs of tangible goods consumed in the delivery of 7 Wg CE services.* Construction material (including wood, paint, glass, etc.) used. Delivery of utilities included the cost of any utilities purchased on behalf of the Wing. Material for the protection of the environment included supplies necessary for the clean-up of, or response to, environmental problems. Fire services material included the foam and other supplies necessary to fight fires.

3. *Contracts – for the delivery of services.* A single payment to a contractor included labour, material and overhead. Tracking contracts separately eliminated the need to separate those costs.

4. *Accommodation infrastructure required to accomplish 7 Wg CE goals and objectives.* This category included office space, furniture, photocopiers, telecommunication services and some utilities.

5. *Transportation – Wing vehicles used by 7 Wg CE.* Costs included a measurement of use (i.e. cost per vehicle mile), fuel and other associated costs (maintenance, repairs, etc.). Transportation also included the cost of 7 Wg CE personnel travel for business purposes or to attend training courses.

6. *Tools and equipment – required in the course of operations.* 7 Wg CE purchased tools and equipment used on an ongoing basis, such as drills, computers, or fire-fighting equipment. Some specialised equipment was rented for specific jobs as needs arose.

7. *Office supplies –* stationery, pens, printed material for training programmes, overhead slides and small office equipment such as calculators.

8. *Other costs that did not fit any other description.*

Information shortfalls

After gathering the information, the CAC/7 Wg CE team believed a number of important costs were missing. The labour costs reported by CEMIS were incomplete as it recorded only direct labour. Supervisors' time and all engineering time, including leave, were charged to engineering overheads (which was recorded on FIS). CEMIS did not capture labour costs for goods or services provided and paid for by other units on the Wing or by AC/NDHQ. Some employees received clothing and footwear allowances, which were not included in the 7 Wg CE budget. As well, the cost of providing personnel to deployed operations was not tracked.

NDHQ and ACHQ paid significant training expenses for both military and civilian personnel. FIS did not report which unit benefited from the training expense. DND had initiated financial accountability in an individual training project that would be able to report these costs, but information from it would not be available for about a year.

The 7 Wg CE budget did not include facility operating costs such as maintenance, janitorial, electricity, heating and supporting infrastructure, such as telephone, fax and photocopiers. Estimates had been supplied only for some of these costs.

The costs in the model prepared by CAC were determined by extracting data manually from various information systems and by calling people and asking for estimates. This was too cumbersome and slow a process to maintain the business model on an ongoing basis. A critical aspect of the project was developing an information system to determine the required costs. A substantial part of Phase 1 was spent on developing software (resource management consumption information interface – RCMII) that would allow a unit to extract its costs from the existing information systems.

The Phase 1 final report for the CCMP concluded that:

- The Cost Center Management concept was feasible.

- It was possible to provide managers with the total cost of running their organisation.

- Although the existing information systems within the armed forces were not designed to provide cost information by business function, they could provide the information needed if put to better use.

Phase 1 had been a success and the Commander of Air Command had given approval for Phase 2, which was to develop a business model for all of 7 Wing. Now 7 Wing was going to be closed. This would be a real test for the model – going ahead with Phase 2 at a different wing.

Discussion questions

1. Despite its apparent uniqueness and complexity, the military has many similarities to other organisations that may be more familiar to you, for example in terms of setting objectives and organisational structure. What is the overall goal of DND? What is the more specific goal of Air Command? Give an example of a line position and a staff position and the chain of command for each.

2. Why did DND manage resources the way it did? What was the motivation for change?

3. Should ABC/ABM be considered as an alternative to the existing cost system? Why?

4. Break down the costs in Exhibit C.5 into the following table:

Cost item	System where cost raised	Amount	Method of cost assignment to Wing			Comment
			Cost incurred and directly charged	Cost incurred but not charged	Cost charged but not incurred	

How much of the total cost is based on information from corporate information systems? How much is controlled by the 7 Wg CE budget?

5. Categorise these costs using the eight cost elements provided in the case. Although this information was not available to the CAC/CE team at the time you may use the following assumptions:

(a) CE's spending tracked by FIS was 75 per cent on civilian salaries and 25 per cent on material (in the maintenance and CE operations accounts).

(b) CE's spending tracked by CCA was 90 per cent on material and 10 per cent on tools and equipment.

6. Preparing the business model for 7 Wg CE involves determining the activities performed under each of the six principal functions. Try to add one or two activities to each of the principal functions. Prepare a matrix showing the relationship between these activities and their cost elements.

7. Could this business model be applied to another Wing?

Glossary

7 Wg CE	7 Wing Construction Engineering
ACHQ	Air Command Headquarters, located in Winnipeg
ADM	Assistant deputy minister, reports directly to a deputy minister
CAC	Consulting and Audit Canada, management consulting service operated by Government Services Canada
CCA	Customer consumption awareness, a stand-alone costing module of the Canadian Forces Supply System used to extract resource consumption from the CFSS
CCMP	Cost Centre Management Project, a project undertaken by Air Command to introduce decentralised resource management
CDS	Chief of Defence Staff, the senior military advisor to the Minister of National Defence
CE	Construction Engineering

CEMIS   Construction Engineering Management Information System, the financial information system used by Construction Engineering throughout the military

CFB   Canadian Forces Base – the role of a base is to provide personnel and material support to operational units

CFM   Cost Factors Manual, provides a common basis for estimating DND personnel, equipment and facility costs

CFSS   Canadian Forces Supply system, an EOQ-based material management inventory supply system that keeps track of quantities and location of material in the supply system and is used to order required supplies

DCC   Defence Construction Canada, a Crown Corporation that contracts for DND on large projects

DM   Deputy minister, the senior public servant in a government department.

DND   Department of National Defence

FIS   Financial Information System of the Department of National Defence

GSC   Government Services Canada, formerly Supply and Services Canada, purchasing agent for federal government

LOMMIS   Land Ordnance Maintenance Management Information System, a forces-wide information system used by Electrical and Mechanical Engineering to track vehicle maintenance costs

Materiel   All public property, other than real property and money, provided for the Canadian Forces, includes any vessel, vehicle, aircraft, animal, missile, arms, ammunition, clothing, stores, provisions or equipment

NDHQ   National Defence Headquarters, located in Ottawa

PS2000   Public Service 2000, an initiative of the federal government to enable the Public Service to function effectively in the context of continuing restraint

Unit	A basic organisation building block of the Canadian Forces (e.g. a ship, battalion, regiment, company, squadron, station or base) Structure at the Department of National Defence

Notes

1. National Defence 1992–93 Estimates, Part III, Expenditure Plan, Ministry of Supply and Services, 1992, p. 10.

2. Ibid., p. 32.

3. Defence 2000: A Vision for Management Through Innovation, November 1992, p. 1.

4. National Defence 1992–93 Estimates, op. cit., p. 10.

5. Material is all public property, other than real property and money, provided for the Canadian Forces.

6. National Defence 1992–93 Estimates, op. cit., p. 10

7. Revenue was generated primarily from the sale of utilities, the rental of single and married quarters to Canadian Forces personnel, the sale of meals to personnel not entitled to receive rations free of charge and the provision of sales of goods and services to NATO countries and other foreign national governments.

8. An operating agency is expected to recover its costs from fees charged.

9. A unit was a basic organisation building block in the Canadian Forces.

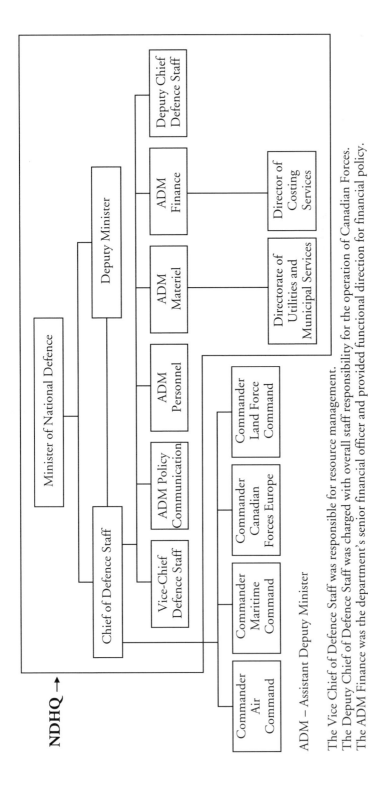

NDHQ →

ADM – Assistant Deputy Minister

The Vice Chief of Defence Staff was responsible for resource management.
The Deputy Chief of Defence Staff was charged with overall staff responsibility for the operation of Canadian Forces.
The ADM Finance was the department's senior financial officer and provided functional direction for financial policy.

Exhibit C.1 Reporting structure at the Department of National Defence.

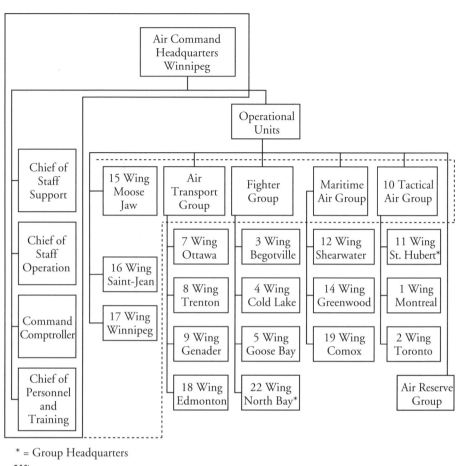

* = Group Headquarters

⌐¬
¦_¦ Reporting to Commander Air Command

☐ Located at ACHQ Winnipeg

Exhibit C.2 Operational and support units in Air Command.

Aim

To introduce a decentralised resource management system, which aligns responsibility, authority and accountability at the lowest practical level and gives the consumer the responsibility for funding and managing his resources.

Objectives

- to determine how and to what extent AIRCOM can adopt a user pay/cost centre programme (user pay means giving the consumer budgetary responsibility for resources consumed);
- to develop the procedures, information systems and training required to implement such a programme.

Scope

- to determine what cost elements should be managed or provided at the unit level;
- to determine whether the applicable cost data required are readily available and if not, how to develop a system to provide them;
- to determine how consumers should interface with suppliers and develop the required electronic interface systems;
- to determine how suppliers should be funded;
- to determine implementation requirements, such as training, historical data, equipment and reorganisation.

Exhibit C.3 Cost centre management project.

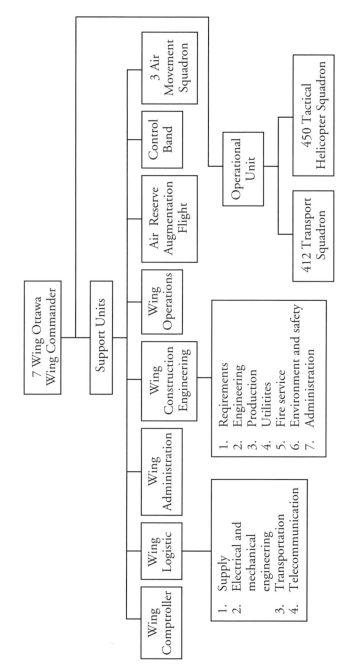

Exhibit C.4 Operational support unit on 7 Wing.

FIS[1] (controlled by 7 Wg CE)	$23,955,450	
FIS[2] (controlled by AIRCOM)	500,000	
CCA[3] (controlled by supply at NDHQ)	314,550	
Total corporate information system		$24,770,090
CEMIS-military salaries[4]	5,368,684	
LOMMIS[5] vehicle and equipment rentals	191,784	
Transportation – vehicle and equipment rentals	41,149	
Total: Functional system		$5,601,773
Construction and maintenance[6]	28,000,000	
Grants in lieu of taxes[7]	13,000,000	
Natural gas	968,749	
Defence Construction Canada contracts	480,000	
Government Service Canada contracts	80,000	
Vehicle uses	227,952	
Vehicle depreciation	154,691	
Contributed material	85,624	
Fire-fighting equipment[8]	75,541	
Urea	10,000	
Chemicals	5,000	
Telecommunication[9]	115,500	
Photocopies[10]	36,465	
Total estimates:		$43,239,522
Total annual 7 Wg costs:		$73,611,385

1. Controlled three FIS accounts: CE Operations, Civilian Pay and Maintenance.
2. The CE Environment and Safety FIS account was controlled by Air Command.
3. Includes supplies, furniture and equipment.
4. CEMIS applied standard costs for military labour using established departmental rates based on rank and level.
5. LOMMIS applied a standard cost, based on market rates, to labour incurred on equipment maintenance projects. By dividing the total cost of labour incurred on each vehicle used by 7 Wg CE by the age of the vehicle, it estimated an annual cost for vehicle and equipment maintenance.
6. Funded by NDHQ/ACHQ.
7. As a federal government department, DND did not pay property taxes. The Department of Public Works paid grants in lieu of property taxes to municipalities on all federal land. As 7 Wg CE was the Wing property manager, property taxes were part of its operation.
8. All fire-fighting equipment, urea and chemicals were paid for by NDHQ.
9. The communications squadron provided costs for telephones, fax machines and cellular phones assigned to CE squadron.
10. Wing Supply estimated photocopier costs for 7 Wg CE based on invoices from a representative month.

Exhibit C.5 1991–92 Annual costs at 7 Wing Construction and Engineering.

Corporate information systems

NDHQ operated several corporate information systems (essentially one for each functional area such as finance, supply, personnel, training, maintenance, etc.). CAC used two of these systems to obtain information for the CCMP: the Department of National Defence Financial Information System (FIS) and the Customer Consumption Awareness (CCA) module of the Canadian Forces Supply System (CFSS). FIS contained budget and spending information for the entire military. However, because spending was recorded by who paid for it (usually NDHQ), rather than who benefited from it, FIS did not provide much useful spending information to the business model. For example, military payrolls were charged to personnel, so wing-level military pay could not be determined from FIS. CFSS was a material management inventory system for ordering supplies. It assigned a distribution account number to any organisation that used supplies from CFSS. CCA used the distribution account number to track actual material consumption by user.

Information from functional systems

Different military-wide functional areas (e.g. Construction Engineering or Electrical and Mechanical Engineering) had their own information systems to serve their specific needs. Construction Engineering tracked its costs using the Construction Engineering Management Information System (CEMIS). Electrical and Mechanical Engineering tracked maintenance costs over the total life of vehicles and equipment using its forces-wide system, the Land Ordnance Maintenance Management Information System (LOMMIS). Transportation kept records on vehicles rented by the Wing. (The Material Group at NDHQ purchased most vehicles used by the military.)

Estimates

Lieutenant Colonel Brown provided estimates for:

- work funded by ACHQ and/or NDHQ;
- grants in lieu of property taxes paid by the Department of Public Works;
- fees paid by NDHQ to Defence Construction Canada (DCC) for major construction and maintenance projects, and to Government Services Canada (GSC) for contracting services;
- the value of material supplied to contractors for use on building projects.

The Directorate of Utilities and Municipal Services at NDHQ purchased natural gas in bulk. It received and paid invoices covering the cost of gas for a number of CFBs. Annually the Directorate provided an approximate cost for natural gas to each CFB. Every year the Directorate of costing services prepared a cost factors manual (CFM) that provided a common basis for estimating DND personnel, equipment and facility costs. The costs were national averages based on several years of historical data. CAC used the CFM to determine 7 Wg CE's vehicle usage cost, such as gas, maintenance and depreciation (on vehicles owned by the military and used by CE). The fire chief provided cost estimates for fire-fighting equipment, urea (fire-fighting foam) and other chemicals.

Exhibit C.6 Sources of cost information.

CASE STUDY D

Target costing: when accounting and marketing collide

(Timothy West prepared this case. Copyright © 1998 by Institute of Management Accountants, Montvale, NJ. Reproduced with permission.)

Introduction

'Good morning, Batdorf & Bronson! How may we help you?' And so starts another day at Batdorf and Bronson (B&B), one of the country's premier coffee roasters. The employees of B&B share three common characteristics: (1) a passion for coffee, (2) an above-average intellect and (3) an interest in a variety of outside activities. In fact, B&B so values these characteristics that they represent the qualifications considered for anyone offered employment with the company. Although B&B employees recognise and value these commonalities, they also share one unexpected characteristic: a general lack of familiarity with accounting and other financial information. Today, those working at B&B have been forced to acknowledge that accounting/operating information is playing a bigger role in their decision-making processes. As a result, B&B's employees have been working hard recently to develop their understanding of the roles marketing and accounting play in operating their growing business.

Almost 85 per cent of B&B's total 1995 sales were to wholesale customers (e.g. cafes, carts, kiosks and restaurants). Retail locations and the mail order catalogue generated the remaining sales. Over the past 10 years, the company's loyal customer base and word-of-mouth marketing have resulted in rapid and continuous growth in wholesale operations (see Exhibit D.1). However, B&B anticipates sustaining growth by opening production facilities in new geographic markets (the Minneapolis roastery opened in 1994) and using new distribution channels (mail-order sales). These strategic initiatives pressure B&B's management/staff to better understand both their potential markets and the costs associated with serving those markets.

B&B's management has identified three aspects of current operations that could affect the feasibility of entering new coffee markets:

- *The highly competitive coffee market.* The coffee market, once dominated solely by supermarket coffee suppliers (Folgers and Maxwell House), has accommodated sales of specialty coffees (premium price/high-quality coffees) as a new market segment. Consumers of specialty coffees represent approximately 12 per cent of the total coffee market and include individuals, cafes and restaurants. B&B tries to appeal to the top 25 per cent of the individual customers in the specialty coffee market segment and the top 33 per cent of cafe/restaurant customers. This market segment has become very attractive to coffee suppliers because of its sales growth and income potential.

- *B&B's current marketing strategy.* In positioning B&B in the specialty coffee market, company management considered four dimensions: price, quality, flexibility and deliverability. These competitive dimensions represent a consistent force affecting B&B's decision-making.[1]

- *B&B's current cost structure.* As B&B's president has said, 'Batdorf & Bronson's profits are a result of providing the best product and service we can. If we focus on roasting coffee and serving our customers, the financial aspects will take care of themselves.' B&B views coffee roasting as an art and their success has depended on their artistic skills. This commitment to roasting excellence has resulted in financial/cost structure issues taking a secondary role within the company. In fact, *the company's current financial information system provides reports to facilitate tax return preparation rather than financial reporting or cost management.*

The competitive coffee market

Three elements of the coffee market are analysed in this section: (1) industry history, (2) B&B's company history within the industry and (3) trade associations within the industry.

Industry history

The US coffee market historically has focused on supplying customers with low-quality, high-caffeine products, using grocery store-based distribution channels. Companies such as Folgers, Maxwell House and Hills Brothers have dominated this segment of the coffee industry. In 1962, American coffee consumption peaked on a per-capita basis at about 3.1 cups per day. From 1963 to 1988, coffee consumption continued to decline overall. Today, coffee consumption is 1.8 cups per person per day.

In the late 1980s, however, specialty coffees began demonstrating significant growth. Using high-quality beans (known as varietals), coffee roasters around the country began producing coffees to serve the expanding specialty coffee market. In addition, many of these roasters began offering coffee drinks such as espresso, cappuccino or variations of them.

The industry leader in specialty coffee is Starbucks, Inc. Starbucks emphasises the importance of varietal quality in the roasting process. They also recognise the potential for retail sales in coffee-house/restaurant settings. Initially operating exclusively in Seattle, Starbucks focused on mail-order sales and word-of-mouth marketing to increase sales. Although sales grew by pursuing that strategy, Starbucks' management believed that more significant sales and profit growth was possible through retail locations. As Ted Tingle of the Specialty Coffee Association of America observed, 'For a long time, the focus was on coffee bean retailing; then Starbucks figured out the real money is in beverage retailing.' Having gone public in 1992, Starbucks now operates more than 600 company-owned retail locations and an additional 50 kiosk sites located in high-traffic areas such as malls and airports (see Starbucks' 1995 Annual Report).

Historically, Starbucks identified locations for future stores by targeting areas that have exhibited a strong mail-order demand for the company's products. (See Exhibit D.2 for an analysis of competitors in the specialty coffee market.)

Company history

B&B began roasting coffee in Olympia, Washington, in 1986 and sales of coffee have grown rapidly since that time. The company is committed to offering the highest-quality coffee (in terms of bean quality and final product freshness) and providing exceptional customer service. As a result, the company has maintained a 'roast-to-order' approach to the roasting process. The roast-to-order philosophy has implications for both marketing and accounting:

- Coffee is shipped within 24 hours of roasting to ensure freshness.

- Customers get the coffee they want, when they want it and in the right quantity.

- H&B maintains virtually no work-in-process inventory.

- Roast-to-order production costs per pound are higher.

Trade associations

Three coffee industry trade associations supply information about trends in coffee production and consumption. Annually, the National Coffee Association (NCA) prepares the Winter Coffee Drinking Study. This study provides the longest available statistical series (since 1950) on consumer drinking patterns related to coffee and other beverages. Until 1991, the International Coffee Organization (ICO) also provided support for this study. More recently, the Specialty Coffee Association of America (SCAA) has provided statistical information concerning customer trends with regard to the specialty coffee industry.

B&B's current marketing strategy

B&B sells moderately priced coffees to wholesale and retail customers by delivery via United Parcel Service (UPS). Management has established a market niche for B&B's products through three strategies: product differentiation, alternative distribution channel utilisation and moderate pricing as opposed to premium pricing.

Product differentiation

As one employee stated 'B&B is the Nordstroms of coffee. We will try and do whatever it takes to please the customer.' B&B has attempted to differentiate their products along three dimensions:

- quality – commitment to both product and customer-service excellence;

- deliverability – shipping to customers within 24 hours of roasting;

- flexibility – adherence to the roast-to-order philosophy.

Distribution channels

B&B operates one retail store and recently has begun offering mail-order/catalogue sales. However, B&B's main focus is on wholesale accounts. At this time, B&B has decided to increase sales through wholesale and mail-order distribution channels rather than to expand their retail store operations through additional company-owned locations or franchises. The company also has avoided offering brewing equipment such as espresso machines because of the difficulty of maintaining the equipment.

As part of B&B's pursuit of new distribution channels, the company opened their new Minneapolis roastery in 1994. The decision to operate a roastery outside the Olympia area reflects the company's commitment to deliver coffee within 24 hours of roasting to any customer. The new Midwest location allows for quicker deliveries to customers on the East Coast and throughout the Midwest.

B&B's pursuit of additional sales through alternative distribution channels has caused company management to rethink their current product packaging, pricing policies and costing system. For example, sales to wholesale customers from either Olympia or Minneapolis follow B&B's 'rule of thumb' pricing model (see below). Wholesale customers receive their product in standard five-pound plastic bags. Retail and mail-order customers, however, buy B&B's products in one-pound or half-pound bags. Retail/mail-order packaging also is more decorative and, accordingly, more expensive. The labour required to prepare five individual one-pound bags is substantially more than the labour associated with preparing a single five-pound bag. Therefore, B&B charges higher prices for their retail and mail-orders, but they are somewhat inconsistent in establishing their various retail price points.

B&B's 'rule of thumb' pricing model

Since B&B began operations in 1986, the company has followed this 'rule of thumb' approach for establishing wholesale prices. The model consists of four parts:

1. *Green bean cost per pound* (Exhibit D.3, Column 1). The 'green' cost is established by coffee brokers and represents the delivered cost of the green coffee beans. As expected, the market cost of green beans varies across varietals. For example, Columbian beans used for the 'Italian roast' cost $2.14 per pound, whereas Costa Rican 'La Minita' beans cost $3.66 per pound. Because a commodity market exists that prices raw materials on a per-pound basis, B&B has always used the green market per-pound price as the first cost component for their pricing model.

2. *Roasting allowance* (Exhibit D.3, Column 2). Once in the roaster, green beans lose approximately 20 per cent of their weight due to water evaporation. This 'up the stack' loss is accounted for by increasing the green bean cost by 25 per cent. The 25 per cent cost allowance represents the weight lost compared to the net roasting weight. For example, if 100 pounds of greens were roasted, the process would yield only 80 pounds of roasted beans. The 20 pounds lost compared to the 80 pounds remaining of roasted coffee result in a 25 per cent (20 lb + 80 lb) cost allowance being added to the initial green cost per pound.

3. *Mark-up for profit and overhead* (Exhibit D.3, Column 3). Historically, B&B has added a flat $3.00 to the per-pound bean cost to 'cover' all other expenses and profit. No changes have been made in this rate since the company's inception ten years ago.

4. *Market adjustment* (Exhibit D.3, Column 4). B&B managers also attempt to reserve 30¢ to 50¢ for adjustment of their final wholesale price to position their products appropriately in the market. Their goal is to price B&B's products in the middle (moderate pricing strategy) of comparable coffees offered by competitors.

Although this pricing model has remained unchanged for the past ten years, both the company's operations and costs have changed radically. Accordingly, B&B is considering revising their pricing model given their rapid sales growth, changing costs and pursuit of sales in alternative markets.

B&B's current cost structure

Three elements of B&B's competitive strategy determine the company's current cost structure:

- First, the roasting process dictates product quality. Therefore, costs associated with the roasting process are viewed as essential and 'worth every penny' because B&B's customers expect high-quality products.

- Second, management's decision to pursue new customers through alternative distribution channels requires a commitment of expenditures for product promotion, new customer identification and continuous customer service. Management considers the costs incurred in these areas essential for B&B's future growth and financial success.

- Third, additional administrative management staff have been required to keep up with the volume of activity generated by rapidly increasing sales (see B&B's income statement, Exhibit D.4).

Roasting process

The four steps in the roasting process include: (1) green coffee bean acquisition, (2) green bean storage, (3) roasting the beans and (4) packing the roasted beans.

1. *Green coffee bean acquisition.* The roasting process starts with the acquisition of the greens – green coffee beans. At B&B, the master roaster purchases the finest arabica beans on the coffee market. To accomplish this task, she deals with brokers in San Francisco and New York City, who in turn deal with importers. These brokers send samples to B&B, which are then roasted and taste-tested for quality. Upon approval, B&B purchases a container of beans (250 bags).

2. *Green coffee bean storage.* Once the beans have been purchased, they are stored by the brokers and later shipped by truck to the two production sites, Olympia and Minneapolis. B&B is charged a storage fee and invoice fee per order. At the production sites, B&B has on hand an average of two to three weeks of inventory. During storage, the greens must he protected from contamination. They need to be kept dry and away from heat since heat accelerates the moisture loss in coffee. In fact, coffee is similar to baking soda in that it absorbs flavours and odours easily. Therefore, extra precautions need to be taken to preserve quality.

3. *Bean roasting.* B&B buys the beans green and sells them roasted. The beans are roasted to order, a unique characteristic of specialty coffees. Bean roasting is an art, not a science. Each lot of beans reacts differently during the actual roasting process, requiring roasters to rely on their eyes, ears and nose to prepare a perfect batch. It takes three months of training to become a full-fledged roaster. Due to the mental and physical demands placed on these artists, roasters roast only 20 hours per week. At B&B, each 'batch' to be roasted typically begins with 100 pounds of green coffee beans being loaded into a hopper, which elevates the beans into the roaster. During the roasting process, the beans undergo two chemical reactions. The first reaction occurs eight minutes into the roast and is known as the first cracking. At this time, the water in the beans boils and puffs up, causing the bean to increase in volume by two-thirds. The second reaction occurs 11 minutes into the roast, when the interior water of the bean expands, thereby forcing the bean oils to the surface. These oils are important because they are later extracted in water to provide the coffee with its flavour. Upon reaching a temperature of 500° Fahrenheit, the beans are discharged from the roaster into a cooling tray. The beans are cooled quickly to prevent them from roasting further or 'overcooking'. The cooling tray is equipped with an arm that stirs the beans over the fans to help them cool. Once cooled, the beans are directed through a device known as a de-stoner, which uses a vacuum system to pull the beans up through a pipe and empty them into large containers. Any objects denser than the beans will fall to the ground, so rocks and other foreign objects are eliminated from the coffee.

4. *Packing the roasted beans.* The final stage in the roasting process is blending or packing. For the orders that request blends of coffee, varietals are blended together in the cooling tray according to a bill of materials that specifies each blend's 'recipe' (mixture of beans). The beans are packed either in five-pound state-of-the-art gas-barrier valve bags (wholesale) or smaller paper bags for more immediate use (retail/mail-order). At this stage, the roasting process is complete and the coffee is ready for distribution.

Product promotion and customer service

B&B has established both a product promotion (new customer support) department and a customer service department to meet the growing customer needs associated with the pursuit of sales through additional distribution channels (see Exhibit D.5). The product promotion department, staffed by three people, focuses on: (1) promotional materials (primarily emphasising B&B's national recognition), (2) mail-order catalogue support, (3) new customer identification and training and (4) ongoing training for existing customers.

The customer service department, staffed by four people, handles existing customer requests involving: (1) standard orders; (2) special orders, including revisions to standard orders; and (3) customer order follow-up, including concerns and complaints. Customer service representatives require nearly a year of training to become sufficiently knowledgeable about the industry and coffee preparation to respond effectively to customers' questions over the phone.

Interviews with the members and managers of each service department revealed their dissatisfaction with the current information system. The typical complaint was that the existing information system was designed for financial (in reality, the information system focused on tax reporting), rather than customer service information. For example, the customer service manager would like a system that identifies customers who had not ordered from B&B in more than three weeks. A list of this type would provide an excellent source for new sales information and information concerning lost sales. Unfortunately, information of this type is not regularly available under the current information system.

Administrative/management staff requirements

B&B's administrative staff consists mainly of persons responsible for accounting functions: chief bookkeeper, accounts receivable clerk and accounts payable clerk. These employees maintain B&B's accounting systems on a day-to-day basis. They also complete monthly financial statements, file payroll reports and provide an outside accountant with the information necessary to complete quarterly and annual income tax filings. The accounting staff has grown in the last four years from one part-time book-keeper to three full-time employees. Company management consists of three managers involved with day-to-day operations and two board member investors who participate in weekly operations committee meetings. The only addition to the group has been Jeanne Pupke, who serves as the chief operating officer for B&B. Recently, these managers have become much more involved in the marketing and accounting of B&B because of the company's growth over the past several years.

B&B's financial performance expectations

This section includes two alternative income statement presentations. The first represents B&B's current income statement, prepared from the existing accounting information system. The alternative provides insight into B&B's cost structure based on a preliminary activity-based costing (ABC) analysis.

Current financial information

As shown in Exhibit D.1, B&B's current financial results reflect an operating profit of $285,762 (7.24 per cent of sales). These results compare favourably with the industry leader, Starbucks, whose operating profit margin was 8.62 per cent in 1995 (see Starbucks 1995 Annual Report). As required by accounting standards, cost of goods sold includes direct material (bean costs, see Exhibit D.6; packaging/shipping supplies costs, see Exhibit D.7; and shipping) direct labour (hourly and supervisory wages and benefits) and manufacturing overhead. B&B assumes that these product costs generally are variable with sales (although facility rent and some other costs remain fixed with volume). Currently, no cost accounting system exists to apply overhead at the product level because B&B has been comfortable with the 'rule of thumb' pricing model used in the past.

The cost categories demonstrating the greatest increases are selling and administrative expenses. With the added volume of sales activity and the additional personnel, costs in these two areas have increased rapidly. The resulting 1995 costs, in fact, show very little resemblance to the selling and administrative costs for 1994. These cost increases reflect management's position that customer service is critical for current and future success.

Case requirements

Using the information presented in the previous sections, you are expected to analyse the 'rule of thumb' product pricing model currently being used by B&B. Compare the resulting prices to comparable prices developed using two alternative pricing methods: target (mark-up) pricing and target costing. As part of your analysis, answer each of the questions in the following three sections.

'Rule of thumb' product pricing model

B&B's current pricing model emphasises simplicity. The model relies on the green bean costs, readily available through the coffee markets, as the basis for establishing product prices. The green bean cost is then adjusted for 'up the stack loss', a standard dollar mark-up and a market adjustment to arrive at a product's price per pound. The pricing formula can be defined as follows:

> Product price = Cost per roasted pound
> + Standard $3.00 mark-up
> + Market adjustment

where:

Cost per roasted pound	= green bean cost per pound × 1.25, the 'up the stack' loss adjustment;
Standard $3.00 mark-up	= the adjustment, used since 1986, to approximate the company's 'other' non-bean costs (or excluded costs) per pound;
Market adjustment	= B&B management will attempt to adjust a product's market price within a range of 30¢ to 50¢ to position the product as moderately priced compared to competitors.

Using B&B'S 'rule of thumb' answer the following questions:

1. Do you agree with B&B's treatment of the 'up the stack' loss occurring in the roasting process?

2. Does the $3.00 mark-up added to the bean cost cover B&B's current cost structure plus an appropriate level of operating profit? *Note*: The 'appropriate level of operating profit' should be sufficient to pay the interest on existing debt and provide a 14.79 per cent after-tax (assume a tax rate of 30 per cent) return on investments (at book value) of $1,500,000.

3. Does the market adjustment (30¢ to 50¢) used by management increase or decrease the dependability of B&B's current pricing model?

4. What changes, if any, would you recommend for establishing retail pricing based upon wholesale costs.

Mark-up pricing

Traditional mark-up pricing or cost-based pricing was developed as a relatively straightforward approach to product pricing. The assumption is that each product's price must: (1) cover all the costs traceable to the product, (2) assist in covering the organisation's common expenses and (3) contribute to the organisation's expected level of income. Under this method, a 'product cost' is determined and a product's price is established by 'marking up' the product cost. The pricing equation for this cost-based approach is:

Target price = Product cost + [Product cost × Mark-up percentage]

where determination of the mark-up percentage is as follows:

$$\frac{(\text{Excluded expenses} + \text{Income required})}{(\text{Product cost per unit} - \text{Sales volume})}$$

where:

Excluded expenses	=	expenses not considered in determining product cost per unit;
Income required	=	required rate of return × investment (or operating assets) product cost per unit;
Product costs per unit	=	costs identified with producing a product;
Sales volume	=	volume of sales expected for the company's products.

Based on this pricing model, answer the following questions:

1. What costs would you include as part of B&B's product costs?

2. What costs would become excluded expenses for the mark-up percentage calculation?

3. Compute the mark-up percentage appropriate for pricing B&B's wholesale products. *Note*: the 'income required' should be sufficient to pay the interest on existing debt and provide a 14.7 per cent after-tax (assume a tax rate of 30 per cent) return on investments (at book value) of $1,500,000. Compute the wholesale prices for B&B's products and compare the resulting prices to B&B's prices determined using their 'rule of thumb' pricing model. What recommendations would you make based on your comparison?

4. What recommendations would you make for developing a 'retail' mark-up of wholesale prices computed with the target pricing strategy?

Target costing

Target costing is a market-based approach that works backwards from a market price to determine an acceptable cost of producing a product or service. In contrast, target pricing represents a cost-based approach for determining the appropriate sales price of products or services. The two techniques are both opposite and complementary.

A computational model for target costing is as follows:

Target cost = Sales − Excluded expenses − Income required

where:

Sales $= \sum$ (sales price per unit × expected sales volume), for all products;

Excluded expenses = all expenses excluded from target cost;

Income required = required rate of return × investment (or operating assets).

The resulting target cost then can be compared to existing product cost estimates to indicate opportunities for cost reduction. For example, if the current product cost exceeds computed target cost, managers have three options: (1) reduce current product costs, (2) eliminate the product based on their company's inability to produce the product at the target cost, or (3) continue offering the unprofitable product because it provides benefits other than those measured by profit (e.g. large customer demands for the product).

The majority of the target costing examples discuss the technique's use during the initial product design process. Target costing, however, can also direct managers towards existing products that may be losing their competitive position because of changing costs associated with the product. As part of the market analysis required for this case, you should complete the worksheet provided in Exhibit D.8 for 3–5 coffee types. Once the worksheet is complete, you should attempt to position B&B's products as the 'moderately priced' product for the selected coffee types. Use the prices you set as the basis for determining target costs for these 3–5 coffee types.

Answer the following questions associated with your target costing analysis:

1. What costs would you include as part of B&B's product costs?

2. What costs would become excluded expenses for the target costing calculation? What are the strengths and weaknesses of excluding these expenses from the target cost?

3. Compute the wholesale prices for B&B's products and compare the resulting prices to the prices determined using B&B's 'rule of thumb' pricing model. What recommendations would you make based on your comparison? *Note*: The 'income required' should be sufficient to pay the interest on existing debt and provide a 14.7 per cent after-tax (assume a tax rate of 30 per cent) return on investments (at book value) of $1,500,000.

4. What recommendations would you make for developing a retail mark-up of wholesale prices computed with the target costing strategy?

Note

1. For additional insight into the elements of product differentiation, see Robin Cooper, *When Lean Enterprises Collide* (Boston: Harvard Business School Press, 1995) and Michael E. Porter, *Competitive Advantage: Creating and Sustaining Superior Performance* (New York: Free Press, 1985).

	1991	1992	1993	1994	1995
Wholesale:					
Olympia	$598,725	$758,089	$996,855	$1,302,004	$1,744,140
Minneapolis	0	0	0	653,103	1,601,560
Retail stores	400,335	420,387	447,390	474,354	568,300
Mail-order	0	11,374	16,585	20,789	3,750
Total sales	$999,060	$1,189,850	$1,460,830	$2,450,250	$3,947,750

Exhibit D.1 Summary of sales by distribution channel.

Competitor	Market strategy
1. Starbucks	1. Retail locations – sales of specialty coffee and coffee drinks
2. Seattle's Best Coffee (SBC)/Torrefazione Italia	2. Wholesale and grocery store sales of coffee beans
3. Coffee Bean, Inc. (CBI)	3. Retail locations
4. Allegro	4. Retail locations
5. Peet's Coffee and Tea	5. Retail drink sales in a coffee-house format
6. Barney's Coffee & Tea	6 Retail sales of coffee beans
7. Gloria Jean's Coffee Bean	7. Retail sales of coffee beans
8. First Colony Coffee & Tea	8. Retail sales of a wide variety of foods and premium coffees in a coffee-house format
9. Folgers and Maxwell House	9. Grocery store sales of standard (low-quality) coffee; plus introduction of limited specialty brands

Exhibit D.2 Analysis of competitors.

Varietal/product type	Green bean cost/lb (1)	Roasting allowance (2)=(1)×1.25	Mark-up for profit and overhead (3)	Market adjust. (4)	Wholesale price (5) $\sum$(1)−(4)	Retail or mail-order price (6)	Price difference (7)=(6)−(5)	% price difference (8)=(7)÷(5)
Columbia decaffeinated	$2.58	$0.64	$3.00	$0.43	$6.65	$9.80	$3.15	47.37
Columbia 'French Roast'	2.27	0.57	3.00	0.31	6.15	9.20	3.05	49.59
Columbia 'Italian Roast'	2.14	0.53	3.00	0.63	6.30	9.40	3.10	49.21
Costa Rica SHB	2.18	0.54	3.00	0.33	6.05	8.90	2.85	47.11
Costa Rica 'La Minita'	3.66	0.92	3.00	0.72	8.30	11.00	2.70	32.53
Estate Java	2.48	0.62	3.00	0.30	6.40	9.60	3.20	50.00
Ethiopia Harrar	2.58	0.64	3.00	0.43	6.65	10.30	3.65	54.89
Guatemala Antigua	2.48	0.62	3.00	0.35	6.45	9.10	2.65	41.09
Kenya AA	2.89	0.72	3.00	0.44	7.05	9.75	2.70	38.30
Kenya AA decaffeinated	2.96	0.74	3.00	0.45	7.15	10.40	3.25	45.45
Mexico Altura Pluma	2.28	0.57	3.00	0.25	6.10	9.65	3.55	58.20
Sumatra Mandheling	2.38	0.59	3.00	0.38	6.35	9.55	3.20	50.39
Sumatra decaffeinated	2.82	0.72	3.00	0.46	7.00	10.85	3.85	55.00
Tanzania Peaberry	2.07	0.52	3.00	0.36	5.95	9.10	3.15	52.94
Yemen Mocha Sanani	3.36	0.84	3.00	0.65	7.85	10.45	2.60	33.12

Exhibit D.3 B&B's product price list based on the 'rule of thumb' pricing model.

Sales (see Exhibit D.5)		
Cost of sales (see Exhibits D.6 andD.7):		$3,947,750
Direct material (beans, scrap and spoilage and packing/shipping)	2,205,775	
Direct labour	437,559	
Manufacturing overheads	281,874	
Total cost of goods sold		925,208
Gross margin		1,022,542
Selling expenses		349,118
Administrative expenses		387,662
Operating income		285,762
Interest expense		35,000
Tax expense		75,650
Net income		$175,112

Exhibit D.4 Current Batdorf & Bronson income statement for the year ended 31 December 1995.

| | Wholesale | | | Retail/mail order | | | |
Varietal/product type	Price (1)	Pounds sold (2)	Total sales (3) = (1) × (2)	Price (4)	Pounds sold (5)	Total sales (6) = (4) × (5)	Total sales (7) = (3) + (6)
Columbia decaffeinated	$6.65	26,824	$178,391	$9.80	2,298	$22,523	$200,914
Columbia 'French Roast'	6.15	91,603	563,371	9.20	12,468	114,704	678,075
Columbia 'Italian Roast'	6.30	26,551	167,287	9.40	1,781	16,739	184,026
Costa Rica SHB	6.05	100,798	609,840	8.90	17,066	151,883	761,723
Costa Rica 'La Minita'	8.30	8,316	69,033	11.00	634	6,971	76,004
Estate Java	6.40	23,032	147,421	9.60	2,655	25,485	172,906
Ethiopia Harrar	6.65	20,657	137,382	10.30	1,969	20,281	157,663
Guatemala Antigua	6.45	10,268	66,240	9.10	416	3,790	70,030
Kenya AA	7.05	28,811	203,134	9.75	1,673	16,310	219,444
Kenya AA decaffeinated	7.15	18,041	129,009	10.40	1,211	12,587	141,596
Mexico Altura Pluma	6.10	20,170	123,054	9.65	994	9,585	132,639
Sumatra Mandheling	6.35	75,746	480,998	9.55	14,605	139,480	620,478
Sumatra decaffeinated	7.00	25,041	175,298	10.85	1,679	18,217	193,515
Tanzania Peaberry	5.95	40,373	240,235	9.10	4,653	42,343	282,578
Yemen Mocha Sanani	7.85	7,005	55,007	10.45	110	1,152	56,159
Total sales: pounds and dollars		523,236	$3,345,700		64,212	$602,050	$3,947,750

Exhibit D.5 Sales by product and distribution channel.

Varietal/product type	Green bean cost per pound (1)	Roasting allowance (2) = (1) × 0.25	Bean cost per roasted pound (3) = (1) + (2)	Roasted pounds sold (4)	Cost of beans sold (5) = (3) × (4)
Columbia decaffeinated	$2.58	$0.64	$3.22	29,122	$93,853
Columbia 'French Roast'	2.27	0.57	2.84	104,071	295,778
Columbia 'Italian Roast'	2.14	0.53	2.67	28,332	75,683
Costa Rica SHB	2.18	0.54	2.72	117,864	319,983
Costa Rica 'La Minita'	3.66	0.92	4.58	8,950	40,968
Estate Java	2.48	0.62	3.10	25,687	79,513
Ethiopia Harrar	2.58	0.64	3.22	22,626	72,918
Guatemala Antigua	2.48	0.62	3.10	10,684	33,043
Kenya AA	2.89	0.72	3.61	30,484	109,888
Kenya AA decaffeinated	2.96	0.74	3.70	19,252	71,018
Mexico Altura Pluma	2.28	0.57	2.85	21,164	60,113
Sumatra Mandheling	2.38	0.59	2.97	90,351	268,273
Tanzania Peaberry	2.07	0.52	2.59	45,026	116,483
Sumatra decaffeinated	2.82	0.72	3.53	26,720	94,053
Yemen Mocha Sanani	3.36	0.84	4.20	7,115	29,833
Total pounds sold and bean costs				587,448	$1,761,400

Exhibit D.6 Cost of beans sold.

Varietal/product type	Pounds sold wholesale (1)	Pounds sold retail/mail-order (2)	5-pound wholesale bags (3)	1-pound retail/ mail-order bags (4)	½-pound retail/ mail-order bags (5)
Columbia decaffeinated	26,824	2,298	5,365	1,532	766
Columbia 'French Roast'	91,603	12,468	18,321	9,974	2,494
Columbia 'Italian Roast'	26,551	1,781	5,310	1,272	509
Costa Rica SHB	100,798	17,066	20,160	14,840	2,226
Costa Rica 'La Minita'	8,316	634	1,663	352	282
Estate Java	23,032	2,655	4,606	1,831	824
Ethiopia Harrar	20,657	1,969	4,131	1,270	698
Guatemala Antigua	10,268	416	2,054	245	171
Kenya AA	28,811	1,673	5,762	1,338	335
Kenya AA decaffeinated	18,041	1,211	3,608	897	314
Mexico Altura Pluma	20,170	994	4,034	765	229
Sumatra Mandheling	75,746	14,605	15,149	12,171	2,434
Sumatra decaffeinated	25,041	1,679	5,008	959	720
Tanzania Peaberry	40,373	4,653	8,075	3,325	1,329
Yemen Mocha Sanani	7,005	110	1,401	59	50
Bags required for product sold	523,236	64,212	104,647	50,830	13,381
Less: allowance for bags wasted: 5 pound (6%) 1 pound (10%) ½ pound (12%)			6,683	5,650	1,824
Total bags consumed in production			111,330	56,480	15,205
Cost per bag			$0.45	$0.80	$0.75
Total packaging costs			$50,100	$45,184	$11,404

Exhibit D.7 Cost of packaging/shipping supplies.

	Competitors						
Coffee type	Starbucks	SBC	Folgers	Maxwell House	Hills Brothers	Brothers	Your choice
Columbian Supreme	$9.75 (16 oz)	$8.99 (16 oz)	$7.33 (36 oz)	$5.05 (24 oz)	$6.05 (36 oz)	$5.85 (13 oz)	?
French roast	?	$8.99	$7.33 (36 oz)	$6.75	$6.75 (36 oz)	?	?
French decaf	?	$8.99 (16 oz)	?	$7.13 (24 oz)	?	?	?
Italian roast	$8.95 (16 oz)		?		?	?	?
Additional coffee types:						?	?

Exhibit D.8 Analysis of competitors' pricing.

CASE STUDY E

Using EVA at OutSource, Inc.

(Paul A. Dierks prepared this case. Copyright © 1998 by Institute of Management Accountants, Montvale, NJ. Reproduced with permission.)

'I've been hearing a lot lately about something called MVA which stands for market value added and I was curious whether it is something we can use at OSI,' Keith Martin said. Keith is president and CEO of OutSource, Inc. His guest for lunch that day was a computer industry analyst from a local brokerage firm. Keith had invited him to lunch so he could get more information on MVA and its uses.

'Yes,' the analyst replied, 'I've heard a great deal about EVA and MVA. EVA is a residual income approach in which a firm's net operating profit after taxes – called NOPAT – is compared to a minimum level of return a firm must earn on the total amount of capital placed at its disposal. MVA represents the difference between the market and book value of a company over a period of time.'

'Have you seen the most recent issue of *Fortune*?' he continued, handing Keith a copy. 'It has an article[1] in it updating Stem Stewart's list of the top 1,000 firms ranked by MVA. You will also be interested in an earlier *Fortune* article[2] on EVA, or economic value added. EVA is closely related to MVA. However, don't be misled by the simplicity of the EVA calculations in that article. The after-tax operating profit – NOPAT, as you called it – and the amount used for capital don't come directly off the financial statements. You have to analyse the footnotes to determine the adjustments that have to be made to come up with those amounts – Bennett Stewart calls them equity equivalents, or "EEs", in his book, *The Quest for Value.*'[3]

'Those articles sound like very interesting reading for me, especially at this point,' Keith said. 'Can you send me copies?'

'Sure,' said the analyst. 'But tell me, what is it about MVA and EVA that piqued your interest in trying them at OSI?'

'In tracking our industry', Keith replied, 'I see the stock prices of some of our key competitors, like Equifax, increasing. Yet when I compare OSI's recent growth in sales and earnings, our return on equity and earnings per share compare well to those firms, but our stock price doesn't achieve nearly the same rate of increase and I don't understand why.'

The analyst replied, 'Some of those firms might be benefiting from using EVA already and the market value of their stock probably reflects the results of their efforts. It has been shown that a higher level of correlation exists between EVA and a stock's market value than has been found with the traditional accounting performance measures, like ROE or EPS.'

'But the MVA 1,000 ranking probably includes only large firms,' Keith observed after looking over the article the analyst gave him. 'Will EVA work in a small service firm like OSI?'

'Most of the largest US firms are in the Stem Stewart MVA ranking,' the analyst said, 'but I've read about EVA being used at smaller firms. And some firms in the ranking are service firms, such as AT&T, McDonald's, Marriott International and Dun & Bradstreet. I'm not an expert on MVA or EVA, but I don't see any reason why it wouldn't work at OSI.'

'I'd like to find out more about MVA and EVA and how we can use them at OSI. For example, we've talked about a new incentive plan – will EVA work in that area? And, if so – will it help us in deciding how we should organise and manage our operations as we expand and grow? Can you get me more information on these things?'

'An application EVA is touted for is its use in incentive plans,' the analyst replied. 'A team of students from Capital University has been assigned to me this fall to do an industry-related project and I was looking for something "meaty" for them to do. This looks like just the ticket. I'll brief them on it and have them come over to get the necessary information and interview you.'

'Great! I look forward to meeting them,' Keith said.

Company information

OutSource, Inc. (OSI) is a computer service bureau that provides basic data processing and general business support services to a number of business firms, including several large firms in their immediate area. Its offices are in a large city in the mid-Atlantic region and it serves client firms in several mid-Atlantic states. OSI's revenues have grown fairly rapidly in recent years as businesses have downsized and outsourced many of their basic support services.

The CorpInfo Data Service (CIDS) classifies OSI as an information services firm (SIC 7374). This group is composed, in large part, of smaller, independent entrepreneurs that provide a variety of often-disparate services to both corporate and government clients. Market analysts feel a continuously healthy economy translates into strong potential for higher earnings by members of this group. A factor sustaining an extended period of growth is the increased attention of firms to controlling costs and outsourcing their non-core functions, such as personnel placement, payroll, human resources, insurance and data processing. This trend is expected to continue to the end of the decade, probably at an increasing rate. Several firms in this industry have capitalised on their growth and geographic expansion to win lucrative contracts with large clients that previously had been awarded on a market-by-market basis.

Although OSI operates out of its own facilities, which include some computing equipment and furniture, the bulk of its computer processing power is obtained from excess computer capacity in the local area, primarily rented time during third-shift operations at a large local bank. To be successful in the long term, however, OSI's management knows it must expand its business considerably and, to ensure full control over its operations, it must set up its own large-scale computing facility inhouse. These items are included in OSI's long-range strategic plan.

As OSI's reputation for an accurate, reliable and quick response service has spread, the firm has found new business coming its way in a variety of data processing and support services. The issue has been deciding which services to take on or stay out of in light of the current limitations on OSI's computing resources, to ensure it can continue to provide high-quality service to its customers. Things definitely are looking up for OSI! and industry market analysts have recently begun to look more favourably on its stock.

In 1993, OSI's board decided to pursue additional opportunities in payroll processing and tax filing services. OSI purchased a medium-sized firm that had an established market providing payroll calculation, processing and reporting services for several Fortune 500 firms on the East Coast. Now OSI is in the midst of developing a new payroll processing system, called PayNet, to replace the outmoded system originally created by the firm it acquired.

Once PayNet is developed, it will give users an integrated payroll solution with a simpler, more familiar graphical user interface. From an administrative perspective, it will allow OSI to reduce its manual data entry hiring, to speed data compilation and analysis and to simplify administrative tasks and the updating of customer files for adds, moves and changes. PayNet will serve as the backbone for OSI's service bureau payroll processing operations in the future but, at present, developmental and programming costs have proved higher than expected and will delay the rollout of the final version of the new payroll engine. Beta testing of the production version of PayNet was delayed from the second to the third quarter of 1996.

OSI's financial statements for 1995 appear in Exhibits E.1 and E.2. The following list of information, extracted from the footnotes to OSI's annual report for 1995 is pertinent to calculating a firm's EVA:

1. Inventories are stated principally at cost (last in, first out), which is not in excess of market. Replacement cost would be $2,796 more than the 1994 inventory balance and $3,613 more than the 1995 inventory balance.

2. Deferred tax expense results from timing differences in recognising revenue and expense for tax and reporting purposes.

3. On 1 July 1993, the company acquired Company, a payroll processing and reporting service firm. The acquisition was accounted for as a purchase and the excess of cost over the fair value of net assets acquired was $109,200, which is being amortised on a straight-line basis over 13 years. One-half year of goodwill amortisation was recorded in 1993.

4. Research and development costs related to software development are expensed as incurred. Software development costs are capitalised from the point in time when the technological feasibility of a piece of software has been determined until it is ready to be put online to process customer data. The cost of purchased software, which is ready for service, is capitalised on acquisition. Software development costs and purchased software costs are amortised using the straight-line method over periods ranging from three to seven years. A history of the accounting treatment of software development costs and purchased software costs follows:

	Expensed	Capitalised	Amortised
1993	$166,430	$9,585	0
1994	211,852	5,362	$4,511
1995	89,089	18,813	5,111
	$467,371	$33,760	$9,622

Additional financial information

OSI's common stock was trading at $2 per share. A preferred dividend of $11 per share was paid in 1995 and the current price of the preferred stock is approximately at its par value. Other information pertaining to OSI's debt and stock follows:

Short-term debt		$8,889	Rate: 8.0%
Long-term debt:			
Current position		$18,411	Rate: 10.0%
Long-term portion		$98,744	Rate: 10.0%
Total long-term debt		$117,155	

Stock market risk-free rate (90-day T-bills) = 5.0%
Expected return on market = 12.5%
Beta value of OSI's common stock = 1.20
Expected growth rate of dividends = 8.0%
Incom tax rate = 35.0%

Case requirements

The management of OutSource, Inc. has asked you to prepare a report explaining EVA (economic value added) and MVA (market value added) and how they are calculated, and they would like to know the advantages and disadvantages of using EVA to evaluate the firm's performance on an ongoing basis, as well as in assessing the performance of individual managers throughout its organisation. As part of your report, calculate EVA and MVA from OutSource, Inc.'s financial statements for 1995, using both the operating approach and the financing approach as described in Bennett Stewart's book, *The Quest for Value*. Finally, OSI's management would like to know if EVA can be used as part of an incentive system for its employees and how it should proceed to implement such an incentive system at OutSource, Inc.

Notes

1. Ronald B. Lieber (1996) 'Who are the real wealth creators', *Fortune*, 9 December, pp. 107–8, 110, 112, 114.

2. Shawn Tully (1993) 'The real key to creating wealth', *Fortune*, 20 September, pp. 38–40, 44–5, 48, 50.

3. G. Bennett Stewart III (1999) *The Quest for Value*. New York: HarperCollins.

OutSource, Inc. – balance sheet 31 December	1995	1994
Assets		
Current assets:		
Cash	$144,724	$169,838
Trade and other receivables (net)	217,085	192,645
Inventories	15,829	23,750
Other	61,047	49,239
Total current assets	$438,685	$435,472
Non-current assets:		
Property, plant and equipment	$123,135	$109,600
Software and development costs	33,760	14,947
Data processing equipment and furniture	151,357	141,892
Other non-current assets	3,650	8,844
	$311,902	$275,283
Less accumulated depreciation	85,018	57,929
Total non-current assets	$226,884	$217,354
Goodwill	88,200	96,600
	$753,769	$749,426
Liabilities and shareholders' equity		
Current liabilities:		
Short-term debt and current portion of long-term note	$27,300	$31,438
Accounts payable	67,085	57,483
Deferred income	45,050	32,250
Income taxes payable	19,936	12,100
Employee compensation and benefits payable	30,155	28,950
Other accrued expenses	28,458	27,553
Other current liabilities	17,192	29,769
Total current liabilities	$235,176	$219,543
Long-term debt less current portion	98,744	117,155
Deferred income taxes	6,784	4,850
Shareholders' equity:		
Cumulative non-convertible preferred stock, $100 par value, authorised 5,000 shares, issued and outstanding 1,000 shares	100,000	100,000
Common stock, $1 par value; 300,000 shares authorised; 219,884 shares issued and outstanding	219,884	219,884
Additional paid-in capital	32,056	32,056
Retained earnings	61,125	55,938
Total shareholders' equity	$413,065	$407,878
	$753,769	$749,426

Exhibit E.1 OutSource, Inc. balance sheet.

OutSource, Inc. – statement of income for the year ended 31 December	1995
Operating revenue	$2,604,530
Costs of services	1,466,350
Gross profit	$1,138,180
Less: operating expenses:	
Selling, general and administrative	$902,388
Research and development	89,089
Other expense (income)	59,288
Write-off of goodwill and other intangibles	13,511
Earnings (loss) before interest and taxes	$73,904
Interest income $1,009 interest expense	12,427
Earnings (loss) before income taxes	62,486
Income tax provision	21,870
Earnings (loss)	$40,616

OutSource, Inc. – statement of cash flows for the year ended 31 December	1995
Cash flows from operating activities:	
Net earnings (loss)	$40,616
Depreciation	21,978
Amortisation of software & development costs	5,111
Decrease (increase) in accounts receivable	(24,440)
Decrease (increase) in inventories	7,921
Decrease (increase) in other current assets	(11,808)
Increase (decrease) in deferred income	9,602
Increase (decrease) in accounts payable	12,800
Increase (decrease) in income taxes payable	7,836
Increase (decrease) in employee compensation and benefits payable	1,205
Increase (decrease) in other accrued expenses	905
Increase (decrease) in other current liabilities	(12,577)
Increase (decrease) in deferred income taxes	1,934
Net cash provided by (used for) operating activities	$61,083
Cash flows from investing activities:	
Expended for capital assets	($36,619)
Goodwill amortised	8,400
Net cash provided by (used for) investing activities	($28,219)
Cash flows from financing activities:	
Payment of long-term note	($4,138)
Payment of short-term note	(18,411)
Preferred dividends	(11,000)
Common stock dividends	(24,429)
Net cash provided by (used for) financing activities	($57,978)
Net cash flows provided (used)	($25,114)
Cash at beginning of year	$169,838
Cash at end of year	$144,724

Exhibit E.2 OutSource, Inc. statement of income.

CASE STUDY F

Dialysis Clinic, Inc.

(Treatment costing in managed care)

(Copyright © 1997 Institute of Management Accountants, Montvale, NJ. Reproduced with permission.)

Clinic overview

Dialysis Clinic, Inc. (DCI) is an independent, non-profit, full-service dialysis clinic in the Midwest. During the current year, DCI earned net income of $225,029 (7.5 per cent). on revenues of just over $3 million (see Exhibit F.1). Dialysis patients suffer from a variety of kidney disorders that result in their kidneys' inability to remove waste build-up in their blood. Dialysis patients cannot be cured by treatment; they can only maintain their current quality of life. As a full-service provider of dialysis treatments, DCI serves approximately 102 haemodialysis (HD) patients at the clinic and 62 peritoneal dialysis (PD) patients in their homes. Patients receiving HD treatments must visit the clinic three times each week where their blood is cleansed by a dialyser machine. Alternatively, PD patients complete a similar blood cleansing process on a daily basis using in-home treatment techniques that are monitored by DCI. HD treatments represent 41 per cent of 34,967 total treatments delivered during the current period. However, HD accounts for approximately 61.8 per cent of the clinic's total revenues. Organisationally, DCI is one of 100 other dialysis clinics composing a national conglomerate. DCI, however, once operated as a captive clinic within a regional hospital until 1979 when it was spun off because hospital management felt the clinic was a 'financial loser'.

Healthcare environment

Healthcare is currently the largest industry in the US composing 14 per cent of gross domestic product (GDP). Since the implementation of Medicare in 1965, the industry has grown rapidly, based upon a fee-for-service, third-party insurance system. Under the retrospective cost-based payment system initially instituted by Medicare, healthcare providers were reimbursed for services delivered at actual cost plus an allowable profit. Using this system, providers could maximise revenues (reimbursements) and profits by increasing either the number of patients served, the average number of treatments per patient or the average intensity of patients' treatments. Little incentive existed to control cost, because the higher the cost, the higher the level of reimbursement. Because employers (health insurance) or the government (Medicare) were responsible for the large majority of medical reimbursements, Americans could distance themselves from the increasing cost of healthcare because 'somebody else was paying'.

In 1983, Medicare implemented a new prospective payment system (PPS) that established fixed reimbursement rates for inpatient services/treatments. Standardised reimbursement rates were determined for treatment categories or diagnosis-related groups (DRGs), independent of a healthcare organisation's cost structure. The goal of the new programme was to standardise treatment delivery, improve service delivery efficiencies and promote cost containment. The implementation of PPS, however, resulted in unexpected consequences, e.g. (1) shifting operating costs to third-party payers (private health insurance companies), (2) decreasing treatment availability for Medicare and indigent patients, and (3) increasing expenditures for treatment alternatives to inpatient care. Furthermore, financial considerations (competition) began challenging treatment quality considerations as the objective of healthcare.

PPS caused healthcare organisations to assess whether their costing systems could accommodate the new fixed price reimbursement structure and the increased competition among healthcare providers. The healthcare industry, historically, emphasised quality of care, but not the cost of care. However, as healthcare facilities faced changing levels of regulation (e.g. Medicare, rate review, certificate of need programmes), facility managers began requiring treatment level cost data that existing internal management information systems were not designed to provide. As regulatory intensity increased, healthcare providers faced increasing pressure to enhance existing costing systems in an effort to identify the most cost-effective way of providing uninterrupted services.

Presently, healthcare is undergoing a third economic revolution because society has concluded that cost containment and managed care are preferable to ever-rising healthcare costs. Increasingly, therefore, insurance companies are negotiating fixed-rate contracts with providers that establish fixed reimbursement rates per patient, regardless of services provided. Rather than providing fixed reimbursements for services rendered, managed care contracts establish a fixed reimbursement rate per patient. These fixed-rate agreements are known as capitation contracts and represent a key element in the healthcare industry's move towards managed care. Health maintenance organisations (HMOs) were developed to service these capitated contracts established between member groups (e.g. university employees often belong to an HMO) and participating physicians. Healthcare providers currently find themselves bidding on more managed care, capitated rate contracts and, as a result, treatment-level costs are now becoming increasingly important. Profitability now depends upon cost containment, because reimbursement revenues are becoming increasingly fixed by contract. Accordingly, management decisions concerning long-term fixed-rate contracts now require increasingly accurate costing at both the treatment level and the patient level.

Alternative treatment costing models

Over the past 40 years, several costing models have been developed to enable healthcare management decisions. Before 1965, healthcare providers adopted a caretaker approach to medical care. During this period, when patients were admitted to hospitals, they were observed with only limited treatment intervention. Corporate employee benefits programmes at that time increasingly provided health insurance, but third-party payments were a relatively recent phenomenon and very little health insurance was available for the elderly. Independent clinics and outpatient ancillary services were rare. Prior to the advances in antibiotics and surgical techniques, medical care primarily involved monitoring patients, making them as comfortable as possible and watching them get better or die.

This relatively passive approach to patient care focused cost systems on the number of patients in a healthcare facility, rather than the quantity or types of treatments provided for any individual patient. Average aggregate costing was sensible because every patient was treated much like all other patients with similar illnesses. They all received approximately the same quality, types and quantity of care. Some lived and some died because of or despite the best care provided, which was much the same regardless of the severity of any specific illness. Healthcare organisations lacked any incentive to examine cost on any level other than the facility as a whole. Instead, they emphasised utilisation of available beds and change in patient count. Costing systems, therefore, focused on aggregate costs and simple computations of average cost-per-patient day or average cost-per treatment.

Two aggregate costing models were developed during this period and they are still commonly used throughout the healthcare industry. These models consider all costs of an organisation as a single pool of indirect costs (complete aggregation), equally assigned to individual patient days or treatments without differentiation. The first model, the ratio of cost per patient day model (RCP) reduces total costs to a cost per patient day. Presently, some facilities (e.g. nursing homes and hospice care) receive reimbursements based upon the number of patient days of service provided. The RCP divides aggregate annual costs by the total number of patient days, regardless of the treatments/procedures provided for any one patient. The second model, the ratio of cost per treatment model (RCT), examines per-treatment costs without distinguishing among treatments delivered, i.e. total annual costs are divided by the total number of treatments provided. Today, the RCT is commonly used in costing ancillary services (e.g. X-ray and laboratory). Using aggregate departmental costs, individual per-treatment costs are estimated (computed) without distinguishing among the relative intensity of individual treatments performed.

With the passage of Medicare in 1965, the costing in healthcare facilities changed dramatically. Following Medicare's cost plus reimbursement policy directive, facilities focused on reimbursement maximisation as a primary objective. Managers maximised reimbursement by allocating overheads to the departments that generated the greatest charges. By 1969, however, costs were allocated increasingly to ancillary departments because patient days in the hospital were limited in terms of both allowable length of stay and reimbursement rate per day. As a result, greater emphasis was placed upon providing both inpatient and outpatient ancillary services (e.g. laboratory and

X-ray procedures) because these services remained fully reimbursable under the old cost-plus Medicare policy. Healthcare providers invested extensively, therefore, in new facilities and technologies that enhanced their diagnostic and treatment capabilities. Throughout this period, virtually any higher medical costs could be recovered through reimbursement if they were charged appropriately to Medicare patients through the Medicare Cost Report.

The Medicare Cost Report required that a 'stepdown' indirect cost allocation method be followed by facilities receiving Medicare reimbursement for delivered services. The resulting ratio of cost to charges (RCC) method was developed as a transitional, hybrid aggregate/allocation cost model that satisfied Medicare reimbursement requirements. RCC allocates aggregate indirect costs to revenue-producing departments, following procedures commonly referred to in accounting as the step-down method of service department cost allocations. The objective of the step-down costing method was the full costing of revenue-producing ancillary departments (e.g. laboratory, X-ray). Although the step-down method provided information at the departmental level, subsequent approximations were required in estimating the cost of individual treatments/procedures performed within the department. Treatment cost information was computed within each department, based upon the department's RCC rate (full costs ÷ total charges). Managers could multiply the resulting RCC rate times the standard charge for a procedure in an effort to approximate that procedure's cost. Accordingly, the RCC model reflects the computation of treatment costs at either the facility level or the department level.

RCC encouraged decision-makers to pursue highly reimbursed treatment types, rather than emphasising efficient cost utilisation, because individual treatment costs were less important as long as a facility/department's aggregate revenues exceeded aggregate costs. When hospitals, clinics or departments as a whole were profitable, for example, RCC would indicate that all individual treatment types within those units were profitable because RCC assumes a constant mark-up (profitability) for each treatment type within the unit.

As healthcare managers began emphasising cost containment and improving treatment costing systems, challenges were made to many of the underlying assumptions associated with their existing RCC-based cost systems established and required by Medicare. Managers began examining how the relationship between costs and treatments/procedures (i.e. activities) affected product line costing precision. Managers recognised that more accurate identification of treatment specific costs could alter the perceived profitability of certain treatment types, previously costed using RCC-based aggregate cost allocations. More accurate costing was expected to improve managers' decisions concerning alternative treatment strategies and the choice of services provided by the facility.

As a result, hospitals and other treatment providers began redesigning their costing systems in an effort to provide more precise treatment-level cost information. Managers have shifted the use of cost information, moreover, from overall financial planning to service pricing and performance measurement decisions. Recently, 97 per cent of the hospitals surveyed attributed the increased sophistication of their cost systems to PPS or managed care capitated contracts that establish fixed reimbursement rates per treatment or per patient, respectively. Managers were now asking their cost systems to provide more accurate measures of a treatment's 'true' cost.

End stage renal dialysis

Although organ transplantation remains the best long-term solution for kidney disease, the shortage of organs forces approximately 200,000 patients a year to choose dialysis as the practical treatment alternative. In 1972, Congress instituted the End Stage Renal Disease Programme which provides that dialysis treatments for patients insured under social security are reimbursed through Medicare. Consequently, Medicare pays for approximately 93 per cent of all dialysis treatments at a fixed reimbursement rate. In effect, Medicare has created a de facto health maintenance organisation for dialysis treatment. Renal dialysis, therefore, represents a window into the future of healthcare (i.e. fixed reimbursement rates and managed care). DCI basically provides an ancillary service under a fixed payment structure that approximates the capitated rates established under managed care contract. Dialysis treatment providers must emphasise cost containment, because reimbursement rates have remained virtually fixed over the past 20 years. In fact, adjusting for inflation, reimbursement rates have effectively declined 161 per cent during the period 1974–89.

The downward pressure on reimbursement rates prompted dialysis providers to consider less costly treatment alternatives. Consequently, two treatment delivery methods are provided by most facilities. First, haemodialysis (HD) treatments require patients to visit a dialysis clinic where they receive treatment using dialyser equipment. Alternatively, peritoneal dialysis (PD) allows patients to administer their own treatments at home. Patients using peritoneal dialysis select a clinic to monitor their status and to assist in ordering/delivering the supplies required for this treatment modality. Haemodialysis represents an equipment-intensive, in-clinic treatment that consumes more of the clinic's durable equipment resources than peritoneal dialysis treatments. The expected difference in treatment costs is reflected in the Medicare reimbursement rates, i.e. HD – $129.70, PD – $55.59.

Cost containment pressures also have caused changes in the organisational structure of dialysis clinics over the past decade. Hospital administrators perceived dialysis departments as very unprofitable because RCC-based cost systems allocated, indirect costs to ancillary departments on a basis that was determined for the hospital as a whole, i.e. allocated costs were not based upon the hospital resources consumed in delivering dialysis services. As shown in Exhibit F.2, in 1980, 58 per cent of the dialysis clinics were hospital-based non-profit facilities. By 1991, only 33 per cent of the nearly 2,100 dialysis clinics were hospital-based non-profit clinics, whereas 56 per cent of the operating clinics had become independent facilities. During this twelve-year period independent clinics (non-profit and for-profit combined) increased nearly 250 per cent compared to an 18 per cent increase in hospital-based clinics during the same period. As indicated by these results, clinic administrators perceive that clinic viability depends upon managing costs within a fixed-reimbursement framework and that cost containment is facilitated by adopting an independent organisation.

Current treatment costing options

The DCI location presented in this case study serves approximately 102 HD patients and 62 PD patients. HD treatments constitute 41 per cent (14,343) of total clinic treatments with PD treatments representing the remaining 59 per cent (20,624) of the total 34,967 treatments delivered through the clinic. The independent clinic provides a much greater level of PD services than typical dialysis clinics because the managers aggressively pursue PD opportunities throughout a broader geographic area.

The cost data were obtained from clinic inventory lists, interviews, accounting and patient records. The supplies typically used for HD and PD were determined by interviewing clinic personnel. Labour, durable equipment and general overhead costs were identified from year-end financial statements. In costing each delivery method, the clinic's cost system recognised only treatment-specific supplies as direct costs. The remaining 60 per cent of total costs represent non-specific or indirect costs (e.g. nursing services, durable equipment and facilities expense). As a result, subsequent identification of indirect costs with individual treatment types depends upon the treatment costing model used when computing alternative treatment delivery method profitability. For example, if 62.2 per cent of indirect costs are allocated to HD (based upon the number of patients receiving a treatment type), then both HD and PD are apparently profitable. On the other hand, if approximately 60 per cent of indirect costs are assigned to PD (based upon total treatments provided), then PD will lose money. In either case, there is considerable uncertainty about which treatment costing method is right and no clear indication whether one or the other treatment alternative is more or less profitable. Additionally, because the clinic as a whole is profitable, approximating treatment costs using an RCC model results in both HD and PD appearing profitable.

Physicians and patients wanted to continue both services. Additionally, the clinic staff do not believe either treatment type (or modality) is a financial loser, despite the costs and losses computed with these two aggregate treatment costing models. The primary differential, of course, is indirect cost (overhead). Furthermore, the effect of clinic cost allocation would be magnified for hospital-based dialysis departments where the department becomes responsible for an added share of general hospital overhead. This may certainly explain why so many hospitals over the past decade sold their dialysis services (which lost them money) to independent clinics (which make a profit on those same services).

The problem perceived by the clinic staff is how to interpret existing cost information to determine the cost-effectiveness of HD and PD. The payments for these services are fixed and known. Aggregate costs are known also. Individual and comparative treatment costs, however, are subject to much interpretation. Management could continue to offer either HD or PD at a loss of course and they are disinclined to reduce either service regardless of the negative financial performance indicated by their costing system. However, management is uncomfortable with the results of its cost analyses. This case study is designed to address this dilemma, i.e. to better estimate treatment costs, evaluate treatment profitability and recommend cost-saving approaches.

Treatment costing refinement process

The existing cost information provided a basis for computing treatment costs under three aggregate costing models: RCP, RCT, RCC. However, each of these traditional methods treated labour (mostly nursing services), durable equipment (depreciation and maintenance) and general overheads (facilities and administration) as fixed expenses, without considering the demand placed on these resources by the treatment alternatives. DCI management and employees understood that the HD and PD treatments placed different burdens on the clinic's resources and staff. They understood that alternative costing systems that emphasised resource consumption instead of expenditure allocation might provide improved insight into the 'true' cost of these treatment alternatives. As a result, DCI began exploring the possibility of using an activity-based costing (ABC) system for cost analysis. Their only available examples, however, emphasised manufacturing and not service organisations. Furthermore, these manufacturing-based examples indicated that increased levels of overhead costs represented one key indicator of when an ABC system might be appropriate. As they examined the potential for ABC at DCI, clinic managers progressed through a two-phase cost-refinement process clinic as they attempted to develop improved treatment-level cost information.

In each phase the standard supply costs and the episodic supply costs were traced to a specific treatment type as presently tracked by the existing cost system. Under the current system, standard supplies represented items exclusively used or fully consumed in providing a treatment type (e.g. drugs, syringes). Episodic supplies included additional materials needed to treat complications (e.g. infections), to monitor health status (e.g. laboratory check-ups) or to manage cases with special problems (e.g. dialysis of haemophiliacs).

Phase 1: Analysis of general overhead

Clinic management initially directed their attention towards an analysis of general overheads. General overhead costs represented 26 per cent of revenues. The detailed expenses in this category were obtained from existing financial records. Overhead costs included expenses associated with occupancy, administration, equipment rental expense and general supplies. In this initial phase of the cost-refinement process, four overhead cost pools, with corresponding activity drivers. were identified as representing the key strategic resources represented by the clinic's overhead expenditures (see Exhibit F.3). The partially completed overhead cost-analysis worksheet in Exhibit F.3 provides a basis for estimating the overhead-related resources consumed by the HD and PD treatment types. Only the identification of an appropriate activity driver for the communications system and medical records cost pool proved controversial. Several clinic staff members believed that the number of treatments provided, regardless of type, should serve as the activity driver for this cost pool. Their reasoning was based on the idea that the resources provided through this cost pool facilitated billing and billing/reimbursement was an activity performed on a treatment-by-treatment basis. However, because medical records and treatment scheduling were maintained on a by-patient basis, the number of patients was selected as the final activity driver.

(Note: The analysis of the communications/medical records cost pool could be conducted with either transactions or patients as the activity driver. However, the resulting treatment costs may prove different with the selection of alternative assumptions.)

At this point, a preliminary computation was made of treatment costs using only the ABC analysis of general overhead expenses. Exhibit F.4 includes a partially completed worksheet indicating how HD and PD treatment costs were computed after Phase One of the cost refinement process. Labour and durable equipment expenses were not analysed in terms of cost pools during the initial phase of the cost refinement process. Instead, these costs were aggregated and allocated to the individual treatment types, based upon the number of treatments. No distinction was made between the resources consumed for HD and PD because clinic staff indicated that 'labour and equipment costs are fixed expenses that do not change regardless of the procedures performed.'

Phase 2: Analysis of labour/nursing services and durable equipment

After completing their analysis of general overhead expenses in Phase 1, clinic management developed a different perspective on cost behaviours. They clarified their understanding of activities performed within the clinic and how costs related to the activities carried out by clinic staff. As a result, they changed their position on labour/nursing services and durable equipment expenses. An agreement was reached that these cost categories also should be analysed from an ABC perspective.

Labour/nursing services represented the single largest expenditure in the clinic. However, because management initially perceived this resource as being too difficult to analyse, examination of the key activities performed in this area was put off until the end. As a result of their Phase 1 experience, clinic management began thinking of payroll as available resources and whether the activities performed by the staff were essential or non-essential. The resulting analysis of labour/nursing services represented an interesting use of ABC in an area previously considered a fixed expense by management. Exhibit F.5 presents a partially completed ABC worksheet for the labour/nursing services resources.

Four cost pools were identified and as occurred during the analysis of general overheads, an appropriate activity driver for one cost pool proved controversial. A question arose concerning the demands placed on the clinic's administration and support staff by the alternative treatment types. The debate came down to a choice between the relative number of patients and the relative number of treatments. Again, the clinic staff selected the number of patients as the activity driver, just as they had done in determining the appropriate activity driver for the communications/medical records cost pool in general overhead. As in the general overhead analysis, the resulting treatment cost computations change significantly if the number of treatments replaces number of patients as the activity driver for the administration and support staff cost pool.

By far, the bulk of the clinic's durable equipment expenses related to the dialysers used in HD treatments. Additionally, HD treatments provided to PD patients (usually the result of a PD complication) are reimbursed as an independent HD treatment and not absorbed as an additional cost of providing PD services. Therefore, durable equipment costs were traced directly to individual treatment types in a manner just like standard and episodic supplies. Exhibit F.6 includes durable equipment expenses as directly traceable costs with $120,600 and $16,446 identified with HD and PD, respectively.

Conclusion

No one purposefully chooses to encourage healthcare delivery methods that squander scarce resources. Unfortunately, given bad costing systems, more costly delivery methods can actually be encouraged. Similarly, more cost-effective treatment alternatives can be wrongfully reduced or discontinued. The assumptions and data classification of any costing method are crucial to accurate costing, because the selection of a costing system can influence managers' decisions to provide or eliminate alternative procedures or delivery methods. If a treatment or delivery method is eliminated for cost reasons, however good or bad the reasons, both physicians and patients may go elsewhere and thereby threaten the financial viability of the organisation as a whole. The solution is to improve treatment costing accuracy and increase the value of cost information to decision-makers. When cost information is accurately identified, healthcare executives can effectively assure the potential long-term profitability of their managed care contracts.

Discussion questions

1.   Identify three major healthcare policy changes during the last 30 years and discuss how those changes impact the cost systems of healthcare organisations.

2.   Compute treatment costs for HD and PD using the aggregate costing models (use the Exhibit F.1 data):
     (a) ratio of cost per patient (non-traceable costs allocated to treatment types based upon the number of patients receiving each treatment);
     (b) ratio of cost per treatment (non-traceable costs allocated to treatment types based upon the relative number of treatments provided for each treatment alternative);
     (c) ratio of cost to charges (all costs allocated based upon a constant allocation rate as determined by dividing total cost by total revenue).

3.   Compute HD and PD treatment costs based upon the Phase 1 cost-refinement process results (see Exhibits F.3 and F.4).

4.   Compute HD and PD treatment costs based upon the Phase 2 results of the cost refinement process (see Exhibits F.5 and F.6).

5.   Discuss the strengths and weaknesses of the alternative cost models. Consider the underlying assumptions associated with each cost model, the shift in cost and the apparent profitability (or loss) associated with HD and PD under the different costing methods and the potential impact of these alternative costing methods on the clinic management's decision-making.

	Clinic-based haemodialysis	Home-based peritoneal dialysis	Clinic totals	
	(102 patients)	(62 patients)	$	%
Revenues:				
Number of treatments	14,343	20,624	34,967	
Charge per treatment	$129.70	$55.59		
Total revenue	$1,860,287	$1,146,488	$3,006,775	100.00
Cost of service:				
Standard supplies	512,619	152,281	664,900	22.11
Episodic supplies	98,680	212,015	310,695	10.33
Contribution margin	1,248,988	782,192	2,031,180	67.56
Fixed expenses:				
Labour/nursing services			883,280	29.38
Durable equipment			137,046	4.56
General overhead			785,825	26.14
Net income			$225,029	7.48

Exhibit F.1 DCI's current period income statement.

	Hospital-based		Independent		
	Non-profit	**For-profit**	**Non-profit**	**For-profit**	**Total**
1980	583 (58.1%)	17 (1.7%)	79 (7.9%)	325 (32.3%)	1,004 (100.0%)
1985	612 (44.0%)	17 (1.2%)	158 (11.4%)	605 (43.7%)	1,392 (100.0%)
1991	687 (33.0%)	19 (0.9%)	217 (10.4%)	1,159 (55.7%)	2,082 (100.0%)

Exhibit F.2 Shift in organisational structure of dialysis providers (number of service providers).

Proposed cost pools	Total	HD	PD
1. Facility costs (e.g. rent, maintenance, depreciation)	$233,226		
2. Administration and support staff salaries, includes benefits	354,682		
3. Communications systems and medical records	57,219		
4. Utilities	40,698		
Total general overhead expense	$785,825		

Proposed activity drivers	Total	HD	PO
Square footage (facility costs)	30,000	18,900	11,100
Number of patients (admin and support salaries)	164	102	62
Number of treatments (communication & medical records)	34,967	14,343	20,624
Estimated kilowatt usage (utilities)	662,700	563,295	99,405

Exhibit F.3 Worksheet for analysis of general overhead identification of cost pools and corresponding activity drivers.

Cost categories	Total	HD	PD
Costs directly traceable to treatments:			
Standard supplies	$664,900	$512,619	152,281
Episodic supplies	310,695	98,680	212,015
Unanalysed costs:			
Labour/nursing services	883,280	362,322	520,958
Durable equipment	137,046	56,216	80,830
Total expenses excluded from ABC analysis	1,995,921	1,029,837	966,084
Costs analysed with ABC:			
General overhead expenses (see Exhibit F.3)	785,825		
Total DCI expenses	$2,781,746		
Divide by number of treatments		÷14,343	÷20,624
Cost per treatment type			

Exhibit F.4 Worksheet for computation of treatment costs – Phase 1 of the treatment costing refinement process.

Proposed cost pools	Total	HD	PD
Nursing services:			
1. RNs	$239,120		
2. LPNs	404,064		
3. Administration and support staff			
(nurse supervisor, pre-dialysis educator,			
scheduling secretary)	115,168		
4. Machine operations (technicians)	124,928		
Total labour/nursing services expense	$883,280		

Proposed activity drivers	Total	HD	PD
Full-time equivalent staff (FTEs)			
RNs	7	6	1
LPNs	19	15	14
Number of patients			
(admin and support salaries)	164	102	62
Number of dialyser treatments			
(machine operations)	14,343	14,343	0

Exhibit F.5 Worksheet for analysis of labour/nursing services – identification of cost pools and corresponding activity drivers.

Cost categories	Total	HD	PD
Costs directly traceable to treatments:			
Standard supplies	$664,900	$512,619	$152,281
Episodic supplies	10,695	98,680	212,015
Durable equipment (Phase 2)	131,046	120,600	16,446
Total traceable expenses	1,112,641	731,899	380,742
Costs analysed with ABC:			
General overhead expenses (see Exhibit F.3)	785,825		
Labour/nursing services (see Exhibit F.5)	83,280		
Total DCI expenses	$2,781,746		
Divide by number of treatments		÷14,343	÷20,624
Cost per treatment type			

Exhibit F.6 Worksheet for computation of treatment costs – Phase 2 of the treatment costing refinement process.

CASE STUDY G

Tempest, Inc.

(The balanced scorecard)

(Copyright © 1997 by Institute of Management Accountants, Montvale, NJ. Reproduced with permission.)

Bill Jennings had a-tough choice to make. Bill was activity-based project manager of Tempest, Inc. a large European manufacturer of industrial and consumer detergents and paints. Joe Smith, his boss and chief financial officer of Tempest, had offered him the position of manager, capital spending. This new position would give Bill responsibility for managing the financial planning and monitoring of Tempest's $415 million capital budget, a position of major importance. However, it would also mean leaving his current role in leading highly visible performance improvement projects involving activity-based management and organisational re-engineering. Furthermore, it was June, and Tempest's lengthy, tedious, capital budgeting process, disliked by many in the company, would begin in about a month.

The entire capital budgeting process took about six months. First, each subsidiary would propose investment in several projects. These proposals would reach the European head office in July and August. They typically represented a significant increase in expenditure over the previous year. Over the next few months, Joe Smith's staff would gather various pieces of information about project costs and specific benefits to prepare for year-end meetings. Held in December, these were a series of annual planning meetings, during which the subsidiary CEOs and CFOs presented projected year-end results and negotiated performance targets for sales, net income, headcount and capital for the new year. Tempest's overall capital target was then established as a percentage of total expected revenues.

January was a very busy month. Each subsidiary would lobby and negotiate for changes in the resources and results targets established in December, even while year-end performance numbers were being finalised. Finally, by mid-February, final targets were established. It seemed that no sooner did one cycle end than it was time for the next one to begin.

Joe Smith believed that Tempest needed a repeatable and reliable capital budgeting process and that Bill Jennings was the right person for the job. After much discussion, Bill accepted the position. He was excited. He now saw this as a highly visible opportunity to apply his process improvement skills to a far-reaching process which had major business impact. Additionally, since his boss was also very interested in improving the process, he would have all the support he needed to get the job done. The sea of life appeared calm and untroubled.

The business climate

Tempest, Inc. had been in business for 30 years at that point. Each of its five subsidiaries (two located in Europe, two in Asia and one in the USA) were organised around product groups (industrial and consumer detergents and paints) and each had its own plants. Each subsidiary's board reported in to the executive board in Europe, with CFOs reporting to Joe Smith. Bill now had responsibility for coordinating worldwide capital budget development activity with the CFOs of the subsidiaries.

For decades, the company had been the market leader in most of the categories in which it competed. With sales of $4 billion, an unshakable reputation with the trade and a large base of customers for its premium priced, high-quality, innovative products, it had operating power that could not be matched by the competition, which, for the most part, had no critical mass to pose a serious threat. In recent years, Tempest had fuelled its growth with heavy investment in the latest manufacturing technology and believed this would be an insurmountable barrier to any new competitor. Tempest's highly automated state-of-the-art plants were the benchmark for the industry and a considerable source of pride for the executive board. Several 'high-tech' projects, which returned less than the cost of capital, were approved by the board, because of the 'strategic value of an investment in new technology'.

The problem had been that the company had no problem. Tempest was incredibly successful. The only group apparently concerned about capital spending was the finance division, which felt that more attention needed to be addressed to cash-flow issues. The company's board had ample experience, very good judgment and an excellent reputation in the industry for aggressive business strategy. There simply was no apparent need to 'overanalyse' things. Nonetheless, in recent years a disturbing trend had emerged.

Small regional manufacturers, whose products matched Tempest's quality at much lower prices, were operating in several key markets. Consumers in these markets had unique needs which Tempest's large-scale production capability could not economically accommodate. The new competition's flexible manufacturing facilities produced small runs of products for the local trade and provided highly customised service to small localised industrial clients. Furthermore, with 'value pricing' becoming an issue in the consumer markets, many of Tempest's retail outlets were beginning to stock their shelves with 'house brands'. The small local producers were the major source of such products.

Individually, these regional manufacturers were no threat to the giant. Collectively, however, they were an increasingly troubling force. Two of the largest of these regional producers had recently merged and the company's strategic planners were now concerned that further consolidation would pose a serious threat to Tempest's position in the marketplace. For the first time in 20 years sales were flat and expected to show no growth in the next three years, despite anticipated continuing market growth. A major business publication, noticing this trend, included it in a major report on the impact of generic manufacturers on major brands. This event crystallised many board concerns and became a catalyst for change within Tempest.

Planned changes to capital spending

In mid-July, Tempest's board, which prided itself on its ability to make quick decisions, responded. It was decided that, given market conditions, price must remain flat. The heavy capital investment programmes had resulted in explosive growth of depreciation expenses. In order to sustain income growth targets (which had to be maintained as a separate issue from sales growth), costs of production would have to be reduced. Simultaneously, return on investment targets was raised to strengthen overall financial performance. Given this 'get better' versus 'get bigger' philosophy, it was agreed that capital investment should be focused on improvement rather than expansion. Capital investment had to decrease as a percentage of sales. Allowing continued growth of capital spending at current rates would lead to depreciation charges which would significantly erode the bottom line. The board hoped that this new focus would yield results in two ways: first, projects that did not yield solid benefits would not be implemented and second, projects that held the promise of very good returns would be implemented without excessive spending. This new focus would allow 'more to get done with less' (capital).

Many people asked Bill what all this meant. Would capital projects already begun be stopped? Were there particular types of projects that would not be funded in the future? What was the target for the new capital budget? Bill was concerned. A storm seemed to be brewing.

Cost-cutting teams were deployed throughout the company. A few examples of the new focus were widely discussed in the company. In one instance, the number of engineers scheduled to visit the USA to evaluate new equipment was reduced from 14 to four. Some managers complained that instead of cutting 'fat', 'muscle' was being sliced away (translation: their budget had the biceps and should not be cut). However, this was an expected reaction to the new lean focus.

Many agreed that this new cost-consciousness was appropriate. It stood in conflict, however, with a major motivator for many managers. Many of Tempest's directors liked the power of having a substantial capital budget. Indeed, at times, it seemed that the size of your capital budget, along with the number of staff in your department, signalled your importance to the rest of the organisation. Thus much attention became focused on the capital budget.

By the end of August, two camps had emerged. The first group consisted of a stream of anxious visitors to Bill Jennings' office. They (and their representatives) had questions about how much would be 'cut' out of the total budget. They emphasised how important their projects were to the success of the company, especially in the face of the emerging competitive threats. They also wanted to know how their obviously superior projects could be guaranteed inclusion in the capital budget. Perhaps there could be two tiers of projects: an 'A' list (which would presumably include many of their own projects) and a 'B' list of inferior projects (of which many seemed to be in a variety of departments other than their own). The second camp seemed to have decided that the power of their influence with the board and the obvious superiority of their projects would make them guaranteed inclusion in the budget. Bill was unhappy. The waters were decidedly choppy.

This wasn't an easy time for Bill. The directors were a formidable group of people with power to impact his career and they all expected that he could recognise the unique value of their projects. He grew thin and pale. He wore a hunted look and took to ducking into the nearest empty office when he saw a director approach, to avoid painful discussions of why a particular project just *had* to be funded. He wished for the old days when he facilitated teams in their pursuit of performance improvement. Joe Smith noticed Bill's pain. 'Surely', said Joe, 'some of those performance improvement principles could be applied to the capital budgeting process.' Bill felt sick. The waves were higher than he had ever seen them.

Strategy and capital planning

In late August the board hired a consultant for advice on issues of strategic importance. She had the board attend a senior management course on 'Competitive Strategy'. This was a change from previous strategy meetings where the board would retire for a week to the sumptuous surroundings of a luxury resort. Directors noted this and commented on it. When they returned, they assembled the company's 6,000 employees in five cities for a satellite broadcast of a meeting at which the chairman discussed the competitive challenges facing Tempest. 'Strategic Intent', 'Competitive Advantage' and 'Critical Capabilities' were addressed, as were 'Cycle Time', 'Delighting the Customer' and 'Empowerment'. When the issues came around to 'refocusing' capital spending, the chairman referred to 'your chief financial officer, Joe Smith and his team, who are working on a solution'. The chairman was 'confident that this revised capital strategy would re-energise the company by allowing it to concentrate on only those opportunities that could deliver the best results.' In no way would the new capital plan impair Tempest's ability to compete. Cycle time would improve and manufacturing processes would become more nimble as a result of this new focus. The chairman said he would have Joe Smith report to the board in November on how the process redesign was progressing and how he intended cutting $65 million from the capital budget. Joe Smith smiled as the camera zoomed in on him. Bill was glad the camera crew did not know who 'Joe's team' was. Bill felt the waves batter at him as he sank under the surface.

That evening Joe and Bill had a long discussion. How would they manage the expectations of the directors with ideas for capital investments? They had to overcome the 'squeakiest wheel gets his/her project funded' syndrome. How would they deliver results to the board? How could they be sure that they could select the 'best' capital investment ideas and reject the rest? Should the value of a capital project be measured only by a discounted cash flow? Should an attempt be made to reflect what value the project could deliver to customers, the trade and the employees? How did these issues relate to each other? Were some more important than others? Were there other issues they were missing? Would this new process take too long to implement? What if it didn't succeed? Should they work with a group of directors to validate their thoughts?

Validation, they decided, was a must on two fronts – first, to test how sound their ideas were, but second and as important, to test the 'political' ramifications of a new approach. Bill recalled an approach he had read about, which may have some application here – the balanced scorecard model.[1] They called in Joyce Shu, the director of strategic planning. Joyce had perhaps the best cross-functional overview of how things should work in the company. The three worked late into the night and when the meeting ended they had a plan.

Over the next few weeks Bill led Joe, Joyce and a small cross-functional team of managers in two meetings where they identified a series of performance factors that capital investments should impact. This brainstorming process ended with close to a hundred such factors. There were too many to use effectively and Bill referred to research papers for a method that would help narrow the list down to a few key performance factors. He found one that worked: the Performance Measurement Questionnaire.[2] The method was a democratic, consensus-oriented way to distil a wide variety of potential measures of performance into a shortlist of the few most important to Tempest. It began with a list of all the performance measures. Each member of the cross-functional team 'voted' for each measure by circling a number on a scale from 1 to 7 where '7' was most important. The measures with the highest average scores became part of a final set of 25 measures.

Bill was amazed at how much he had contributed to the tool. He was back in a mode of improving the performance of a process – in this case, the capital budgeting process. He was happy. The waves were rough, but he was riding them well.

Implementing the process

A series of videoconferences with key subsidiary VPs and directors followed, explaining the new capital evaluation process. The new process included a decision tool which evaluated each project on the basis of the value it was expected to deliver. 'Value' was defined from the perspectives of several 'stakeholders' including 'Customers', 'Shareholders', 'Internal Business Processes' and 'Innovation and Learning'. Each of these stakeholders was represented by specific performance factors. Projects would be valued on the basis of how much they could contribute to these factors and therefore 'value'. Initially, many directors were sceptical – only they really knew their project. Only they were therefore qualified to decide whether it should be funded or not. How could anyone else know this better? Besides, it was argued, nobody was genuinely unbiased in their recommendations. People would obviously rate their projects ahead of everyone else's.

Bill responded to the concerns with confidence. He believed that the new process was theoretically and practically sound and, because of the sound logic backing his conviction, opposition to the process gradually weakened. The subsidiaries proceeded to gather project proposals as they always had. Joe Smith asked for the subsidiary CFOs' support in rolling out the new process in mid-October.

Each subsidiary formed a capital evaluation committee (CEC) consisting of key board members. Directors submitted lists of recommended capital investment projects, which the CEC rated (scored) according to the 'value' they promised to deliver. The maximum score a project could earn was 1,000 points. Projects were ranked by their scores and an estimate of the capital required for each was made. Each subsidiary was told to assume they had 20 per cent less capital than the previous year. When the capital available 'ran out', the expectation was that other projects could not be funded. Given the current capital budget of $415 million, this would result in planned investment of $332 million and allow some flexibility in meeting the $350 million target established by the board. These ranked lists of projects were sent by the subsidiaries to Tempest headquarters during November. Bill consolidated the information into a single ranking for the year-end meetings and found that when $332 million was assigned completely, 215 projects fell 'below the line' – they could not be funded.

One point of contention was that the final list of projects differed from a simple pooling of the separate subsidiary level lists. For instance, eight of the projects that were below the line for the Asian subsidiary had higher scores than accepted projects at the European subsidiary. Thus, in the final list, these eight Asian projects were ranked as fundable, while several previously accepted European subsidiary projects fell below the line. In the past, choices about which projects to implement had not been a critical issue since most capital projects had been approved. Now the board had to reach an understanding as to whether the European projects had priority, given that region's rapidly changing environment. The political ramifications of this discovery could not be addressed by the new capital evaluation process alone. Instead, they required management judgment. However, the list of projects for which discussion was now necessary was much smaller and could be examined in depth.

The CEC meetings proceeded smoothly when participants realised that the process was actually very sound – it did not allow individuals' biases to overvalue a project. For instance, a project that did nothing to help the 'Customer' could not get a high score from the 'Customer' perspective. Weak projects were exposed for what they really were now that there was a consistent basis of evaluation. People even withdrew projects that only weeks before 'just had to be funded'. Bill felt he was getting his 'sea legs' now.

Despite the progress made, there were those who grumbled about the process in the washrooms. It took too long. Judgment and creativity were being stifled. How could they be expected to do their jobs if they didn't get the resources to function? They would talk with their board if they had to. The grapevine conveyed these things to Bill and he grew concerned – but not for long.

Joe Smith and Bill met with the chairman and introduced the new process to him. He was delighted. He led the executive board in an active discussion of the process, with the CEOs and CFOs of the subsidiaries participating via videoconference. At the end of the meeting the chairman announced that he was well-satisfied with the new process and its results. He was especially pleased with the focus provided by the process. As a direct result, the time required for senior management to review capital projects had been reduced by 50 per cent to 75 per cent. He congratulated Joe Smith and Bill on their excellent work. He also recommended using a similar approach for other areas in the company where priority calls, once made, locked the company on a course of action that was expensive to change. With this, many of those who had recently expressed dissatisfaction with the new process re-examined their positions. Bill was pleased. He had found his core competence. He began thinking seriously about taking up sailing.

Required

1. How does the 'balanced scorecard' approach described in Exhibit G.1 differ from a more traditional discounted cash flow method of evaluating capital proposals? Which approach is better suited to Tempest's situation? Why?

2. Bill seems to feel that the logic of the proposed capital rationing system won over its detractors. Do you agree? What were the critical determinants of success for Bill's proposal?

3. What aspects of Bill's problem in this case required knowledge of financial and accounting management techniques?

4. What were the conflicts Bill faced between his personal career objectives and the needs and objectives of Tempest?

Notes

1. See Exhibit G.1.

2. Dixon, J. Robb, Nanni, Alfred J. and Vollman, Thomas E. (1990) *The New Performance Challenge*. Homewood, IL: Business One-Irwin.

To:	Joe Smith, CFO
From:	Bill Jennings
Subject:	Internal Memo: THE BALANCED SCORECARD AT TEMPEST, INC.
Date:	December 3

Background

The new capital evaluation process (The Balanced Scorecard*) is a flexible management tool which helps define and execute business strategy. Designed correctly, it provides a balance for the entire organisation, focusing it in a structural manner on key results, without stifling creativity and judgement. Best of all, once designed, its application is simple and consistent. It also has the capacity to evolve quickly, growing with management experience and absorbing the best emerging business practices and academic thinking. Companies like Apple Computer, Advanced Micro Devices, Analog Devices and FMC Corporation are pioneering its use with great results. Temp Inc. is solidly in this category of advanced, successful users.

What needs it serves

The tool provides a remarkably simple and comprehensive approach to address critical issues for which no coherent alternatives exist. First, it clarifies strategic focus by requiring definition of the relative importance of the company's key stakeholders. Second, it helps define and set targets for the results management expects to deliver as the direct result of the chosen strategy. Third, it provides a structure which channels investments and resource assignments into divisions and departments such that the strategy is executed well.

Not having this clarity results in mixed signals to managers and forces them to make trade-offs between different aspects of performance. Such trade-offs are made by different managers in different ways, resulting in a lack of operating consistently over time and between divisions. This dilution of the organisation's capability to focus on a few key areas and deliver superior results in them is undesirable and, although often recognised as such, is managed ineffectively.

What it is

The tool establishes a limited number of critical performance indicators for the entire company which are directly derived from the organisation's strategic objectives and competitive demands. In Tempest, the scorecard requires 'business value' to be defined from four key 'stakeholders' perspectives: (1) the 'customers'; (2) 'internal business processes'; (3) the 'shareholder'; and (4) innovation and learning. These perspectives of what 'good' performance means are crystallised into a few specific performance measures and are given weights reflecting the company's intent to satisfy its different stakeholders' needs.

A simple scoring process follows. Each project or investment scores points for its potential to succeed in each chosen performance measure. Projects are ranked on their scores and investments are prioritised on that basis. Management decisions can override this ranking allowing for the guidance of judgement and experience.

Since the scores provide a ranking, top projects and very weak projects are generally not debated. Instead, only projects at the 'cutoff' point (the limit at which resources to implement run out) are scrutinised. The method is remarkably robust and does not allow an individual's biases to override what 'value' means (e.g. a project that does nothing for the 'customer' cannot receive a high score in the 'customer' category).

Interesting possibilities

1. This tool begs the use of a top management *quarterly review* book that contains four sections – one for each 'stakeholder'. Each section would map Tempest's progress since the last review in a few critical performance areas. Divisions that are key contributors to these areas would be accountable for specific aspects of performance.
2. It offers a specific and rational vehicle for the *post audit investments*. As such, it can be used to encourage project champions to focus on specific project performance targets. This could avoid unfortunate instances where an individual's project responsibility ends with successful project justification.
3. Performance targets could be set for stakeholder measures to focus streamlining and redesigning activity. This focus also provides a basis for concentrating on only a few key improvement efforts at one time.

Conclusion

This new approach has received refreshingly enthusiastic response because of its greatest strength – its ability to very clearly translate a 'strategy' into operating terms which are commonly understandable, communicable, actionable and measurable. In this context, it is flexible enough to operate with any acronym (BPR, TQM, ABM, etc.), and, in fact, significantly strengthens them all. It focuses the enterprise.

* Kaplan, R.S. and Norton, D.P. (1992) 'The Balanced Scorecard – Measures that Drive Performance', *Harvard Business Review*, January/February and Kaplan, R.S. and Norton, D.P. (1993) 'Putting the Balanced Scorecard to Work', *Harvard Business Review*, September/October.

Exhibit G.1 The balanced scorecard at Tempest, Inc.

CASE STUDY H

East River Manufacturing

(Implementing ABC and ABM)

(Copyright © 1997 Institute of Management Accountants, Montvale, NJ. Reproduced with permission.)

> The Tube Shop of the East River plant was once an outdated manual tube shop. But now it is a modern computer-integrated tube manufacturing facility. Its technology allows East River to increase productivity, work capacity and market share. The innovations have also made the plant more efficient, with less downtime for maintenance and reduced span time. The Tube Shop now boasts an impressive array of new machinery including an automatic storage and retrieval system, and a fully automated tube processing line.
>
> (Bob Kitchen, Manager of Engineering, Power Services Industries)

The Tube Shop's manual production process had been redesigned and full operational implementation of the new $13 million computer-integrated manufacturing line (CIM) was complete. The bay's fabrication operations were automated in order to cut costs, reduce raw tube to finished product time by up to 80 per cent, provide superior quality and ship orders on schedule. 'In today's highly competitive arena we must become the front runner of innovation, quality, cost/value, delivery and service', said Wayne Dreher, manager, Manufacturing/Process Engineering, Tube Shop.

Background information

Power Services Industries (PSI) was founded in 1907. PSI has been a major supplier of boilers, components, power generation equipment and expert services to customers worldwide. PSI's East Rivers' service-related replacement parts and equipment has increased from just under 40 per cent of revenues to approximately 70 per cent.

The market rewards suppliers who can deliver a quality product with quick turnaround at a reasonable cost. That means suppliers will have to deliver lead-time reductions of 50 per cent or more in the near future. Therefore, East River's continued focus will be on achieving dramatic reductions in throughput time and keeping continual pressure on costs.

Prior to installation of the CIM system, the major concern was the efficiency of the manual production process. Marketing often complained that contract cost proposals were excessive and led to uncompetitive quotes. On occasion, their concerns could be documented by evaluation of open public bids or other information gathered by sales personnel. Manufacturing was frequently dissatisfied because a key performance indicator, E/A (estimated manhours/actual manhours), was often unfavourable and there were frequent cost overruns on contracts, even though no changes had been made in the detailed engineering design. And engineering was looking to improve their ability to evaluate numerous design and manufacturing alternatives (tooling, machine constraints and cost) at the tube and feature level, early in the design cycle.

While there had been some question about the adequacy of the labour-focused cost system in place before automation of the Tube Shop, the plant accounting staff felt the system was acceptable and didn't see any pressing need to change it as long as the labour-paced manual line was still in place. Recently however, the cost system was beginning to come under greater scrutiny. There was now concern that the labour-based overhead allocations did not reveal important differences in the cost of projects, some of which could take three to five years to complete and run into millions of dollars. With implementation of the CIM line, there was little doubt that the prior labour-based cost system would be incapable of providing the kind of reliable cost information that engineering, marketing and operations would need.

Cost estimation and product engineering

Sales personnel generate requests for quotations (RFQs) for entire steam generation systems, replacement boiler components and loose tubes from potential customers. The RFQs are initially processed at PSI's Dallas, Texas headquarters. If the order is for replacement parts on a power system originally designed and built by PSI, then detailed blueprints are available and cost estimators can prepare their bids from these blueprints. However, if the customer wants a new power-generation system or has equipment made by another manufacturer and wants to replace a component (a complex subassembly consisting of many parts), then product engineering will prepare preliminary tube designs from historical data on similar products produced before by PSI. There are enough similarities to previously fabricated tube variations that customer RFQs can be developed on a timely basis by querying the parts database. Cost estimators use these preliminary tube designs to prepare estimates of the tube's manufacturing and material cost.

There are several problems associated with the manner in which cost estimates are prepared. First, preliminary engineering designs of new systems and, to a lesser degree, replacement components can only be described at a fairly general level of detail. Firms bidding on projects must prepare quotes without knowing the final design of the project or what demands it will place on the production process. Second, the base-estimating data used by cost estimators was developed from industrial engineering time studies completed in the early 1970s. Mistakes in estimating projects of this magnitude can prove to be very costly. If a project's cost is underestimated, then sizeable cost overruns can occur and the contract will be unprofitable. If a project's cost is overestimated, the contract will likely be won by a competitor.

If the proposal is accepted and becomes a contract, the proposal becomes the base-line or 'as-sold' estimate (i.e. the budgeted cost) for cost monitoring and measuring actual performance. Once a proposal is accepted, product design engineers 'start from scratch' and prepare detailed part and component designs on computer-aided design (CAD) systems. They also determine the materials composition for all tubes. This product structure and tube geometry, which describes the physical characteristics of the tube, is then transferred to draftsmen who transform the product structure into detailed graphics (blueprints). Draftsmen manually load information on the tube's geometry into three different computer systems: (1) the bill of material system; (2) the CAD drawing system; and (3) the tube detail file which converts tube geometry along with design, process, machine and tooling constraints data into process plans. This information is downloaded to East River's mainframe computer.

Computer-integrated manufacturing process

Benefits from implementing the CIM system were expected to result in:

- reduction of manpower;

- increase in throughput;

- decrease in work-in-process inventory;

- reduction in maintenance costs;

- shortening of lead-times;

- increased quality;

- increased capacity;

- increased market share.

Complete automated operations commenced with the integration of all work cells with the Tube Shop controller and plant mainframe computer in April 1992. Product flow philosophy is to pull a part through the Tube Shop without undue build-up of work-in-process inventory between workstations. Most material handling will be by V-roll conveyors and cascades (a buffer storage in front of a workstation). Once a part has been studded or bent, it will be transported by radio-operated crane.

An automatic storage and retrieval system is the first stop for tubes entering the Tube Shop. The system orders and stores tubes in bins until they are needed. When the schedule calls for them, the automatic storage and retrieval system locates the required tubes and transports them directly into the Tube Shop and through the automatic shotblast, which cleans the tubes. From the shot-blast, the tubes are fed directly onto automatic conveyor and cascade systems – these systems are used to perform materials handling wherever possible.

Tubes are then routed to the Bardons & Oliver, a new double-end milling station where tubes are weld-prepped and cut to length. A probe automatically inspects the dimensions of the tube, compares the readings to the programmed dimensions and either accepts or rejects the part. This machine also automatically bar codes each end of the tube with its own unique identification, marking its shop order, part number and manufacturing process information. Bar-code readers located at each work cell continuously update the Tube Shop controller as to the status of each tube in the system. This machine also applies the layout lines for stud patterns and bend tangents. Although much of the work downstream will be performed automatically, the layout lines help operators to subsequently verify that bending and studding equipment is performing to specifications.

Tubes discharged from weld prep will move onto either the tube-to-tube weld line or the line that feeds the studding and bending machines. Tubes that require bending or studding transit down the main line where they will go to either a flat studder, pin studder or a bender. Once all the studding is complete, the tubes are sent via conveyor to the end of the line, where they are deposited in a drop rack until they are needed. Tubes that need to be welded to one or more other tubes travel to the new tube-to-tube welding system where it may take anywhere from 50 seconds to 2.5 minutes to weld two tubes. Next, they go to the NDE (non-destructive examination) station where the welds are X-rayed to ensure product integrity. Tubes that pass inspection are then conveyed to a drop rack to await manual handling.

The only manual handling or set-up required is with the stud welders and certain types of bending machines. This involves changing of the dies and cleaning of feeder systems. Tool and die changes have been made more efficient by locating tooling near machines, staging in the order needed and by eliminating the need to bolt dies in place.

The CIM control system is the heart of the Tube Shop automation. It integrates the information flow within the shop. The control system has an internal model of the shop floor with its machines, queues, material, tooling, consumables and personnel. In addition, it has a list of the work performed, work currently underway and completed work. The control system is responsible for downloading all the information required to process tubes to each machine's computer-numerical control (CNC) system. It ties together all the information for a given work order, from staging of the raw material through to completion of all manufacturing processes and inspection. Each order is tracked in real-time with the use of the advanced bar-coding system described above, which provides critical monitoring and control information, and detects costly errors before they impact product integrity or scheduled shipments. All individual machine control systems serve as shop-floor data collectors and upload information on an order's status to the Tube Shop supervisory controller. Factory Link, the systems application software, is used to manage shop-floor activities for each manufacturing order.

The Tube Shop utilises an IBM manufacturing resource planning system (MAPICS II), a computer-based resource planning and control system, which generates bills of materials, process routings, order quantities and required shipping dates from customer order information entered into East River's mainframe. As part of the CIM investment, the archaic and inefficient manual scheduling system was discarded and a computerised production floor scheduler, known as FACTOR, was integrated into the computer-integrated manufacturing system. FACTOR creates a detailed shop-floor schedule. Both the CIM control system and FACTOR feed information into the higher-level MAPICS II system. Orders are produced on a priority basis. Tubes are run in batches of ten to facilitate any emergency orders that must be immediately interjected into the process. Bar coding is an integral part of the computer-controlled process, providing not only routing and processing instructions, but also allowing other systems, including accounting, to capture real-time data on an order's status as it moves through the Tube Shop. In this way, timely, reliable and inexpensive analyses can be performed and feedback provided.

The production schedule developed by FACTOR, plus the engineering design requirements from the tube detail file and loose tube fabrication program are transferred to the CIM control/integration system where Factory Link manages an order through the factory. The control system should keep material flowing through the Tube Shop in as close to an optimum manner as possible, and consistent with meeting production schedule and cost objectives. Scheduling is accomplished in five to ten minutes – enough time to allow inquiries and subsequent rescheduling. Examples of inquiries include: the effect of adding overtime or a second shift; the result of adding a high priority order; or the result of totally dedicating a particular machine to one large order until it is completed. Output will include, not only the schedule impact of these changes, but also the cost implications. Exhibit H.1 provides an outline of the sequence of high-level activities from proposal preparation to contract completion and shipment.

Electronic Data Interchange (EDI) is utilised to provide a paperless data flow through all operations. 'These high-tech computer systems virtually eliminate the need for paperwork within the Tube Shop,' noted Kitchen. 'They also give us better control. They allow us to predict the impact of rush orders and plan them through without having to put buffers in [the schedule]. They let us run the business better and smarter,' he said.

The Tube Shop was restructured to provide for two modes of operation in the processing of loose tubes. The first mode is the CIM line which processes the loose tubes required for repair and replacement parts, and the fabricated tubes needed as component parts of other assemblies completed at East River. The second mode is a smaller manually operated line that can accommodate unique configurations which cannot be processed on the automated line. Exhibit H.2 shows the Tube Shop layout, including the CIM and manual lines, together with headcount and number of machines in the shop.

To make the transition successful, management had to have the acceptance and participation of employees and their union – a cooperative effort between the state, the union and East River management, necessary for operating the sophisticated computer-controlled equipment in a particular area. The number of job classifications was reduced from 13 to three and workforce requirements were reduced by half. Workers no longer needed in the Tube Shop were reassigned to other parts of the plant.

With the change to self-managed teams and the introduction of automation to the tube line, John Phillips, manager of manufacturing accounting at PSI's Dallas, Texas headquarters, knew there would be even less assurance that the numbers coming out of the existing cost system would be reliable. A different cost system would be needed to accommodate the new process and more accurately measure the costs of activities on the manual line, if the cost system were to provide operating personnel with more reliable contract cost estimates and performance data. Plus Phillips was aware that the plant-wide assignment of overhead costs created cross-subsidies for un-profitable components. With automation, the labour-focused cost system would be all but irrelevant to bid proposals and project management. Phillips had the additional assurance of high-level support from Dan Stevens, President of PSI, who understood the need to change the cost-accounting system to accommodate the new manufacturing system, which resulted in extensive training to enhance computer and mathematics skills.

Activity-based costing project team

The make-up of the activity-based costing (ABC) team would prove to be critical to acceptance of the ABC system throughout its design and implementation phases. It was important that the ABC system be perceived as a system designed by operating personnel to improve decisions with respect to product design, the production process and marketing strategy. It would be a mistake if the ABC system was designed by accounting staff only. Therefore, the ABC project team would have a strong operational orientation and a good understanding of the new automated process.

The ABC team was chosen from members of the CIM implementation team and consisted of a mix of accounting, information systems, engineering, manufacturing and cost-estimating people, knowledgeable of East River's products and processes. For example, a cost estimator was part of the team, since it was crucial to be able to prepare cost estimates for a contract in the same way that accounting would accumulate costs for the contract. If a conflict arose, operational considerations took precedence over standard accounting practices. Prior to the actual start of system design, Phillips held an on-site seminar, which outlined the limitations of the labour-based system described in ABC systems, enumerated the objectives and information requirements for implementing ABC at East River and proposed an implementation plan.

At all times during the design phase, engineering, production and marketing personnel were kept informed of what the ABC team was doing. The team wanted to improve the chances that the ABC system would play an integral part in decisions affecting marketing strategy, product design and the production process. They were not about to let communication breakdowns undermine the credibility of the ABC system. If the channels of communication were kept open and the team could get users to buy in throughout the design and implementation stages, then the likelihood that ABC information would be viewed as essential to project management and future improvement initiatives would be greater. Throughout the CIM/ABC analysis, design and implementation, a major effort was made at cooperating with and satisfying those who would be using the output of the ABC system,

Activity-based costing design objectives

The goal of the ABC project was to design a system that could function as a management tool by providing timely and accurate measurements of which resources were used, how resources were used and how much it cost to use those resources. The ABC system would provide more accurate measures of resources consumed by each contract and could be used to 'drill down' to the component and part level for more detailed costing information. This would satisfy the concerns of marketing people and cost estimators for more reliable product/component information. But the intention was to make it more than just a better part or contract costing system. Phillips recognised that engineering and manufacturing personnel had little interest in product cost data. They were more interested in identifying the cost of various design alternatives and opportunities for cost reduction and permanent cost savings.

Specifically, the following objectives were expected from implementing ABC.

- Identify high-cost activities throughout the manufacturing process.

- Highlight those high cost activities whose cost could be reduced by:

    - reducing the need for an activity (e.g. reducing the number of moves); or

    - reducing the time to perform an activity and, therefore, increasing throughput.

- Identify the costs of low-value and waste activities and establish priorities for improvement or elimination.

- Use the activity reports as a basis for establishing ongoing cost reduction programmes in engineering, purchasing and manufacturing.

- Provide more accurate cost data to Dallas marketing/estimating personnel so they can quote projects with better, more reliable cost numbers.

- Build a file of historical data to load into a simulation model for scheduling and manpower forecasting.

- Expand the study to include plant support costs not included in this phase.

Ultimately, the usefulness of ABC information would be judged on its ability to provide reliable ex ante as well as accurate ex post information. ABC objectives were equally focused on achieving cost estimating, cost reduction and contract cost control goals by linking the ABC system to the automated collection of activity information. The new cost system was designed to place a premium on generating timely information. The CIM system made this possible. The intention was for the cost system to function in more than a scorekeeping or attention-directing capacity. The hope was that by integrating ABC into engineering and production systems, ABC would be flexible enough to be an integral part of product design and process-related decisions.

ABC direct and indirect costs

Because the cost system of the Tube Shop was so closely tied to that of the other four bays, where operations are still largely labour-intensive, Phillips decided not to expand the scope of the project to include East River's or Dallas's support services. Instead, the ABC team focused on the Tube Shop direct costs – labour, fringe benefits, set-up, repairs and maintenance, depreciation and supplies – plus support costs allocated from works – general (i.e. plant support services) and operating-all-works (i.e. central support services located in Dallas).

The contract is the primary cost object in a project management environment. The cost system charges materials directly to the contract and to the part. Product design engineering and drafting/graphics costs are also directly charged to contracts. Burden rates are based upon practical capacity. A material burden rate of 5 per cent of material cost covers the cost of the purchasing and material control costs.

Works include general overheads consisting of production control, maintenance, quality assurance, payroll, accounting and other support services charged to contracts at the rate of 40 per cent of labour cost. In addition, operating-all-works (OAW) costs associated with Dallas support services are charged at the rate of 15 per cent of labour cost. OAW consists of manufacturing engineering support and the resource allocation group, which plans and monitors plant loads, product mix and production volume. In total, the combined works – general and OAW – costs allocated to the Tube Shop amount to less than 30 per cent of the Tube Shop's direct costs.

The Tube Shop's direct costs can be clearly identified with one of 22 process-related cost pools associated with the automated line, the manual line and labour-intensive activities. Exhibit H.3 lists these 22 processes or operations and their associated cost drivers. A cost driver rate is determined for each activity cost pool and serves as the basis for charging contracts and components with the Tube Shop's direct and allocated costs. The Tube Shop costs and cost rates are provided in Exhibit H.4.

Computer simulation of major activities

The ABC project team used now-familiar interviewing techniques to gather activity-based costing information about the manual line. But interviewing was of limited use for organising cost pools and determining cost drivers for the new CIM process. The first step was to identify major activities at each workstation and work cell. Many of the activities performed in the Tube Shop – the human and technology-related resources that would ultimately perform the activities and the cost of these resources, particularly for the manual line – were well-known to operating personnel. For the CIM line, manufacturing engineers had carefully assessed the performance capabilities of the new equipment during the project's evaluation stage. With this information in hand, the ABC team consulted with the operations research group in the Fort Worth Research Division in order to determine the capacities of the major activities.

The research group ran an off-the-shelf computer simulation of the automated line which incorporated known constraints of the automated line, inputs required, outputs that would be generated and the constraints of each part. Utilising a typical 12-month product mix, engineering provided part geometry data – size of the tube, inside diameter, wall thickness, the number of bends, the type and number of studs applied and any other activities which would be performed on a particular tube.

The simulation was a computerised miniaturisation of the entire automated line. It clearly identified each machine, all conveyors connecting the different machines, any cascades where the tubes could be off-loaded, all manning requirements and other elements of the CIM line. As a tube progressed down the line, calling on the different resources needed according to the hypothetical production schedule and tube geometry, the simulation identified unanticipated bottlenecks where tubes started to build up and machines could not operate fast enough to meet the throughput target. For example, if set-up for a tube bender could require from one-half hour to four hours of set-up time, changing over from one set of dies to another set in order to make a different type bend, even in an automated line, would severely restrict the throughput on the line. That was unacceptable. Plus, it would be extremely costly to correct such a deficiency once the automated line was in place, since the equipment and transfer lines were so tightly wedded together. So, in addition to identifying major activities for the ABC study, the simulation provided information about where additional equipment was required before the CIM capital investment decision was finalised.

Information from the simulation was supplemented with information gathered from interviews of hourly people and supervisors to further identify their activities – what they did, how the process worked, some of the process drawbacks and constraints and an initial determination of the non-value-added and value-added activities involved in the Tube Shop operations. After several months, a complete list of activities and their appropriate cost drivers was developed.

The ABC team wanted to utilise the computer-integrated control system to supply all the data for the cost drivers, which would serve as surrogates for the activities previously identified. Each cost driver had to be measurable, readily available and easily understood. The information was going to be used as much for cost-management purposes (e.g. evaluating alternative routings) as it was for product design for manufacturability evaluations and component costing purposes. Therefore, fast communication to decision-makers was critical. If it wasn't in the control system, then it was eliminated from the list of potential cost drivers. Information from the computer simulation, the interviews and historical engineering data available in the control system was very helpful at this stage of the analysis.

Also, automated collection of activity data during production by means of the integrated shop-floor control system permits timely measurement of operating performance and signals operators when to intervene and make necessary corrections. Work cell schedulers automatically collect feedback on process activities (e.g. number of studs applied, number of bends made and other activity-related data) and compare this data with information generated by the computer-controlled production scheduler, which maintains data on each product's requirements. Accumulating actual cost driver data at cost driver rates allows shop supervisors to make frequent contract progress (cost-to-date) comparisons to evaluate how well the contract is progressing against promised delivery dates and as-sold cost estimates (the original bid prices accepted by customers). Any deviations are spotted almost immediately.

The ABC team tried to maximise the amount of the Tube Shop resource cost that could be identified with the major activities. Labour, fringe benefits, welding supplies, repairs and maintenance and depreciation became activity-cost pools. Traditional labour-based methods were used to charge a portion of cost allocated from the general plant overhead pool (works-general) and the OAW pool to the new activity-cost pools. A cost profile of the Tube Shop before and after implementation of the CIM is provided in Exhibit H.5. As anticipated, not only was the absolute dollar cost down significantly, but the mix of costs had changed drastically. The Tube Shop line headcount was reduced from 129 to 63, labour cost was cut in half from $5.5 million to $2.8 million and conversion cost decreased from $7.3 million to $5.2 million. While labour cost had been largely variable before modernisation, the demands of the CIM system required manning with relatively fixed teams of workers, regardless of output. Each operator was trained to perform a wider variety of activities than before, including interpreting engineering data and running multiple machines. Conversion costs were now relatively fixed.

How would the ABC system be used?

There were two overriding objectives in the design of the ABC system. First, ABC should provide a more accurate assignment of costs to contracts, components and parts. The combined benefits of lower costs attributable to the automated line and more reliable ABC cost estimates should result in more competitive bids and an increase in market share for the replacement parts business unit. Plus, they could be more confident that contracts accepted would result in a positive impact on the unit's P&L statement. Also, proposals lost could be analysed to determine where costs were not competitive.

In turn, cost estimators would need to develop cost estimates that emulated the new cost system. It was important that the cost estimators' job not be made more difficult. With an estimator on the ABC team, the team was able to continually review the new set of cost drivers and how activities were going to be costed. Exhibit H.6 provides comparative cost data for selected contracts. In most cases, ABC estimates of the cost to produce a job on the CIM line were significantly less than what it would have cost to manufacture on the old manual line.

The second, more difficult objective for ABC was to improve East River's ability to better manage the overall process from product design through to product delivery. That meant using ABC data to evaluate and select the best designs and processes. Engineers and operating personnel could see the potential for using activity management and activity costing to improve both the design process and the production process. In addition, through the CIM system, East River is extending the existing database of operational information so that it can be utilised to develop new evaluative capabilities and performance measures. By keeping ABC's design and operational uses foremost in mind, management hopes to create an environment where informed decision-making can be accomplished with confidence through the use ABC feedback.

Possible assignment questions

1. What was the competitive environment for power generation equipment in the early 1990s?

2. What factors led to the need for an ABC system?

3. What are the objectives of the plant's activity-based costing system?

4. Construct a diagram of the ABC system and explain how products are costed in a computer-integrated environment.

5. How were the cost drivers determined?

6. Nine of the ten different cost drivers refer to the number of times an activity or operation is performed. Only one of the ten cost drivers relates to processing or machine time. Discuss the advantages and disadvantages of selecting the quantity of a cost driver to assign costs as opposed to utilising the time used to perform an activity when assigning costs.

7. How has the computer-integrated manufacturing system made the Tube Shop more efficient?

8. Capacity utilisation remains stuck in the 45–50 per cent area. How does that affect product costs under the ABC system? Explain the conceptual basis for your answer.

9. What other areas of project design, marketing or manufacturing could be reviewed for continuous process improvement?

10. What role could the ABC system play in East River's continuous improvement efforts?

11. Evaluate the process of developing and implementing the ABC system? Why wasn't ABC implemented across the entire plant?

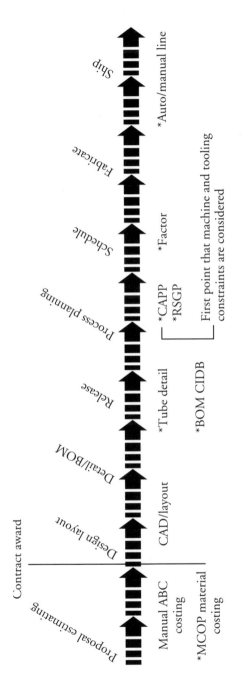

Exhibit H.1 East River plant (B) – proposal-to-shipment process.

Proposal estimating · Design layout · Detail/BOM · Release · Process planning · Schedule · Fabricate · Ship

Contract award

Manual ABC costing

*MCOP material costing

CAD/layout

*Tube detail

*BOM CIDB

*CAPP
*RSGP

First point that machine and tooling constraints are considered

*Factor

*Auto/manual line

Key

ABC	Activity-based costing
MCOP	Materials cost optimisation program
CAD	Computer-aided design
BOM	Bill of materials
CIDB	Contract and information database
CAPP	Computer-aided process planning
RSGP	Route sheet generation program

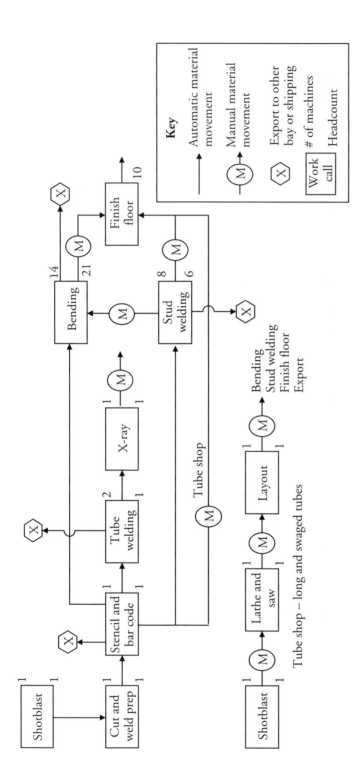

Exhibit H.2 East River plant (B) – Tube Shop manual line.

Activities and activity cost pools: automated line	Cost driver description
Retrieval	No. of lifts
Shotblast – auto	No. of linear feet
Mill B&O – auto	No. of end mills
(Weld prep and bar code)	
Layout – auto	No. of layout lines
Weld – STW – auto	No. of joints welded
Weld – auto pin	No. of studs
Weld – auto flat	No. of studs
CNC bend – auto & check	No. of bends

Activities and activity cost pools: manual line	Cost driver description
Shotblast – manual	No. of linear feet
Mill B&O – manual	No. of end mills
(Weld prep and bar code)	
Lathe – manual	No. of end mills
Saw in shop manual	No. of cuts
Layout – manual	No. of lines
Tube Weld – STW – manual	No. of joints welded
Weld – manual stud	No. of studs
Bend – press	No. of bends
Bend – #2 pines	No. of bends
Bend – #4 pines	No. of bends
Bend – conventional	No. of bends
Swage	No. of reductions

Non-machine activities and activity cost pools: labour driven operations	Cost driver description
Bend – hot	No. of bends
Tube finish	Minutes
Hand operated	

Exhibit H.3 East River Plant (B) – Bay 7 manufacturing – major activities and cost drivers.

Activities and activity cost pools: automated line	Cost driver description	Budgeted annual cost driver	Bay 7 Direct cost of activity	Bay 7 Direct cost per activity	Wks gen allocated cost	Wks gen cost per activity	OAW allocated cost	OAW cost per driver
Retrieval	No. of lifts	28,080	$127,200	$4.530	$0	$0	$0	$0
Shotblast – auto	No. of linear feet	4,193,280	177,500	$0.042	16,200	$0.004	$6,100	$0.001
Mill B&O – auto	No. of end mills	149,760	318,600	$2.127	16,200	$0.108	$6,100	$0.041
(Weld prep and bar code)								
Layout – auto	No. of layout lines	1,198,080	184,300	$0.154	16,200	$0.014	$6,100	$0.005
Weld – STW – auto	No. of joints welded	88,750	402,600	$4.536	48,600	$0.548	$18,200	$0.205
Weld – auto pin	No. of studs	590,400	312,100	$0.052	48,600	$0.008	$18,200	$0.003
Weld – auto flat	No. of studs	5,990,400	312,00	$0.052	48,600	$0.008	$18,200	$0.003
CNC bend – auto and check	No. of bends	59,900	306,600	$5.119	48,600	$0.811	$18,200	$0.304
Activities and activity cost pools: manual line			2,141,000		$243,000		$91,100	
Shotblast – manual	No. of linear feet	1,048,320	100,300	$0.096	24,300	$0.023	$9,100	$0.009
Mill B&O – manual	No. of end mills	68,380	97,800	$1.430	24,300	$0.355	$9,100	$0.133
(Weld prep and bar code)								
Lathe – manual	No. of end mills	12,780	41,900	$3.279	12,200	$0.955	$4,600	$0.360
Saw in shop – manual	No. of cuts	11,810	48,300	$4.090	12,200	$1.033	$4,600	$0.390
Layout – manual	No. of lines	427,890	98,000	$0.229	24,300	$0.057	$9,100	$0.021
Tube weld – STW – manual	No. of joints welded	11,070	180,900	$9.837	24,300	$2.195	$9,100	$0.822
Weld – manual stud	No. of studs	3,010,180	215,200	$0.071	48,600	$0.016	$18,200	$0.006
Bend – press	No. of bends	14,530	152,800	$10.516	48,600	$3.345	$18,200	$1.253
Bend – #2 pines	No. of bends	40,860	372,500	$9.116	145,800	$3.568	$54,700	$1.339
Bend – #4 pines	No. of bends	57,410	480,300	$8.366	194,400	$3.386	$72,900	$1.270
Bend – conventional	No. of bends	14,190	251,700	$17.738	72,900	$5.137	$27,300	$1.924
Swage	No. of reductions	93,100	160,500	$1.722	24,300	$0.261	$9,100	$0.098
Non-machine activities and activity cost pools: labour driven operations								
Bend – hot	No. of bends	4,860	$56,400	$11.605	$18,200	$3.745	$6,800	$1.399
Tube finish	Minutes	1,573,730	836,500	$0.532	249,100	$0.158	$93,400	$0.059
Hand operated			$892,900		$267,300		$100,200	
Total			$5,162,200		$1,166,500		$437,300	

Exhibit H.4 East River Plant (B) – Bay 7 manufacturing – major activities and cost drivers – FY94 costing rates.

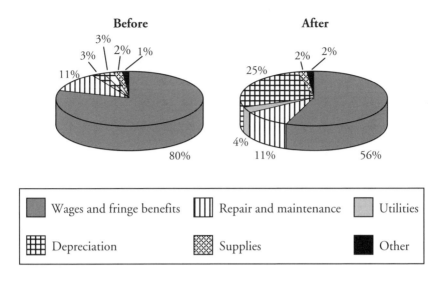

Before

3%
3%
2% 1%
11%
80%

After

25%
2% 2%
4%
11%
56%

▨ Wages and fringe benefits	▥ Repair and maintenance	▨ Utilities
▦ Depreciation	▨ Supplies	■ Other

Exhibit H.5 East River Plant (B) – tube shop expense profile.

Customer	Contract	ABC estimate	Actual cost	VAR	Labour-based estimate	Actual cost	VAR
Amer Paper Products	100-112345	$742	$999	($257)	$1,680	$999	$681
Amer Paper Products	100-112298	58	36	22	490	36	454
Midwest Electric	200-163113	271	234	37	471	234	237
American Power	100-177819	572	402	170	560	402	158
General Pulp	200-243654	802	665	137	1,120	665	455
Pittsburgh Steel	100-211105	12,569	11,852	717	16,520	11,852	4,668
TOTAL		$15,014	$14,188	$826	$20,841	$14,188	$6,653

Exhibit H.6 East River Plant (B) – Bay 7 automated line – conversion cost estimate comparison on selected contracts.

CASE STUDY I

Precision System, Inc.

(Quality costing)

(Suresh S. Kalagnanam and Ella Mae Matsumura prepared this case. Copyright © 1998 by Institute of Management Accountants, Montvale, NJ. Reproduced with permission.)

Precision System, Inc. (PSI) has been in business for more than 25 years and has generally reported a positive net income. The company manufactures and sells high-technology instruments (systems). Each product line at PSI has only a handful of standard products, but configuration changes and add-ons can be accommodated as long as they are not radically different from the standard system.

Faced with rising competition and increasing customer demand for quality, PSI adopted total quality management (TQM) in 1998. Many employees received training and several quality initiatives were launched. Like most businesses, PSI concentrated on improvement in the manufacturing function and achieved significant improvement. However, little was done in departments.

In early 1992, PSI decided to extend TQM to its order entry department, which handles the critical functions of preparing quotes for potential customers and orders. Order processing is the first process in the chain of operation after the order is received from a customer. High-quality output from the order entry department improves quality later in the process and allows PSI to deliver higher quality systems both faster and cheaper, thus meeting the goals of timely delivery and lower cost.

As a first step, PSI commissioned a cost of quality (COQ) study in its order entry department. The study had two objectives:

- to develop a system for identifying order entry errors;

- to determine how much an order entry error costs.

PSI's order entry department

PSI's domestic order entry department is responsible for preparing quotations for potential customers and taking actual sales orders. PSI's sales representatives forward requests for the order entry department, though actual orders for systems are received directly from customers. Orders for parts are also received directly from customers. Service-related orders (for parts or repairs), however, are generally placed by service representatives. When PSI undertook the QOC study, the order entry department consisted of nine employees and two supervisors, who reported to the order entry manager. Three of the nine employees dealt exclusively with taking parts orders, while the other six were responsible for system orders. Before August 1992, the other six were split equally into two groups: one was responsible for preparing quotations and the other was responsible for taking orders.

The final outputs of the order entry department are the quote and the order acknowledgement or 'green sheet'. The manufacturing department and the stockroom use the green sheet for the further processing of orders.

The order entry department's major suppliers are: (1) sales or service representatives; (2) the final customers who provided them with the basic information to process further; and (3) technical information and marketing departments, which provide configuration guides, price masters and similar documents (some in printed form and some online) as supplementary information. Sometimes there are discrepancies in the information available to order entry staff and sales and representatives with respect to price, part number or configuration. These descriptions often cause communication gaps between the order entry staff, sales representatives and manufacturing.

An order entry staff member provided the following example of lack of communication between sales representatives and manufacturing with respect to one order:

> If the sales reps have spoken to the customer and determined that our standard configuration is not what they require, they may leave a part of the order. [In one such instance] I got a call from manufacturing saying when this system is configured like this, it must have this part added. It is basically a no-charge part and so I added it (charge order # 1) and called the sales rep and said to him, 'manufacturing told me to add it'. The sales representative called back and said, 'No, the customer doesn't need that part; they are going to be using another option…so they don't need this'. Then I did another change-order (#2) to take it off because the sales rep said they don't need it. Then manufacturing called me back and said, 'we really need [to add that part] (change order #3). If the sales rep does not want it, then we will have to do an engineering special and it is going to be another 45 days lead time.' So, the sales rep and manufacturing not having direct communication required me to do three change-orders on that order; two of them were probably unnecessary.

A typical sequence of events might begin with a sales representative meeting with a customer to discuss the type of system desired. The sales representative then fills out a form and faxes it or phones it in to an order entry employee, who might make several subsequent phone calls to the sales representative, the potential customer, or the manufacturing department to prepare the quote properly. These phone calls deal with such questions as exchangeability for parts, part numbers, current prices for parts or allowable sales discount. Order entry staff then key in the configuration of the desired system including part numbers and inform the sales representatives of the quoted price. Each quote is assigned a quotation number. To smooth production, manufacturing often produce systems with standard configurations for obtaining orders from recent quotes. The systems usually involve adding on special features to the standard configuration. Production in advance of orders sometimes results in duplication in manufacturing. However, because customers often fail to put their quotation number on their orders, when order entry receive an order, the information on the order is re-entered into the computer to produce an order acknowledgement. When the order acknowledgement is sent to the invoicing department, the information is received again to generate an invoice to send to the customer.

Many departments in PSI use information directly from the order entry department (these are the internal customers of order entry), because the user included manufacturing, service (repair), stockroom, invoicing and sales administration. The sales administration department prepares commission payment and tracks performance. The shipping, customer support (technical support) and collections department (also internal customers) indirectly use order entry information. After a system is shipped, related paperwork is sent to customer support to maintain a service-installed database in anticipation of technical support questions that may arise. Customer support is also responsible for installation of systems. A good acknowledgement (i.e. one with no errors of any kind) can greatly reduce errors downstream within the process and prevent later non-value-added costs.

Cost of quality

Quality costs arise because poor quality may – or does – exist. For PSI's order entry department, poor quality non-conforming 'products' refer to poor information for further processing of an order or quotation (see Exhibit I.1 for examples). Costs of poor quality here pertain to the time spent by order entry staff and concerned employees in other departments (providers of information such as sales or technical information) to rectify the errors.

Class I failures

Class I failure costs are incurred when non-conforming products (incorrect quotes or orders) are identified as non-conforming before they leave the order entry department. The incorrect quotes or order may be identified by the order entry staff or supervisor during inspection of the document. An important cause of class I failures is lack of communication. Sample data collected from the order entry staff show that they encountered more then 10 types of problems during order processing (see Exhibit I.1 for examples). Analysis of the sample data suggests that, on average, it takes 2.3 hours (including waiting time) to rectify errors on quotes and 2.7 working days for correction on orders. In determining costs the COQ study accounted only for the time it actually takes to solve the problem (i.e. excluding waiting time). Waiting time was excluded because employees use this time to perform other activities or work on other orders. The total class I failure costs, which include only salary and fringe benefits for the time it takes to correct errors, amount to more then 4 per cent of order entry's annual budget for salaries and fringe benefits (see Exhibit I.2).

Class II failures

Class II failures are incurred when non-conforming materials are transferred out of the order entry department. For PSI's order entry department, 'non-conforming' refers to an incorrect order acknowledgement as specified by its users within PSI. The impact of order entry errors on the final (external) customer is low because order acknowledgements are inspected in several departments. So most errors are corrected before the invoice (which contains some information available on the order acknowledgement) is sent to the final customer. Correction of the order entry errors does not guarantee that the customer received a good quality system, but order entry's initial errors do not then affect the final customer. Mistakes that affect the final customer can be made by employees in other departments (e.g. manufacturing or shipping).

Sample data collected from PSI's users of order entry department information show that more than 20 types of error can be found on the order acknowledgement (see Exhibit I.1 for examples). The cost of correcting these errors (salary and fringe benefits of order entry person and a concerned person from another PSI department) accounts for approximately 7 per cent for order entry's annual budget for salaries and fringe benefits (see Exhibit I.2).

In addition to the spend on correcting the errors, the order entry staff must prepare a change order for several of the class II failures. Moreover, a change order is required for several other reasons not necessarily controllable by order entry. Examples include: (1) changes in ship-to or bill-to address customers or sales representatives; (2) cancelled orders; and (3) changes in invoicing instructions. Regardless of the reason for the change order, the order entry department incurs cost. The sample data suggests that for every 100 new orders, order entry prepares 71 change orders; this activity accounts for 2.6 per cent of order entry's annual budget for salaries and fringe benefits (see Exhibit I.2)

The order entry staff also spend considerable time handling return authorisations when final customers send their shipment back to PSI. Interestingly, more than 17 per cent of the goods are returned because of defective shipments, and more than 49 per cent fall into the following categories: (1) ordered in error; and (2) 30-day return rights. An in-depth analysis of the letter categories suggest that the majority of returns can be tracked to sales or service errors. The order entry department incurs costs to process these return authorisations, which account for more than 1.9 per cent of the annual budget (see Exhibit I.2). The total class I and class II failure costs account for 15.7 per cent of the order entry department's annual budget for salary and fringe benefits. Although PSI users of order entry information were aware that problems in their departments were sometimes caused by errors in order entry, they provided little feedback to order entry about the existence or impact of the errors.

Changes in PSI's order entry department

In October 1992, preliminary results were presented to three key persons who had initiated the study: the order entry manager, the vice president of manufacturing and vice president of service and quality. In March 1993, the final result was presented to PSI's executive council, the top decision-making body. Between October 1992 and March 1993, PSI began working toward obtaining the International Organisation for Standardisation's ISO 9002 registration for order entry and manufacturing practices, which it received in June 1993.

The effort to obtain the ISO 9002 registration suggests that PSI gave considerable importance to order entry and invested significant effort towards improving the order entry process. Nevertheless, as stated by the order entry manager, the change would not have been so vigorously pursued if cost information had not been presented. COQ information functioned as a catalyst to accelerate the improvement effort. In actually making changes to the process, however, information pertaining to the different types of errors was more useful than the cost information.

Required questions

1. Describe the role that assigning costs to order entry errors played in quality improvement efforts at Precision Systems, Inc.

2. Prepare a diagram illustrating the flow of activities between the order entry department and its suppliers, internal customers (those within PSI) and external customers (those external to PSI).

3. Classify the failure items in Exhibit I.1 into internal failures (identified as defective delivery to internal or external customers) and external failures (non-conforming 'products' delivered to internal or external customers) with respect to the order entry department. For each external failure item, identify which of order entry's internal customers (i.e. other departments within PSI that use information from the order acknowledgement) will be affected.

4. For the order entry process, how would you identify internal failure and external failure? Who would be involved in documenting these failures and their associated costs? Which individuals or departments should be involved in making improvements to the order entry process?

5. What costs, in addition to salary and fringe benefits, would you include in computing the costs of correcting errors?

6. Provide examples of incremental and breakthrough improvements that could be made in the order entry process. In particular, identify prevention activities that can be undertaken to reduce the number of errors. Describe how you would prioritise your suggestions for improvement.

7. What non-financial quality indicators might be useful for the order entry department? How frequently should data be collected or information be reported? Can you make a statement about the usefulness of cost of quality information in comparison to non-financial indicators of quality?

1.	Incomplete information on purchase order.
2.	Transposition of prices on purchase order.
3.	More than one part number on order acknowledgement when only one is required.
4.	Incorrect business units code (used for tracking product line profitability) on the order acknowledgement.
5.	Freight terms missing on the purchase order.
6.	Incorrect part number on order acknowledgement.
7.	Incorrect shipping or billing address on order acknowledgement.
8.	Credit approval missing (all new customers have accredit approval before an order is processed).
9.	Missing part number on order acknowledgement.
10.	Customer number terminated on the computer (an order cannot be processed if number is missing).
11.	Incorrect sales tax calculation on the order acknowledgement.
12.	Part number mismatch on purchase order.

Exhibit I.1 Examples of failures.

	Order entry	**Other department**	**Total cost**
Class I failure costs			
Quotations	1.1%	0.4%	1.5%
Orders	0.9%	1.7%	2.6%
Total class failure	2.0%	2.1%	4.1%
Class II failure costs			
Order acknowledgement	2.6%	4.4%	7.0%
Change order	2.6%	–	2.6%
Final customer	0.02%	0.1%	0.1%
Return authorisation	1.9%	–	1.9%
Total class II failure	7.12%	4.5%	11.6%
Total failure costs	9.1%	6.6%	15.7%

Exhibit I.2 Estimated annual failure costs (as a percentage of order entry's annual salary and fringe benefits budget).

References

Abdel-Khalik, A.R. and Lusk, E.J. (1974) 'Transfer pricing – a synthesis', *Accounting Review*, vol. 49, no. 1, pp. 8–23.

Abernethy, M.A. and Guthrie, C.H. (1994) 'An empirical assessment of the "fit" between strategy and management information system design', *Accounting and Finance*, November, pp. 49–66.

Albright, T.L. and Roth, H. (1992) 'The measurement of quality costs: an alternative paradigm', *Accounting Horizons*, June, pp. 15–27.

Amey, L.R. (1979) *Budgeting Planning and Control Systems*. London: Pitman.

Anandarajan, A. and Christopher, M.G. (1986) 'A mission approach to customer profitability analysis', *International Journal of Physical Distribution and Material Management*, vol. 17, no. 7, pp. 55–68.

Anderson, S.W. (1995) 'A framework for assessing cost management system changes: the case of activity-based costing implementation at General Motors, 1986–993', *Journal of Management Accounting Research*, vol. 7, pp. 1–51.

Ansari, S.L. (1977) 'An integrated approach to control systems design', *Accounting, Organisations and Society*, vol. 2, pp. 101–12.

Anthony, R.N. (1965a) *Management Control – Text and Cases*. Homewood, IL: Richard D. Irwin.

Anthony, R.N. (1965b) *Planning and Control Systems: A Framework for Analysis*. Boston, MA: Graduate School of Business Administration, Harvard University.

Anthony, R.N., Dearden, J. and Vancil, R.F. (1965) *Management Control Systems: Cases and Readings*. Homewood, IL: Richard D. Irwin.

Argyris, C. and Kaplan, R.S. (1994) 'Implementing new knowledge: the case of activity-based costing', *Accounting Horizons*, vol. 8, no. 3, pp. 83–105.

Ashby, W.R. (1956) *An Introduction to Cybernetics*. London: Chapman & Hall.

Atkinson, A.A., Balakrisnan, R., Booth, P., Cote, J.M., Groot, T., Malmi, T., Roberts, H., Uliana, E. and Wu, A. (1997) 'New directions in management accounting research', *Journal of Management Accounting Research*, vol. 9, pp. 80–108.

Baddon, L., Hunter, L., Hyman, J. Leopold, J. and Ramsay, H. (1989) *People's Capitalism*. London: Routledge.

Banker, R., Potter, G. and Srinivasan, D. (2000) 'An empirical investigation of an incentive plan that includes nonfinancial performance measures', *Accounting Review*, vol. 75, no. 1, pp. 65–92.

Bell, W.D. and Hansen, C.G. (1987) *Profit Sharing and Profitability*. London: Kogan Page.

Bendell, T., Boulter, L. and Goodstadt, P. (1998) *Benchmarking for Competitive Advantage*. London: FT Pitman Publishing.

Berry, A.J., Capps, T., Cooper, D., Ferguson, P., Hopper, T.M. and Lowe, E.A. (1985) 'Management control in an area of the NCB: rationales of accounting practices in a public enterprise', *Accounting, Organisations and Society*, vol. 10, no. 1, pp. 3–28.

Besterfield, D.H. (1986) *Quality Control*. Englewood Cliffs, NJ: Prentice-Hall International.

Birnberg, J.G. and Snodgrass, C. (1988) 'Culture and control: a field study', *Accounting, Organisations and Society*, vol. 13, no. 5, pp. 447–64.

Blackburn, J.D. (1988) 'Trends in manufacturing', in Capettini, R. and Clancy, D.K. (eds) *Cost Accounting, Robotics and the New Manufacturing Environment*. Sarasota, FL: American Accounting Association.

Borkowski, S.C. (1990) 'Environmental and organizational factors affecting transfer pricing: a survey', *Journal of Management Accounting Research*, vol. 2, pp. 78–99.

Brinker, B.J. (ed.) (1995) *Handbook of Cost Management*. New York: Warren Gorham Lamont.

Broadbent, J. and Guthrie, J. (1992) 'Changes in public sector: a review of recent "alternative" accounting research', *Accounting, Auditing and Accountability Journal*, vol. 5, no.2, pp. 3–31.

Bromwich, M. (1990) 'The case for strategic management accounting: the role of accounting information for strategy in competitive markets', *Accounting, Organisations and Society*, vol. 15, nos. 1 and 2, pp. 27–45.

Brownell, P. (1985) 'Budgetary systems and the control of functionally differentiated organizational activities', *Journal of Accounting Research*, Autumn, pp. 502–12.

Burns, T. and Stalker, G.M. (1961) *The Management of Innovation*. London: Tavistock.

Burstein, M. (1988) 'Life-cycle costing', in NAA, *Cost Accounting for the '90s*. Montvale, NJ: National Association of Accountants, pp. 257–72.

Carnall, C.A. (1990) *Managing Change in Organisations*. Englewood Cliffs, NJ: Prentice Hall International.

Chandler, A.D. (1962) *Strategy and Structure*, Cambridge, MA: MIT Press.

Chapman, C.S. (1997) 'Reflections on a contingent view of accounting', *Accounting, Organisations and Society*, vol. 22, no. 2, pp. 189–205.

Chenhall, R.H. (1997) 'Reliance on manufacturing performance measures, total quality management and organisational performance', *Management Accounting Research*, vol. 8, pp. 187–206.

Chenhall, R.H. and Langfield-Smith, K. (1998) 'The relationship between strategic priorities, management techniques and management accounting: an empirical investigation using a systems approach', *Accounting, Organisations and Society*, vol. 23, no. 3, pp. 243–64.

Chenhall, R.H. and Morris, D. (1986) 'The impact of structure, environment, and interdependence on the perceived usefulness of management accounting systems', *Accounting Review*, vol. 61, January, pp. 16–35.

Chua, W.F. (1989) 'Interpretive sociology and management accounting review', *Accounting, Auditing and Accountability Journal*, vol. 1, no. 2, pp. 59–79.

Cobb, I. (1993) *JIT and the Management Accountant – A Study of Current UK Practice*. London: Chartered Institute of Management Accountants.

Codling, S. (1996) *Best Practice Benchmarking – An International Perspective*. Houston, TX: Gulf Publishing.

Coombs, H.M. and Jenkins, D.E. (1995) *Public Sector Financial Management*. London: Chapman & Hall.

Cooper, D.J. and Sherer, M.J. (1984) 'The value of accounting reports: arguments for a political economy of accounting', *Accounting, Organisations and Society*, vol. 9, no. 3/4, pp. 207–32.

Cooper, R. (1989) 'The rise of activity-based costing – part 4: what do activity-based costing systems look like?', *Journal of Cost Management*, Spring, pp. 41–2.

Cooper, R. (1990) 'ABC: a need, not an option', *Accountancy*, September, pp. 86–8.

Cooper, R. (1995a) *When Lean Enterprises Collide: Competing through Confrontation*. Boston, MA: Harvard Business School Press.

Cooper, R. (1995b) 'Activity-based costing for improved product costing', in Brinker, B.J. (ed.), *Handbook of Cost Management*. New York: Warren Gorham Lamont, B1-1–B1-33.

Cooper, R. (1996) 'Activity-based costing and the lean enterprise', *Journal of Cost Management*, Winter, pp. 6–14.

Cooper, R. and Kaplan, R.S. (1988) 'How cost accounting distorts product cost', *Management Accounting* (USA), April, pp. 34–40.

Cooper, R. and Kaplan, R.S. (1991) *The Design of Cost Management Systems*. Englewood Cliffs, NJ: Prentice Hall.

Cooper, R. and Kaplan, R.S. (1992) 'Activity-based systems: measuring the costs of resource usage', *Accounting Horizons*, September, pp. 1–13.

Costello, S.J. (1994) *Managing Change in the Workplace*. Homewood, IL: Irwin Professional Publishing.

Cummings, T.G. and Worley, C.G. (1997) *Organisational Development and Change*. Cincinnati, OH: South-Western College Publishing.

Cyert, R.M. and March, J.G. (1963) *A Behavioral Theory of the Firm*. Englewood Cliffs, NJ: Prentice Hall.

Daft, R.L. (1992) *Organisation Theory and Design*, 4th edn. St Paul, IN: West.

Dewe, P., Dunn, S. and Richardson, R. (1988) 'Employee share option schemes: why workers are attracted to them', *British Journal of Industrial Relations*, vol. 26, no. 1, pp. 1–21.

Digman, L.A. (1999) *Strategic Management: Concepts, Processes, Decisions*. Houston, TX: Dame Publications.

Dorhan, W.M. and O'Connor, K. (1998) 'Competitor analysis can give your association the edge', *Association Management*, vol. 50, no. 1, pp. 103–6.

Drury, C. (1992) *Cost and Management Accounting*, 3rd edn. London: Chapman & Hall.

Duncan, R.B. (1972) 'Characteristics of organizational environment and perceived environmental uncertainty', *Administrative Science Quarterly*, vol. 17, pp. 313–27.

Eccles, R.G. (1985) *The Transfer Pricing Problem*. Lexington, MA: Lexington Books.

Emmanuel, C., Otley, D.T. and Merchant, K. (1990) *Accounting for Management Control*, 2nd edn. London: Chapman & Hall.

Ezzamel, M. (1991) 'Transfer pricing', in Ashton, D., Hopper, T. and Scapens, R.W. (eds), *Issues in Management Accounting*. London: Prentice Hall International, pp. 61–81.

Ezzamel, M. (1994) 'From problem solving to problematization, relevance revisited', *Critical Perspectives on Accounting*, vol. 5, pp. 269–80.

Feldman, M.S. and March, J.G. (1981) 'Information as a signal and symbol', *Administrative Science Quarterly*, vol. 26, pp. 171–86.

Flavel, R. and Williams, J. (1996) *Strategic Management: A Practical Approach*. London: Prentice-Hall International.

Foster, G. and Swenson, D.W. (1997) 'Measuring the success of activity-based cost management and its determinants', *Journal of Management Accounting Research*, vol. 9, pp. 109–42.

Foster, G., Gupta, M. and Sjoblom, L. (1996) 'Customer profitability analysis: challenges and new directions', *Journal of Cost Management*, Spring, pp. 5–17.

Fox, A. (1985) *Man Management*, 2nd edn. London: Hutchinson.

Francis, D. (1994) *Step by Step Competitive Strategy*. London: Routledge.

Funnell, W. and Cooper, K. (1998) *Public Sector Accounting and Accountability in Australia*. Sydney: University of New South Wales Press.

Galbraith, J.R. (1977) *Organization Design*. Reading, MA: Addison-Wesley.

George, G. (1983) 'Financial reporting to employees', *Accounting Forum*, September, pp. 17–25.

Gilmour, P. and Hunt, R.A. (1995) *Total Quality Management: Integrating Quality into Design, Operations and Strategy*. Melbourne: Longman.

Goldman, S.L., Nagel, R.N. and Preiss, K. (1995) *Agile Competitors and Virtual Organizations*. New York: Van Nostrand Reinhold.

Gordon, L.A. (1998) *Managerial Accounting – Concepts and Empirical Evidence*. New York: Primis Custom Publishing.

Gordon, L.A. and Naryanan, V.K. (1984) 'Management accounting systems, perceived environmental uncertainty and organizational structure: an empirical investigation', *Accounting, Organisations and Society*, vol. 19, no. 1, pp. 330–48.

Gosse, D. (1993) 'Cost accounting's role in computer-integrated-manufacturing: an empirical field study', *Journal of Management Accounting Research*, vol. 5, pp. 43–77.

Govindarajan, V. (1984) 'Appropriateness of accounting data in performance evaluation: an empirical examination of environmental uncertainty as an intervening variable', *Accounting, Organisations and Society*, vol. 9, no. 2, pp. 125–35.

Govindarajan, V. and Gupta, A.K. (1985) 'Linking control systems to business unit strategy: impact on performance', *Accounting, Organisations and Society*, vol. 10, no. 1, pp. 51–66.

Govindarajan, V. and Shank, J.K. (1992) 'Strategic cost management: tailoring controls to strategies', *Journal of Cost Management*, vol. 6, no. 3, pp. 14–25.

Greenberg, J. (1996) *Managing Behaviour in Organisations*. Upper Saddle River, NJ: Prentice Hall.

Guilding, C. (1999) 'Competitor-focused accounting: an exploratory note', *Accounting, Organisations and Society*, vol. 24, pp. 583–95.

Guilding, C. (2000) 'An international comparison of strategic management accounting practices', *Management Accounting Research*, vol. 11, pp. 113–35.

Guilding, C., Kennedy, D.J. and McManus, L. (2001) 'Extending the boundaries of customer accounting: applications in the hotel industry', *Journal of Hospitality and Tourism Research*, vol. 25, no. 2, pp. 173–94.

Guthrie, J. (1995) *Trends and Contradictions in Public Sector Financial Management Developments in Australia and Britain*, Recent Public Sector

Financial Management Developments Conference, 5th CIGAR Conference, Paris, 4–5 May.

Guthrie, J. (1999) 'A critique of the application of accrual accounting to the public sector', in Clark, C. and Corbett, D. (eds), *Reforming the Public Sector: Problems and Solutions*. Sydney, NSW: Allen & Unwin.

Hamel, G. and Prahalad, C.K. (1994) *Competing for the Future*. Boston, MA: Harvard Business School Press.

Hansen, D.R. and Mowen, M.M. (1997) *Management Accounting*, 4th edn. Cincinnati, OH: South-Western College Publishing.

Hansen, T.A and Riis, J.O. (1996) 'Developing performance networks to improve the benchmarking process – action research for productivity improvement', in Rolstadas, A. (ed.), *Benchmarking – Theory and Practice*. London: Chapman & Hall.

Heagy, C.D. (1991) 'Determining optimal quality costs by considering cost of lost sales', *Journal of Cost Management for the Manufacturing Industry*, Fall, p. 67.

Healy, P.M. (1985) 'The effect of bonus schemes on accounting decisions', *Journal of Accounting and Economics*, vol. 7, pp. 85–107.

Hirst, M.K. (1983) 'Reliance on accounting performance measures, task uncertainty, and dysfunctional behavior: some extensions', *Journal of Accounting Research*, Autumn, pp. 596–605.

Hofstede, G. (1981) 'Management control of public and not-for-profit activities', *Accounting, Organisations and Society*, vol. 6, no. 3, pp. 193–216.

Hood, C. (1995) 'The "new public management" in the 1980s: variations on a theme', *Accounting, Organisations and Society*, vol. 20, no. 2/3, pp. 93–109.

Hopper, T. (1997) *Cost Accounting in Small and Medium Sized Japanese Companies*. Paper presented at the British Accounting Association Conference, Birmingham, March.

Hopper, T. and Kato, Y. (1995) Editorial: 'Japanese management accounting', *Management Accounting Research*, vol. 6, pp. 307–12.

Hopper, T.M. and Powell, A. (1985) 'Making sense of research into organizational and social aspects of management accounting: a review of its underlying assumptions', *Journal of Management Studies*, vol. 22, no. 5, pp. 429–36.

Hoque, Z. (2000a) 'Just-in-time production, automation, cost allocation practices and importance of cost information: an empirical investigation in New Zealand-based manufacturing organizations', *British Accounting Review*, vol. 32, pp. 133–59.

Hoque, Z. (2000b) 'Matching productivity measures with business mission and uncertainty', *Advances in Management Accounting*, vol. 9, pp. 109–25.

Hoque, Z. (2001) 'Strategic management accounting in the value chain framework: a case study', *Journal of Cost Management*, vol. 15, no. 2, March/April, pp. 21–7.

Hoque, Z. and Alam, M. (1999) 'TQM adoption, institutionalism and changes in management accounting systems: a case study', *Accounting and Business Research*, vol. 29, no. 3, Summer, pp. 199–210.

Hoque, Z. and James, W. (2000) 'Linking balanced scorecard with size and market factors: impact on organisational performance', *Journal of Management Accounting Research*, vol. 12, pp. 1–17.

Hoque, Z. and Mia, L. (2001) *Management Information Needs within the New Public Management Context: Findings from an Australian Local Government Entity*, Working Paper. Griffith University School of Accounting and Finance, Gold Coast, Australia.

Hoque, Z., Lokman, M. and Alam, M. (2001) 'Market competition, computer-aided manufacturing and use of multiple performance measures: an empirical study', *British Accounting Review*, vol. 33, no. 1, March, pp. 23–46.

Horngren, C.T. (1977) *Cost Accounting: A Managerial Emphasis*. Englewood Cliffs, NJ: Prentice Hall.

Horngren, C.T., Foster, G. and Datar, S. (2000) *Cost Accounting – A Managerial Emphasis*, 10th edn. Englewood Cliffs, NJ: Prentice Hall.

Hronec, S.M. (1986) 'The effects of manufacturing productivity on cost accounting and management reporting', in NAA, *Cost Accounting for the '90s*. Montvale, NJ: National Association of Accountants.

Ijiri, Y. (1965) *Management Goals and Accounting for Control*. New York: North Holland.

Imai, M. (1986) *Kaizen: The Key to Japan's Competitive Success*. New York: McGraw-Hill.

Imberman, W. (1995) 'Is gainsharing the wave of the future?', *Management Accounting* (USA), November, pp. 35–9.

Ireland, G. (1992) 'Government in business: the measurement of financial performance from the perspective of an analyst', *1992 Public Sector Conventions*, New Zealand Society of Accountants, 1–4 November.

Ittner, C.D. and Larcker, D.F. (1995) 'Total quality management and the choice of information and reward systems', *Journal of Accounting Research*, vol. 33 (Supplement), pp. 1–34.

Ittner, C.D. and Larcker, D.F. (1998) 'Innovations in performance measurement: trends and research implications', *Journal of Management Accounting Research*, vol. 10, pp. 205–38.

Ittner, C.D., Larcker, D.F. and Rajan, M.V. (1997) 'The choice of performance measures in annual bonus contract', *Accounting Review*, vol. 2, no. 2, April, pp. 231–56.

James, W. and Hoque, Z. (1999) 'Balancing the scorecard: beyond the bottom line', *Australian Accountant,* November, pp. 46–7.

Jensen, M. and Meckling, W.H. (1976) 'Theory of the firm: managerial behaviour, agency costs and ownership structure', *Journal of Financial Economics*, pp. 305–60.

Johnson, H.T. (1990) 'Performance measurement for competitive excellence', in Kaplan, R.S. (ed.), *Measures for Competitive Excellence*. Boston, MA: Harvard Business School Press.

Johnson, H.T. (1992) *Relevance Regained: From Top-Down Control to Bottom-Up Improvement*. New York: Free Press.

Johnson, H.T. (1994) 'Relevance regained, total quality management and the role of management accounting', *Critical Perspectives on Accounting*, vol. 5, pp. 259–67.

Jones, L. (1988) 'Competitor analysis at Caterpillar', *Management Accounting* (USA), October, pp. 32–8.

Jones, R. and Pendlebury, M. (2000) *Public Sector Accounting*. London: FT Prentice Hall.

Jonsson, P. (2000) 'An empirical taxonomy of advanced manufacturing technology', *International Journal of Operations and Production Management*, vol. 20, no. 12, pp. 1146–474.

Kaplan, R.S. (1983) 'Measuring manufacturing performance: a new challenge for managerial accounting research', *Accounting Review*, October, pp. 686–705.

Kaplan, R.S. (1994) 'Management accounting (1984–1994): development of new practice and theory', *Management Accounting Research*, vol. 5, pp. 247–60.

Kaplan, R.S. and Atkinson, A. (1989) *Advanced Management Accounting*, 2nd edn. Englewood Cliffs, NJ: Prentice Hall.

Kaplan, R.S. and Norton, D.P. (1992) 'The balanced scorecard – measures that drive performance', *Harvard Business Review*, January–February, pp. 71–9.

Kaplan, R.S. and Norton, D.P. (1993) 'Putting the balanced scorecard to work', *Harvard Business Review*, September–October, pp. 134–47.

Kaplan, R.S. and Norton, D.P. (1996a) *The Balanced Scorecard: Translating Strategy into Action*. Boston, MA: Harvard Business Press.

Kaplan, R.S. and Norton, D.P. (1996b) 'Using the balanced scorecard as a strategic management system', *Harvard Business Review*, January–February, pp. 75–85.

Kaplinsky, R. (1984) *Automation*. Harlow: Longman.

Kelaher, M. (1991) 'Designing commercial enterprises in government', *Australian Accountant*, March, pp. 44–50.

Kelder, R. (1988) 'Era of cost accounting changes', in Capettini, R. and Clancy, D.K. (eds), *Cost Accounting, Robotics and the New Manufacturing Environment*. Sarasota, FL: American Accounting Association, pp. 3.1–3.25.

Kennedy, P.W. (1995) 'Performance pay, productivity and morale', *Economic Record*, vol. 71, no. 214, pp. 240–7.

Kermally, S. (1997) *Total Quality Management*. Oxford: Butterworth Heinemann.

Koontz, H. and O'Donnell, C. (1972) *Principles of Management*. London: McGraw-Hill.

Kotler, P., Ang, S.H., Leong, S.M. and Tan, C.I. (1999) *Marketing Management – An Asian Perspective*. Englewood Cliffs, NJ: Prentice-Hall International.

Langfield-Smith, K. (1997) 'Management control systems and strategy: a critical review', *Accounting, Organisations and Society*, vol. 22, no. 2, pp. 207–32.

Lawrence, P.R. and Lorsch, J. (1967) *Organization and Environment*. Boston, MA: Harvard Business School Division of Research.

Lei, D. and Goldhar, J.D. (1991) 'Advanced manufacturing technology: organisational design and strategic flexibility', *Organizational Studies*, vol. 17, no. 3, pp. 501–23.

Lele, M.M. and Sheth, J.N. (1987) *The Customer is Key*. Chichester: John Wiley & Sons.

Libby, T. and Waterhouse, J.H. (1996) 'Predicting change in management accounting systems', *Journal of Management Accounting Research*, vol. 8, pp. 137–50.

Lindblom, C.E. (1959) 'The science of "muddling through"', *Public Administrative Review*, vol. 19, pp. 79–88.

Lothian, N. (1987) *Measuring Corporate Performance*, CIMA Occasional Papers Series. London: Chartered Institute of Management Accountants.

Lynch, R.L. and Cross, K.F. (1991) *Measure Up!* Cambridge, MA: Blackwell Publishers.

MacArthur, J.B. (1996) 'Performance measures that count: monitoring variables of strategic importance', *Journal of Cost Management*, Fall, pp. 39–45.

Macintosh, N.B. (1985) *The Social Software of Accounting and Information Systems*. New York: John Wiley & Sons.

Macintosh, N.B. (1994) *Management Accounting and Control Systems: An Organizational and Behavioral Approach*. Chichester: John Wiley & Sons.

McNair, C.J., Mosconi, W. and Norris, T. (1989) *Beyond the Bottom Line*. New York: Dow Jones-Irwin.

Maisel, L.S. (1992) 'Performance measurement: the balanced scorecard approach', *Journal of Cost Management*, vol. 6, no. 2, pp. 47–52.

March, J.G. (1989) *Decisions and Organisations*. Oxford: Basil Blackwell.

March, J.G. and Olsen, J.P. (1989) *Rediscovering Institutions: The Organisational Basis of Politics*. New York: Free Press.

March, J.G. and Simon, H.A. (1958) *Organizations*. New York: John Wiley & Sons.

Marks, D. (1995) 'More complex, year by year', *Accountancy*, vol. 116, no. 1226, pp. 86–7.

Mellors, J. (1995) *Running Business in Government: Lessons from the DAS Experience*. Paper presented at the July Conference for the Institute of Public Administration Australia.

Merchant, K.A. (1981) 'The design of the corporate budgeting system: influences on managerial behavior and performance', *Accounting Review*, vol. 56, pp. 813–29.

Merchant, K.A. (1982) 'The control function of management', *Sloan Management Review*, Summer, pp. 43–55.

Merchant, K.A. (1984) 'Influences on departmental budgeting: an empirical examination of a contingency model', *Accounting, Organisations and Society*, vol. 9, no. 3/4, pp. 291–307.

Meredith, J. (1987) 'The strategic advantage of the factory of the future', *California Management Review*, vol. 29, no. 3, pp. 27–41.

Mia, L. (1993) 'The role of MAS information in organizations: an empirical study', *British Accounting Review*, vol. 25, pp. 269–85.

Mia, L. and Chenhall, R.H. (1994) 'The usefulness of management accounting systems, functional differentiation and managerial effectiveness', *Accounting, Organisations and Society*, vol. 19, no. 1, pp. 1–13.

Miles, R.E. and Snow, C.C. (1978) *Organizational Strategy, Structure and Process*. New York: McGraw-Hill.

Mintzberg, H. (1978) 'Patterns in strategy formulation', *Management Science*, May, pp. 934–48.

Mintzberg, H., Quinn, J.B. and Voyer, J. (1995) *The Strategy Process*. Englewood Cliffs, NJ: Prentice-Hall.

Moll, J. (2000) *Accounting for Managing Change in Local Government Organisations: A Case Study of Management Control Systems in a Local Government Water Authority*, BBus(Hons) Dissertation, School of Accounting and Finance, Griffith University, Gold Coast, Australia.

Moll, J. and Hoque, Z. (2000) *Rationality, New Public Management and Changes in Management Control Systems: A Case Study of Managing Change in an Australian Local Government Setting.* Paper presented at the Interdisciplinary Perspectives on Accounting Conference, Manchester, UK, July.

Mongomery, D.C. (1991) *Introduction to Statistical Quality Control,* 2nd edn. New York: John Wiley & Sons.

Morgan, C. and Murgatroyd, S. (1994) *Total Quality Management in the Public Sector.* Buckingham, UK: Open University Press.

Morse, W.J., Roth, H.P. and Psoton, K.M. (1987) *Measuring, Planning, and Controlling Quality Costs.* Montvale, NJ: National Association of Accountants.

Mouritsen, J. (1994) 'Rationality, institutions and decision making: reflections on March and Olsen's rediscovering institutions', *Accounting, Organisations and Society,* vol. 19, no. 2, pp. 193–211.

Newing, R. (1995) 'Wake up to a balanced scorecard', *Management Accounting* (UK), vol. 73, no. 3, pp. 22–3.

Ogden, S.G. (1992) 'The limits of employee involvement: profit sharing and disclosure of information', *Journal of Management Studies,* vol. 29, no. 2, pp. 229–48.

Ogden, S.G. (1993) 'The limitations of agency theory: the case of accounting based profit sharing schemes', *Critical Perspectives on Accounting,* vol. 4, no. 2, pp. 179–206.

Ogden, S.G. (1995) 'Profit sharing and organisational change: attempts to promote employee commitment in the newly privatised water industry in England and Wales', *Accounting, Auditing and Accountability Journal,* vol. 8, no. 4, pp. 23–47.

Otley, D.T. (1980) 'The contingency theory of management accounting: achievement and prognosis', *Accounting, Organisations and Society,* vol. 5, no. 4, pp. 413–28.

Otley, D. (1987) *Accounting Control and Organisational Behaviour.* London: William Heinemann.

Otley, D. and Berry, A.J. (1980) 'Control, organisation and accounting', *Accounting, Organisations and Society,* vol. 5, no. 2, pp. 231–46.

Parker, C. (2001) *Accounting Handbook 2001*. Melbourne: CPA Australia and Institute of Chartered Accountants in Australia.

Parker, L.D. (1976) *The Reporting of Company Financial Results to Employees*, Research Committee Occasional Paper No. 12. London: Institute of Chartered Accountants in England and Wales.

Patton, A. (1972) 'Why incentive plans fail?', *Harvard Business Review*, May–June.

Perera, S., Harrison, G. and Poole, M. (1997) 'Customer-focused manufacturing strategy and the use of operations-based non-financial performance measures: a research note', *Accounting, Organisations and Society*, vol. 22, no. 6, pp. 557–72.

Poland, J.D. (1996) 'New comparability: a new concept in profit sharing plan design', *Journal of Compensation and Benefits*, vol. 12, no. 1, pp. 54–6.

Poole, M. (1988) 'Factors affecting the development of employee financial participation in contemporary Britain: evidence from a national survey', *British Journal of Industrial Relations*, vol. 24, no. 2, pp. 233–50.

Porter, M.E. (1980) *Competitive Strategy: Techniques for Analysing Industries and Competitors*. New York: Free Press.

Porter, M.E. (1985) *Competitive Strategy: Creating and Sustaining Superior Performance*. New York: Free Press.

Powell, T.C. (1995) 'Total quality management as competitive advantage: a review and empirical study', *Strategic Management Journal*, vol. 16, pp. 15–37.

Procter, S., McArdle, L., Hassard, J. and Rowlinson, M. (1993) 'Performance related pay in practice: a critical perspective', *British Journal of Management*, vol. 4, pp. 153–60.

Raffish, N. (1991) 'How much does that product really cost?', *Management Accounting* (USA), March, pp. 36–9.

Reed, M. (1989) *The Sociology of Management*. London: Harvester Wheatsheaf.

Rivlin, A.M. (1996) *Ministerial Symposium on the Future of Public Services*. Paris: OECD.

Rotch, W. (1993) 'Management control systems: one view of components and their interdependence', *British Journal of Management*, vol. 4, pp. 191–203.

Ryan, C. (1998) 'The introduction of accrual reporting in the Australian public sector', *Accounting, Auditing and Accountability Journal*, vol. 11, no. 5, pp. 518–39.

Sansom, G. (1997) *Reinventing Australian Local Government: Community, Innovation and Reform. Speeches and Press Releases.* URL: http://www.psmpc.gov.au/media/sessiona6.htm

Saunders, I.W. and Preston, A.P. (1995) *The Assessment of TQM Performance in Organisations: Applying the S-P Model,* Quality Program Research Report. Australian Centre in Strategic Management.

Scapens, R.W. (1994) 'Never mind the gap: towards an institutional perspective on management accounting practice', *Management Accounting Research*, vol. 5, pp. 301–21.

Schneier, C.E. (1995) *Managing Strategic and Cultural Change in Organisations.* New York: Human Resource Planning Society.

Schuller, T. (1989) 'Financial participation', in Storey, J. (ed.), *New Perspectives on Human Resource Management.* London: Routledge.

Schwartz, H. and Davis, S.M. (1981) 'Matching corporate strategy and business strategy', *Organisational Dynamics*, Summer, pp. 30–48.

Senior, B. (1997) *Organisational Change.* London: Pitman Publishing.

Shank, J.K. and Govindarajan, V. (1988) 'Strategic cost analysis: a case study', *Journal of Cost and Management*, vol. 3, no. 3, pp. 25–32.

Shank, J.K. and Govindarajan, V. (1989) *Strategic Cost Analysis: The Evolution from Managerial to Strategic Accounting.* Homewood, IL: Irwin.

Shank, J.K. and Govindarajan, V. (1992a) 'Strategic cost management: the value chain perspective', *Journal of Cost and Management*, vol. 4, no. 1, pp. 179–97.

Shank, J.K. and Govindarajan, V. (1992b) 'Strategic cost management and the value chain', *Journal of Cost and Management*, vol. 5, no. 4, pp. 5–21.

Shank, J.K. and Govindarajan, V. (1993) *Strategic Cost Management: The New Tool for Competitive Advantage.* New York: Free Press.

Shank, J.K. and Govindarajan, V. (1994) 'Measuring the "cost of quality": a strategic cost management perspective', *Journal of Cost Management*, Summer, pp. 5–17.

Sharma, U. and Hoque, Z. (2001) 'Implementing the balanced scorecard in a government entity: a case study of the housing authority of Fiji', *Journal of Cost Management*, vol. 15, no. 4, July/August, pp. 37–41.

Siegal, G. and Ramanauskas-Marconi, H. (1989) *Behavioural Accounting*. Cincinnati, OH: South-Western College Publishing.

Sim, K.L. and Killough, L.N. (1998) 'The performance effects of complementarities between manufacturing practices and management accounting systems', *Journal of Management Accounting Research*, vol. 10, pp. 325–46.

Simmonds, K. (1981) 'Strategic management accounting', *Management Accounting*, vol. 59, no. 4, pp. 26–9.

Simons, R. (1987) 'Accounting control systems and business strategy', *Accounting, Organisations and Society*, vol. 12, pp. 357–74.

Simons, R. (1990) 'The role of management control systems in creating competitive advantage: new perspectives', *Accounting, Organisations and Society*, vol. 15, no. 1/2, pp. 127–43.

Simons, R. (1995) *Levers of Control*. Boston, MA: Harvard Business School Press.

Simons, R. (2000) *Performance Measurement and Control Systems for Implementing Strategy – Text and Cases*. Englewood Cliffs, NJ: Prentice Hall.

Sloan, A.D. Jr (1963) *My Years with General Motors*. New York: McFadden-Bartell.

Smith, G.R. (1986) 'Profit sharing and employee share ownership in Britain', *Employment Gazette*, vol. 85, pp. 380–5.

Smith, M., Swaffer, A. and Gurd, B. (1998) *The Impact of Organisational Culture of Accounting Lag*. Paper presented at the Interdisciplinary Perspectives on Accounting Symposium, Osaka, Japan.

Smith, P. (1993) 'Outcome-related performance indicators and organizational control in the public sector', *British Journal of Management*, vol. 4, pp. 135–51.

Stevens, R.E., Louden, D.L., Wrenn, B. and Warren, W.E. (1997) *Marketing Planning Guide*. New York: Haworth Press.

Stoner, J.A.F. (1982) *Management*, 2nd edn. Englewood Cliffs, NJ: Prentice Hall International.

Swift, F.W., Gallwey, T. and Swift, J.A. (1996) 'Benchmarking – the neglected element in total quality management', in Rolstadas, A. (ed.), *Benchmarking – Theory and Practice*. London: Chapman & Hall.

Tannenbaum, A.S. (1968) *Control in Organisations*. New York: McGraw-Hill.

Taylor, F.W. (1947) *Scientific Management*. New York: Harper & Row.

Thomas, J.M. (1996) 'Profit sharing plans: new options for an old favourite', *Compensation and Benefits Management*, vol. 12, no. 3, pp. 1–8.

Thompson, J.D. (1967) *Organizations in Action*. London: McGraw-Hill.

Thompson, P. (1990) 'Crawling from the wreckage', in Knights, D. and Wilmott, H. (eds), *Labour Process Theory*. London: Macmillan.

Thorne, H. (1995) 'Performance measures in manufacturing: lessons from the balanced scorecard and dynamic model', *Accounting Forum*, vol. 18, no. 4, pp. 27–44.

Tinker, T., Merino, B.D. and Neimark, M.D. (1982) 'The normative origin of positive theories, ideology and accounting thought', *Accounting, Organisations and Society*, vol. 7, no. 2, pp. 167–200.

Tocher, K. (1970) 'Control', *Operational Research Quarterly*, June, pp. 159–80.

Tuckman, A. (1994) 'The yellow brick road: Total Quality Management and the restructuring of organizational culture', *Organization Studies*, vol. 15, pp. 727–51.

Viljoen, J. and Dann, S. (2000) *Strategic Management*, 3rd edn. Sydney: Longman.

Ward, K., Wendy, H. and Sri, S. (1992) 'Accounting for the competition', *Management Accounting* (UK), vol. 70, no. 2, pp. 19–23.

Watson, D.J. (1975) 'Contingency formulations of organizational structure: implications for managerial accounting', in Livingston, J.L. (ed.), *Managerial Accounting: The Behavioural Foundations*. Columbus, OH: Grid, pp. 65–80.

Weber, M. (1947) *The Theory of Social and Economic Organization*. New York: Oxford University Press.

Wensing, E. (1997) 'The process of local government reform: legislative change in the states', in Dollery, B. and Marshall, N. (eds), *Australian Local Government: Reform and Renewal*. Melbourne: Macmillan Education Australia, pp. 89–102.

Wheelen, T.L. and Hunger, J.D. (1998) *Strategic Management and Business Policy: Entering 21st Century Global Society*. New York: Addison-Wesley.

Whittington, R. (1993) *What is Strategy and Does It Matter?* London: Routledge.

Wilkinson, A. and Willmott, H. (eds) (1995) *Making Quality Critical: New Perspectives on Organizational Change*. London: Routledge.

Wilkinson, A. and Witcher, B. (1993) 'Holistic total quality management must take account of political processes', *Total Quality Management*, vol. 4, no. 1, pp. 47–56.

Wilson, R.M.S. (1991) 'Strategic management accounting', in Ashton, D., Hopper, T. and Scapens, R.W. (eds), *Issues in Management Accounting*. Englewood Cliffs, NJ: Prentice Hall.

Wilson, R.M.S. (1994) 'Competitor analysis', *Management Accounting* (UK), vol. 72, no. 4, pp. 24–8.

Wilson, R.M.S. and Gilligan, C. (1998) *Strategic Marketing Management: Planning, Implementation and Control*. Oxford: Butterworth Heinemann.

Wood, S. (1996) 'High commitment management and payment systems', *Journal of Management Studies*, vol. 33, no. 1, pp. 53–77.

Woodward, J. (1965) *Industrial Organization – Theory and Practice*. London: Oxford University Press.

Yamin, S. and Gunasekaran, A. (1999) 'Organisational quality – a cognitive approach to quality management', *TQM Magazine*, vol. 11, no. 3, pp. 180–7.

Young, S.M. and Selto, F.H. (1991) 'New manufacturing practices and cost management: review of the literature and directions for research', *Journal of Accounting Literature*, vol. 10, pp. 265–98.

Index